SEX ED 120%

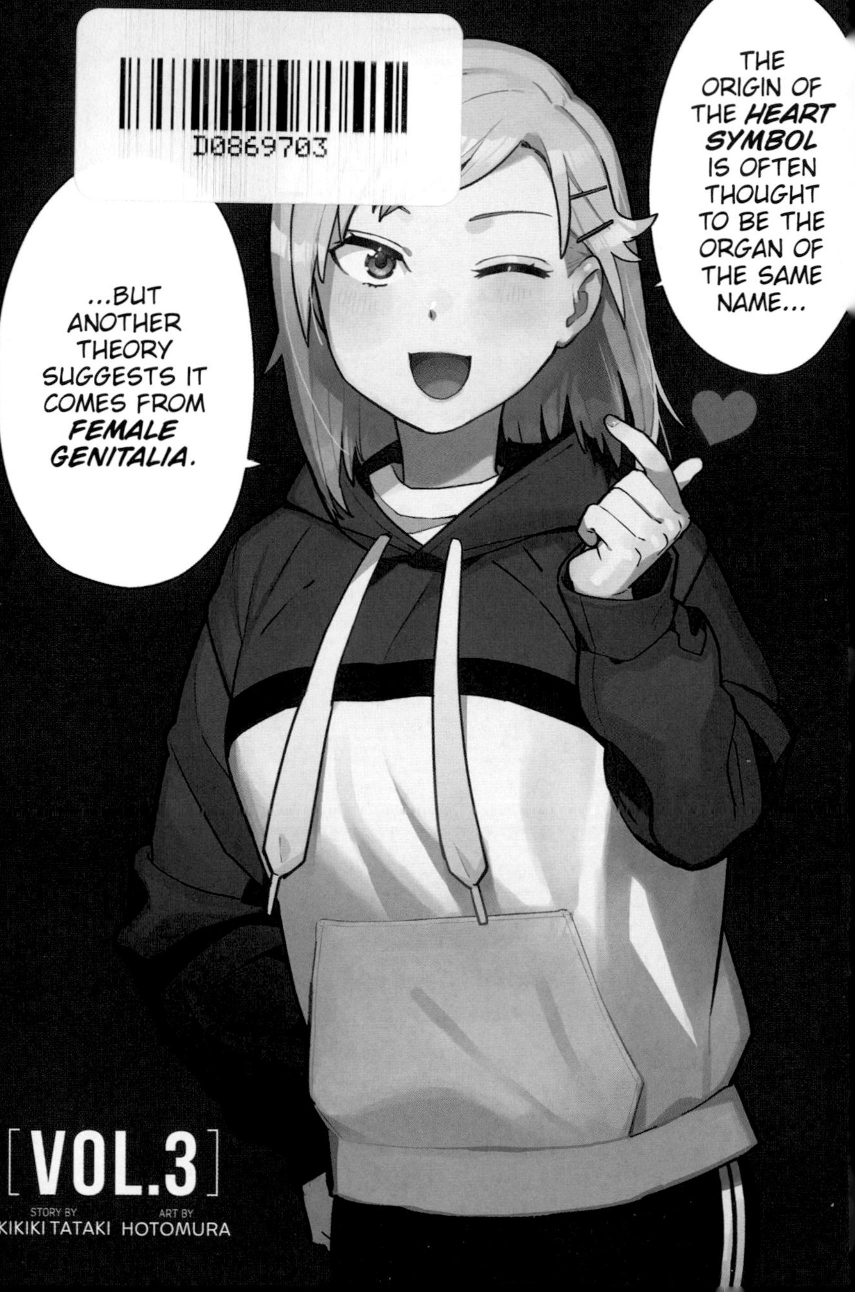

THE ORIGIN OF THE ***HEART SYMBOL*** IS OFTEN THOUGHT TO BE THE ORGAN OF THE SAME NAME...
...BUT ANOTHER THEORY SUGGESTS IT COMES FROM ***FEMALE GENITALIA.***

[VOL.3]

STORY BY KIKIKI TATAKI
ART BY HOTOMURA

CONTENTS

[Class 13]
Pregnancy and Abortion
-003-

[Class 14]
Transgender
-021-

[Class 15]
LGBT History
-039-

[Class 16]
Bisexual
-057-

[Class 17]
Sexual Diversity
-077-

[Class 18]
Sex Ed into the Future
-099-

[Special Lesson]
Date
-125-

SEX ED 120%

[Class 13] **Pregnancy and Abortion**

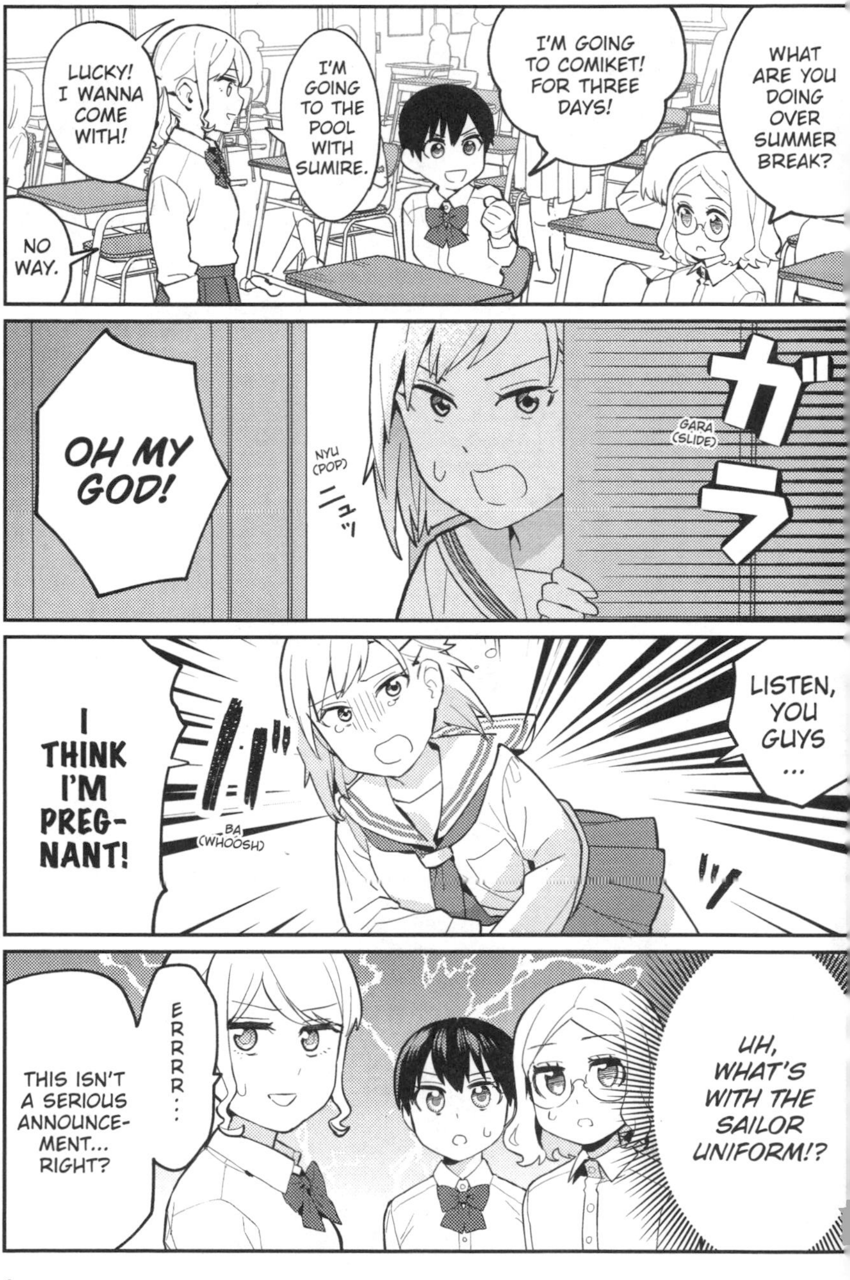
WHAT ARE YOU DOING OVER SUMMER BREAK?
I'M GOING TO COMIKET! FOR THREE DAYS!
I'M GOING TO THE POOL WITH SUMIRE.
LUCKY! I WANNA COME WITH!
NO WAY.
ガラ
GARA (SLIDE)
NYU (POP)
ニュッ
OH MY GOD!
LISTEN, YOU GUYS...
バッ
BA (WHOOSH)
I THINK I'M PREG-NANT!
UH, WHAT'S WITH THE SAILOR UNIFORM!?
ERRRR...
THIS ISN'T A SERIOUS ANNOUNCE-MENT... RIGHT?

Class 13

Pregnancy and Abortion

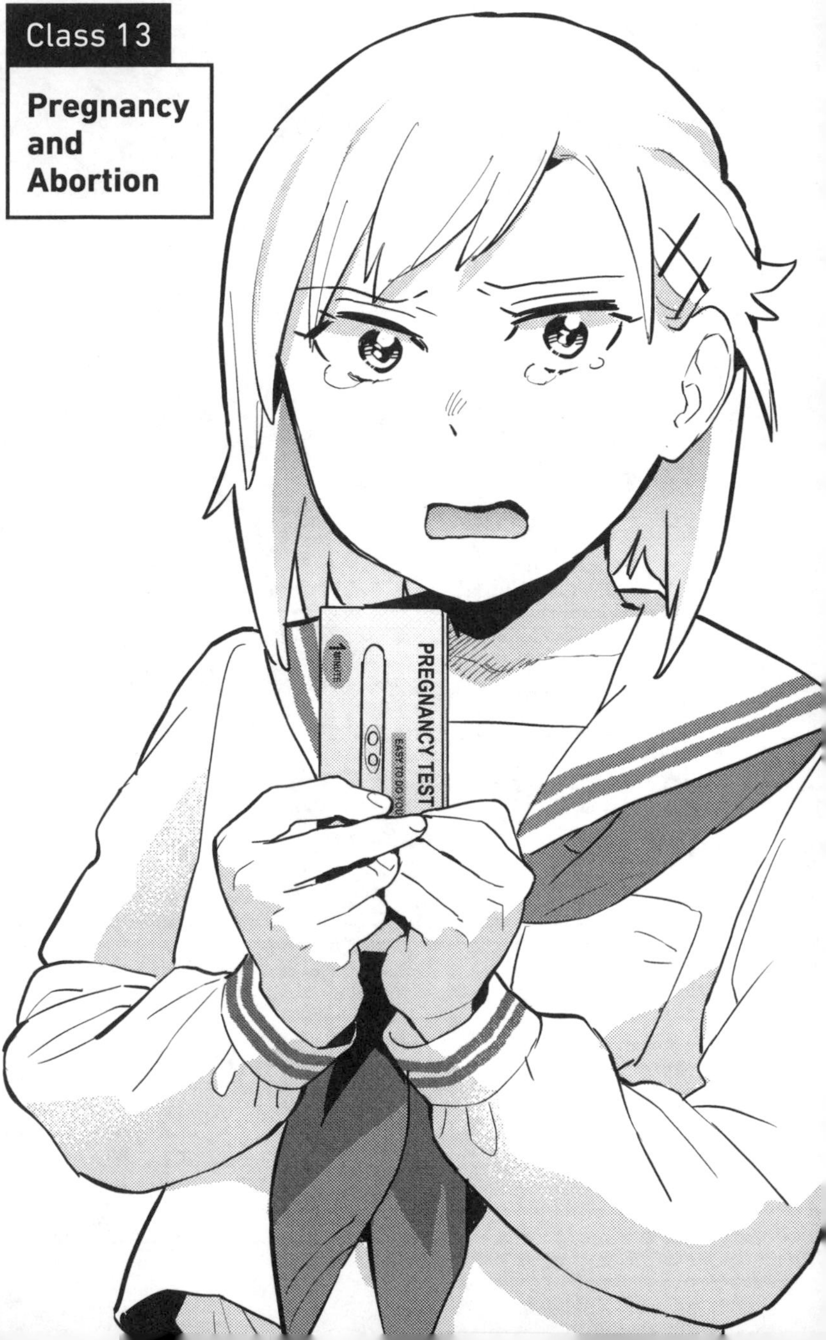

PREGNANCY TEST
1 MINUTE

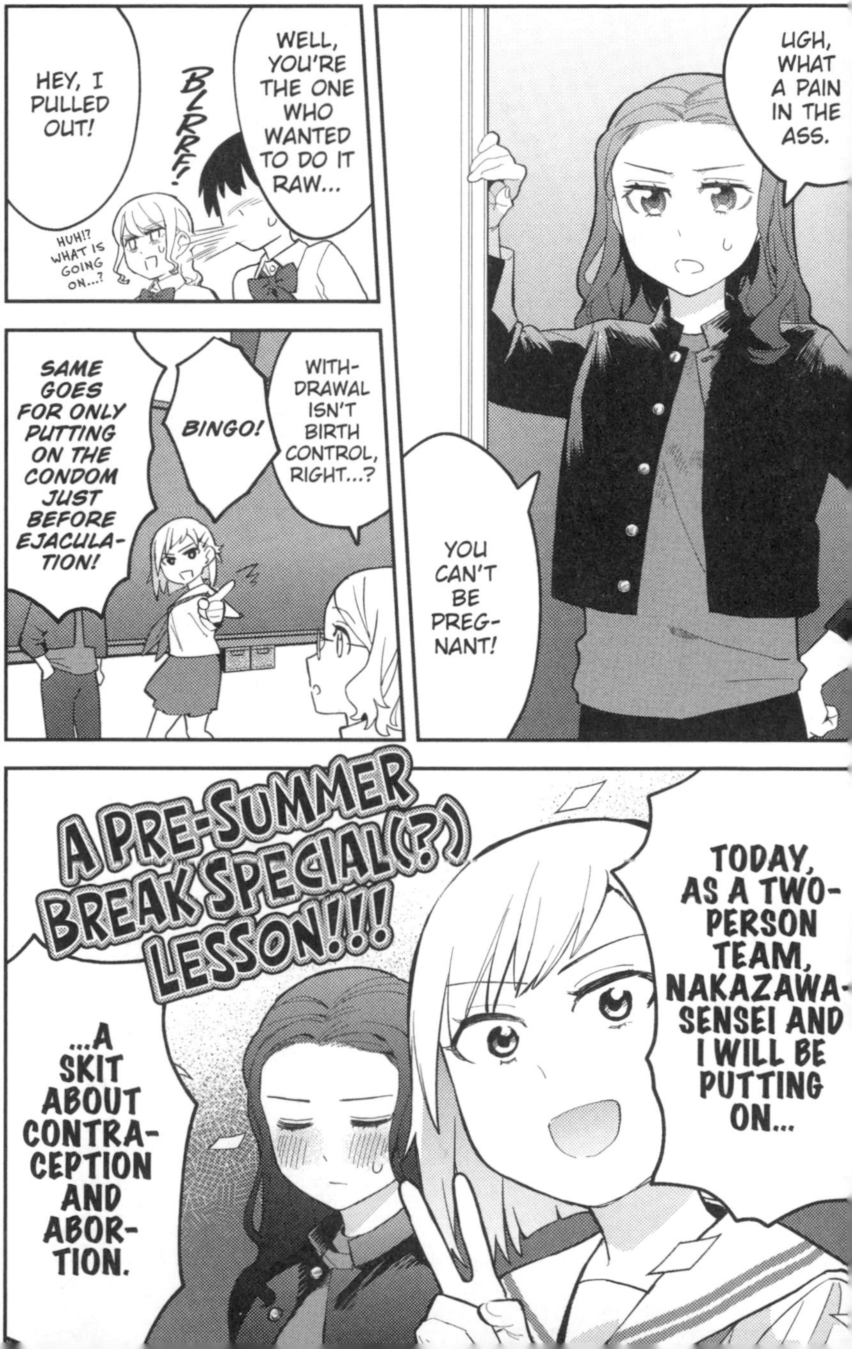
UGH, WHAT A PAIN IN THE ASS.
YOU CAN'T BE PREGNANT!
WELL, YOU'RE THE ONE WHO WANTED TO DO IT RAW...
BLRRF!
HEY, I PULLED OUT!
HUH!? WHAT IS GOING ON...?
WITHDRAWAL ISN'T BIRTH CONTROL, RIGHT...?
BINGO!
SAME GOES FOR ONLY PUTTING ON THE CONDOM JUST BEFORE EJACULATION!
TODAY, AS A TWO-PERSON TEAM, NAKAZAWA-SENSEI AND I WILL BE PUTTING ON...
A PRE-SUMMER BREAK SPECIAL(?) LESSON!!!
...A SKIT ABOUT CONTRACEPTION AND ABORTION.

Morning-After Pill

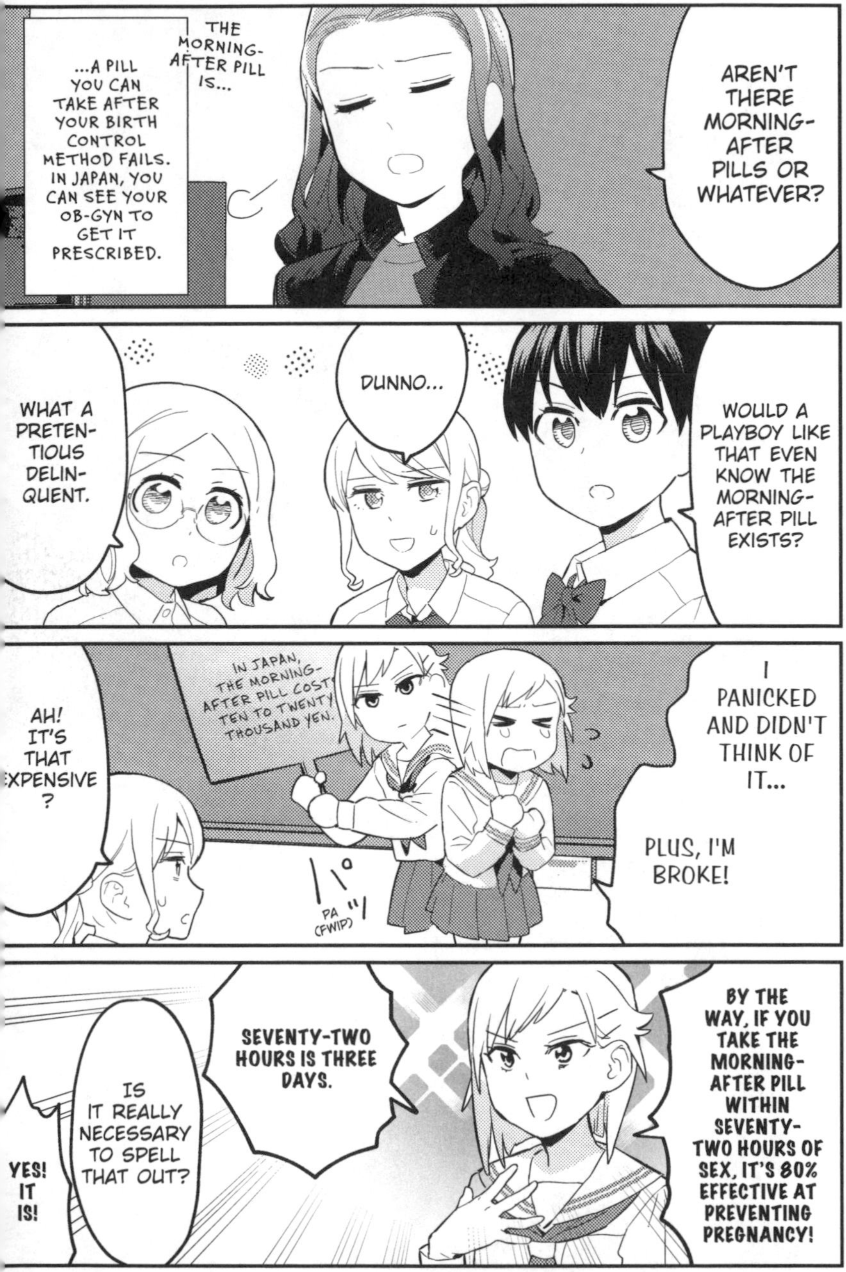
AREN'T THERE MORNING-AFTER PILLS OR WHATEVER?
THE MORNING-AFTER PILL IS...
...A PILL YOU CAN TAKE AFTER YOUR BIRTH CONTROL METHOD FAILS. IN JAPAN, YOU CAN SEE YOUR OB-GYN TO GET IT PRESCRIBED.
WOULD A PLAYBOY LIKE THAT EVEN KNOW THE MORNING-AFTER PILL EXISTS?
DUNNO...
WHAT A PRETENTIOUS DELINQUENT.
I PANICKED AND DIDN'T THINK OF IT...
PLUS, I'M BROKE!
IN JAPAN, THE MORNING-AFTER PILL COST TEN TO TWENTY THOUSAND YEN.
パッ
PA (FWIP)
AH! IT'S THAT XPENSIVE ?
BY THE WAY, IF YOU TAKE THE MORNING-AFTER PILL WITHIN SEVENTY-TWO HOURS OF SEX, IT'S 80% EFFECTIVE AT PREVENTING PREGNANCY!
SEVENTY-TWO HOURS IS THREE DAYS.
IS IT REALLY NECESSARY TO SPELL THAT OUT?
YES! IT IS!

Pregnancy Tests

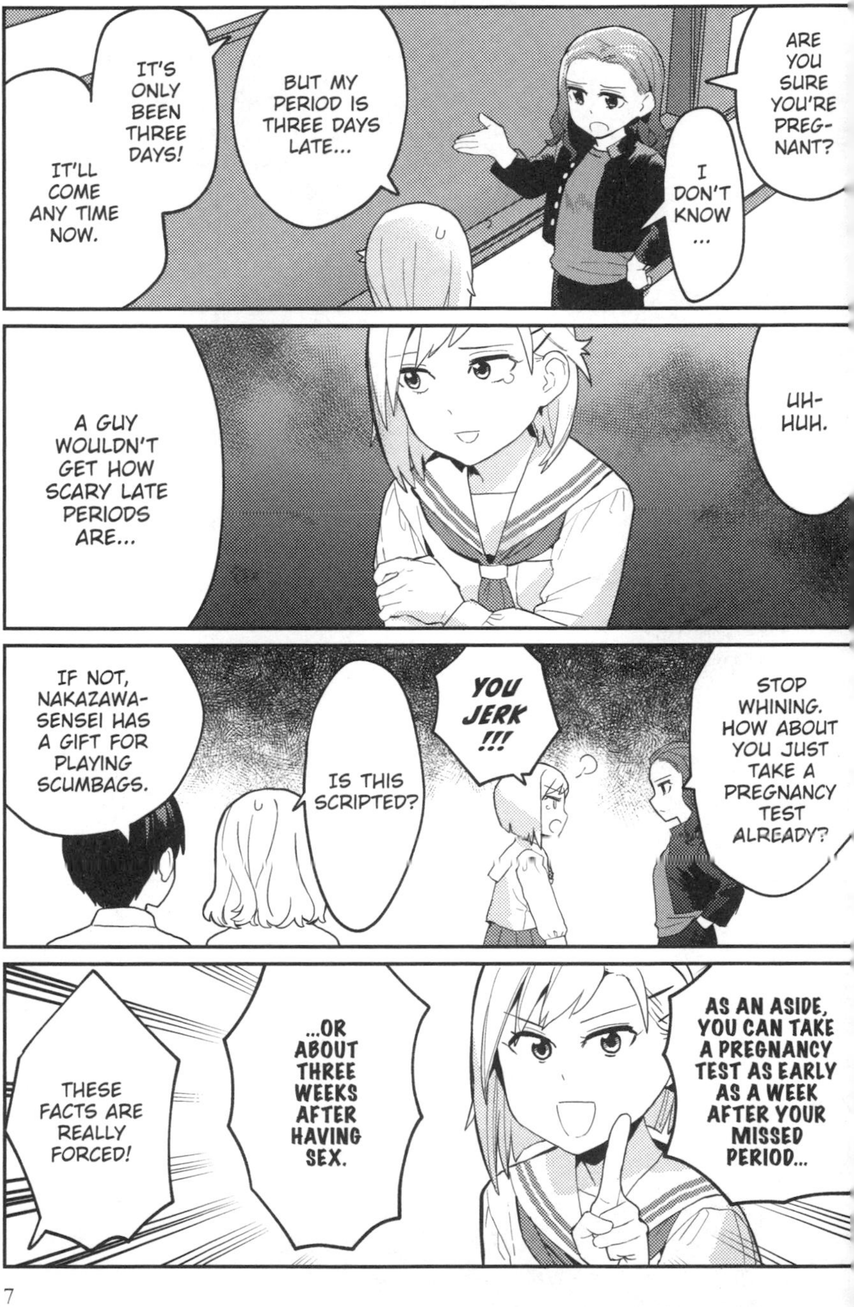
ARE YOU SURE YOU'RE PREGNANT?
I DON'T KNOW ...
BUT MY PERIOD IS THREE DAYS LATE...
IT'S ONLY BEEN THREE DAYS!
IT'LL COME ANY TIME NOW.
UH-HUH.
A GUY WOULDN'T GET HOW SCARY LATE PERIODS ARE...
STOP WHINING. HOW ABOUT YOU JUST TAKE A PREGNANCY TEST ALREADY?
YOU JERK!!!
IS THIS SCRIPTED?
IF NOT, NAKAZAWA-SENSEI HAS A GIFT FOR PLAYING SCUMBAGS.
AS AN ASIDE, YOU CAN TAKE A PREGNANCY TEST AS EARLY AS A WEEK AFTER YOUR MISSED PERIOD...
...OR ABOUT THREE WEEKS AFTER HAVING SEX.
THESE FACTS ARE REALLY FORCED!

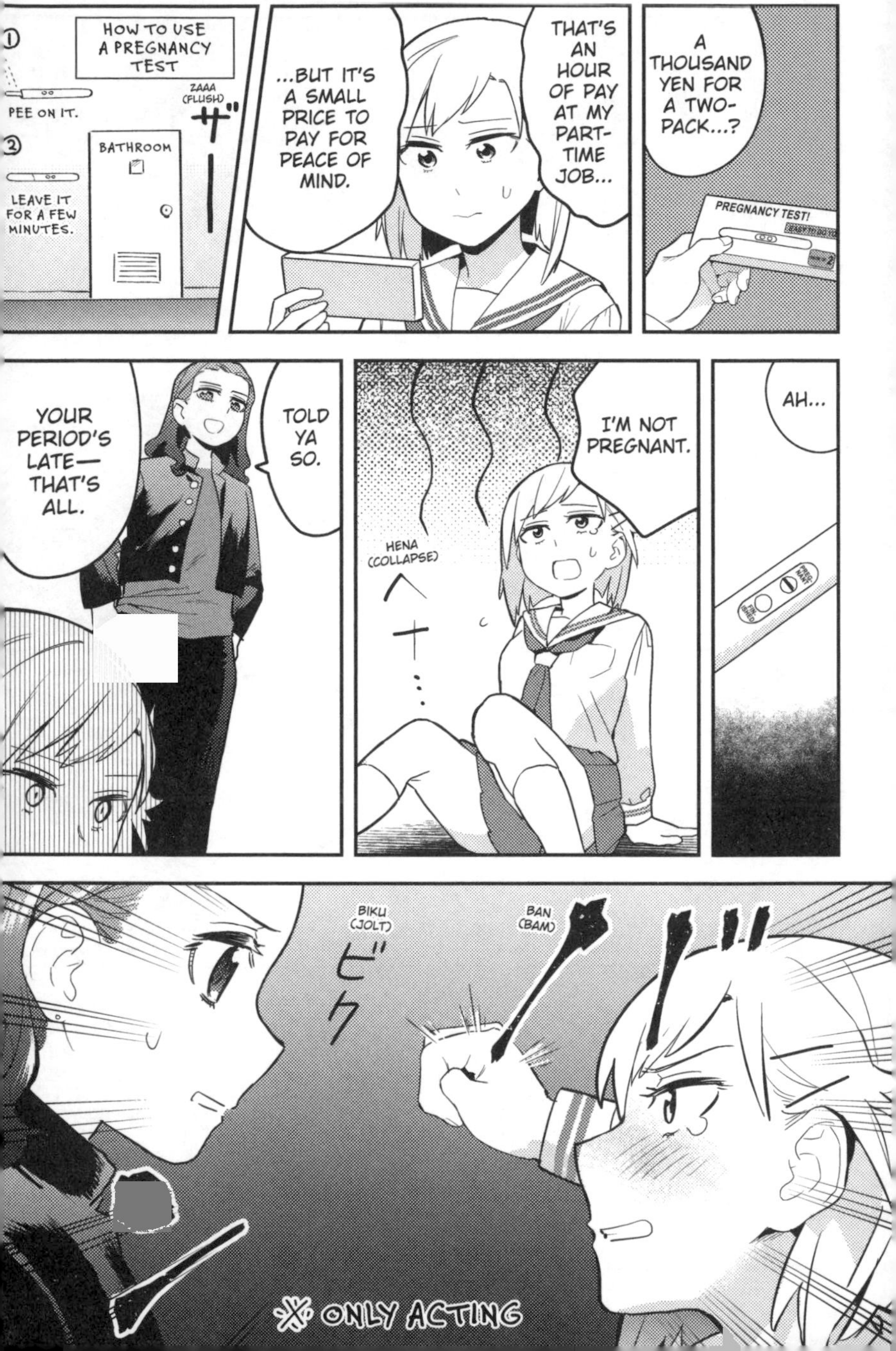
A THOUSAND YEN FOR A TWO-PACK...?
PREGNANCY TEST!
THAT'S AN HOUR OF PAY AT MY PART-TIME JOB...
...BUT IT'S A SMALL PRICE TO PAY FOR PEACE OF MIND.
ZAAA (FLUSH)
HOW TO USE A PREGNANCY TEST
① PEE ON IT.
② LEAVE IT FOR A FEW MINUTES.
BATHROOM
AH...
PREG-NANT
FIN-ISHED
I'M NOT PREGNANT.
HENA (COLLAPSE)
TOLD YA SO.
YOUR PERIOD'S LATE—THAT'S ALL.
BAN (BAM)
BIKU (JOLT)
※ ONLY ACTING

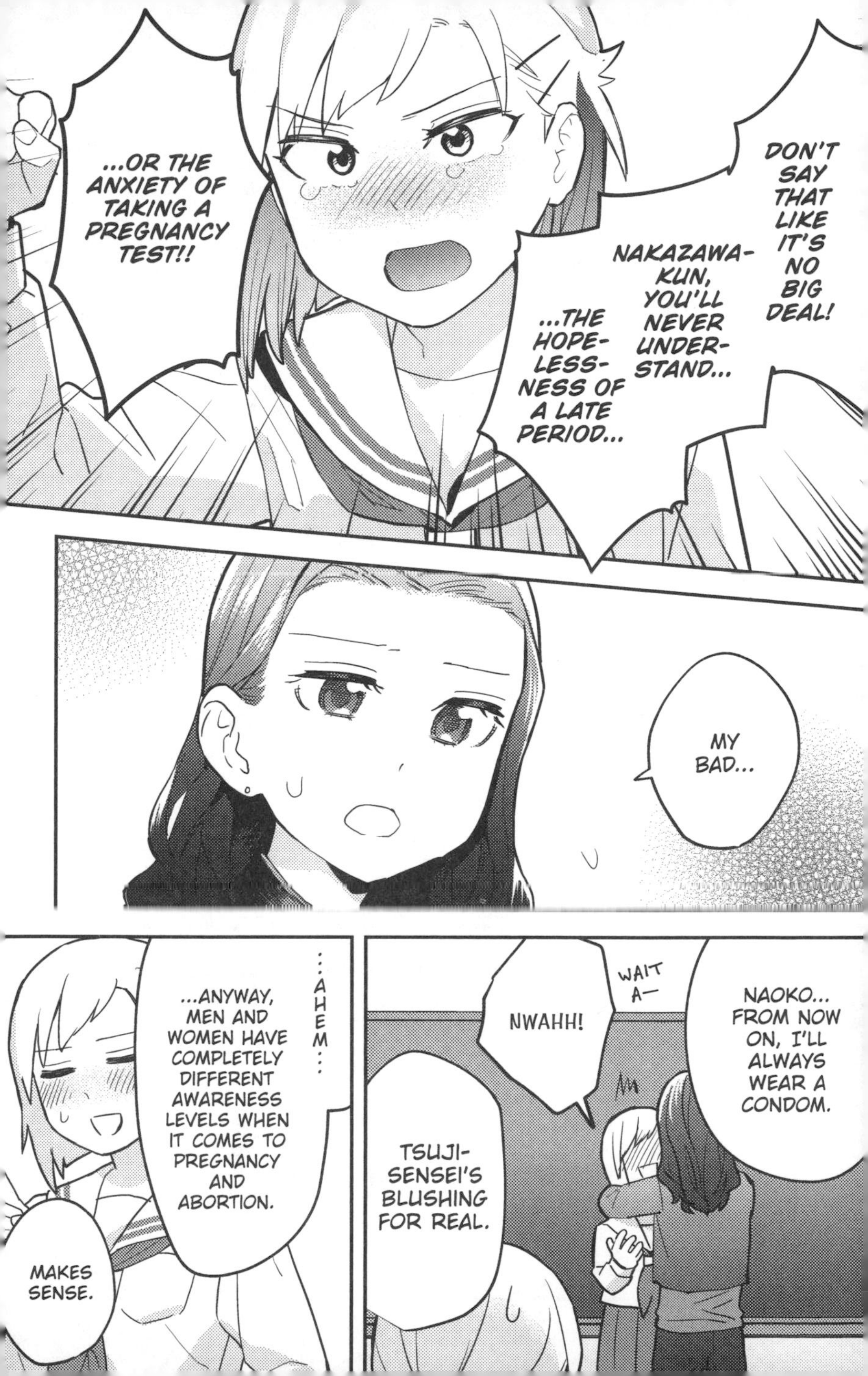
DON'T SAY THAT LIKE IT'S NO BIG DEAL!
NAKAZAWA-KUN, YOU'LL NEVER UNDERSTAND...
...THE HOPELESSNESS OF A LATE PERIOD...
...OR THE ANXIETY OF TAKING A PREGNANCY TEST!!
MY BAD...
NAOKO... FROM NOW ON, I'LL ALWAYS WEAR A CONDOM.
WAIT A—
NWAHH!
TSUJI-SENSEI'S BLUSHING FOR REAL.
...AHEM...
...ANYWAY, MEN AND WOMEN HAVE COMPLETELY DIFFERENT AWARENESS LEVELS WHEN IT COMES TO PREGNANCY AND ABORTION.
MAKES SENSE.

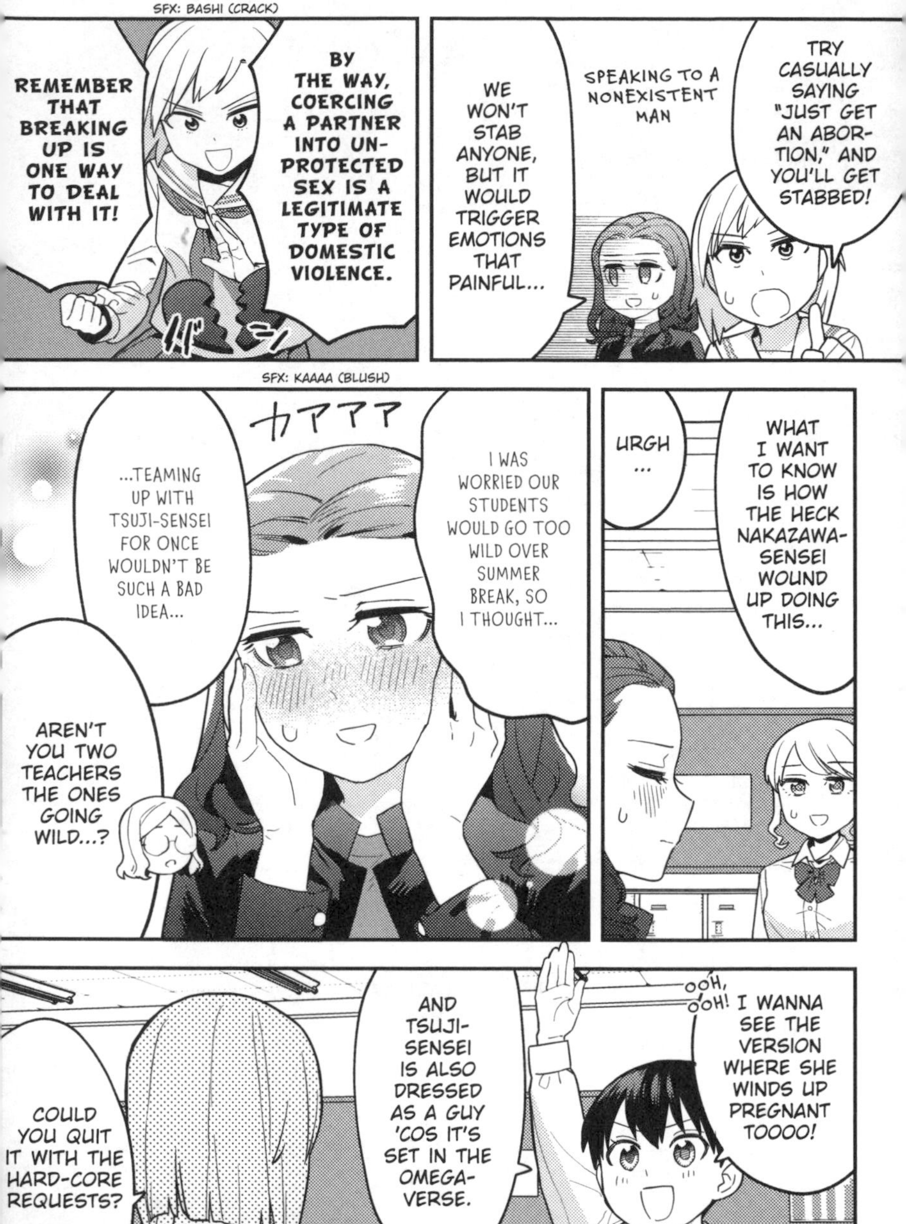
TRY CASUALLY SAYING "JUST GET AN ABORTION," AND YOU'LL GET STABBED!
SPEAKING TO A NONEXISTENT MAN
WE WON'T STAB ANYONE, BUT IT WOULD TRIGGER EMOTIONS THAT PAINFUL...
SFX: BASHI (CRACK)
BY THE WAY, COERCING A PARTNER INTO UNPROTECTED SEX IS A LEGITIMATE TYPE OF DOMESTIC VIOLENCE.
REMEMBER THAT BREAKING UP IS ONE WAY TO DEAL WITH IT!
WHAT I WANT TO KNOW IS HOW THE HECK NAKAZAWA-SENSEI WOUND UP DOING THIS...
URGH ...
SFX: KAAAA (BLUSH)
カアアア
I WAS WORRIED OUR STUDENTS WOULD GO TOO WILD OVER SUMMER BREAK, SO I THOUGHT...
...TEAMING UP WITH TSUJI-SENSEI FOR ONCE WOULDN'T BE SUCH A BAD IDEA...
AREN'T YOU TWO TEACHERS THE ONES GOING WILD...?
OOH, OOH! I WANNA SEE THE VERSION WHERE SHE WINDS UP PREGNANT TOOOO!
AND TSUJI-SENSEI IS ALSO DRESSED AS A GUY 'COS IT'S SET IN THE OMEGAVERSE.
COULD YOU QUIT IT WITH THE HARD-CORE REQUESTS?

I DON'T KNOW WHAT THAT IS.

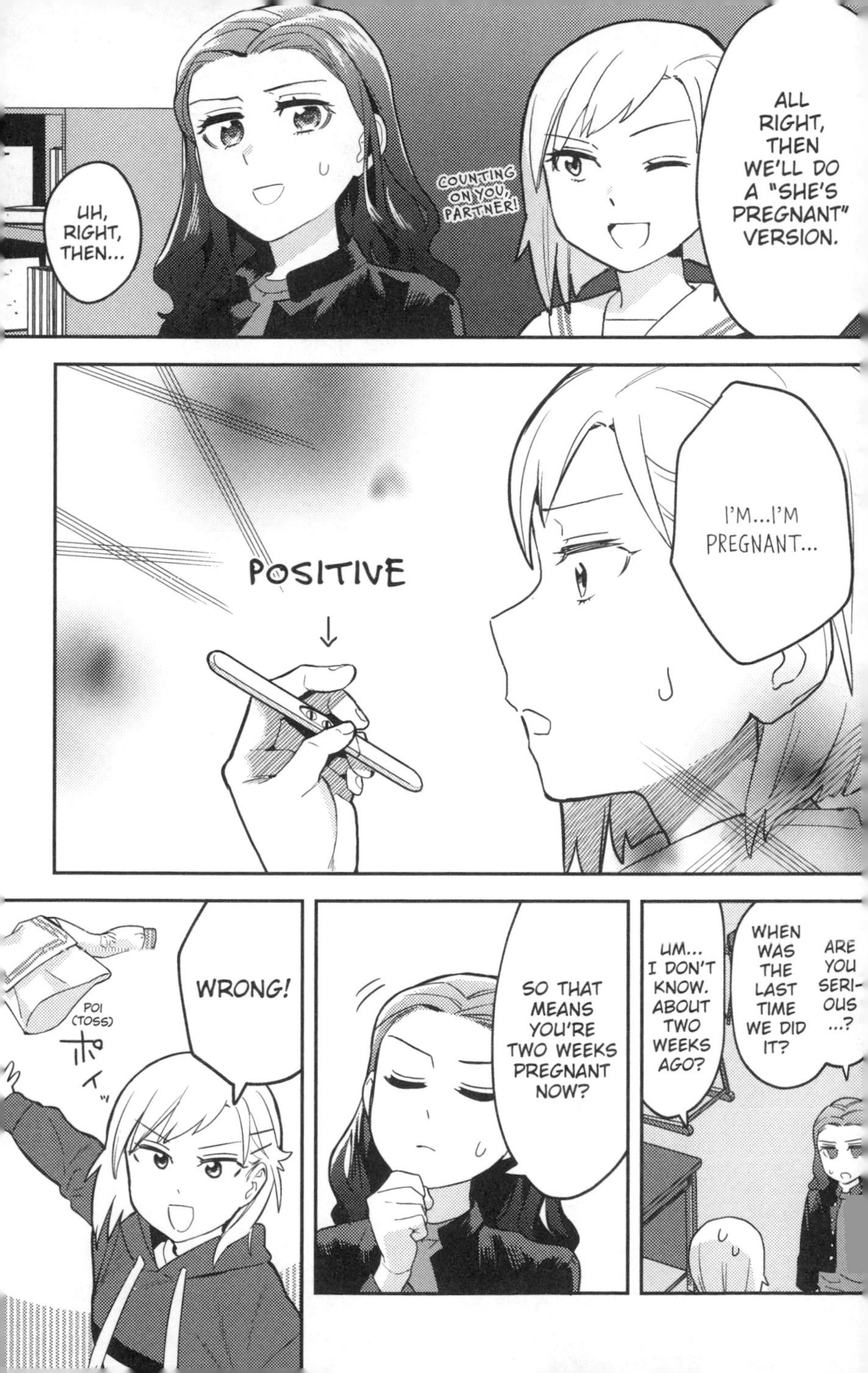
ALL RIGHT, THEN WE'LL DO A "SHE'S PREGNANT" VERSION.
COUNTING ON YOU, PARTNER!
UH, RIGHT, THEN...
I'M...I'M PREGNANT...
POSITIVE
ARE YOU SERI-OUS ...?
WHEN WAS THE LAST TIME WE DID IT?
UM... I DON'T KNOW. ABOUT TWO WEEKS AGO?
SO THAT MEANS YOU'RE TWO WEEKS PREGNANT NOW?
WRONG!
POI (TOSS)
ポイッ

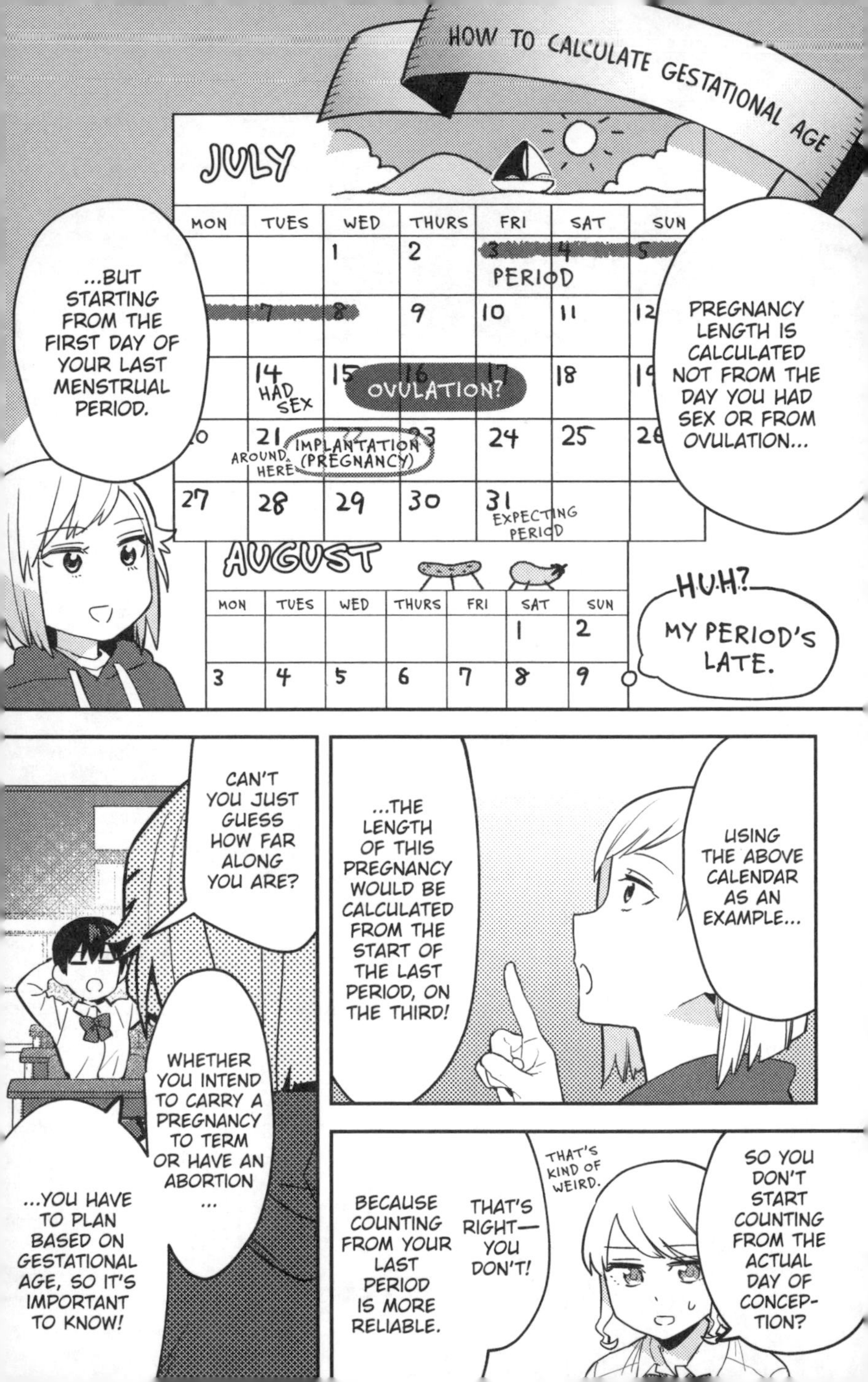
HOW TO CALCULATE GESTATIONAL AGE
PREGNANCY LENGTH IS CALCULATED NOT FROM THE DAY YOU HAD SEX OR FROM OVULATION...
...BUT STARTING FROM THE FIRST DAY OF YOUR LAST MENSTRUAL PERIOD.
JULY
MON TUES WED THURS FRI SAT SUN
PERIOD
14 HAD SEX
OVULATION?
21 AROUND HERE
IMPLANTATION (PREGNANCY)
31 EXPECTING PERIOD
AUGUST
MON TUES WED THURS FRI SAT SUN
HUH?
MY PERIOD'S LATE.
USING THE ABOVE CALENDAR AS AN EXAMPLE...
...THE LENGTH OF THIS PREGNANCY WOULD BE CALCULATED FROM THE START OF THE LAST PERIOD, ON THE THIRD!
SO YOU DON'T START COUNTING FROM THE ACTUAL DAY OF CONCEP-TION?
THAT'S KIND OF WEIRD.
THAT'S RIGHT— YOU DON'T!
BECAUSE COUNTING FROM YOUR LAST PERIOD IS MORE RELIABLE.
CAN'T YOU JUST GUESS HOW FAR ALONG YOU ARE?
WHETHER YOU INTEND TO CARRY A PREGNANCY TO TERM OR HAVE AN ABORTION ...
...YOU HAVE TO PLAN BASED ON GESTATIONAL AGE, SO IT'S IMPORTANT TO KNOW!

Abortion

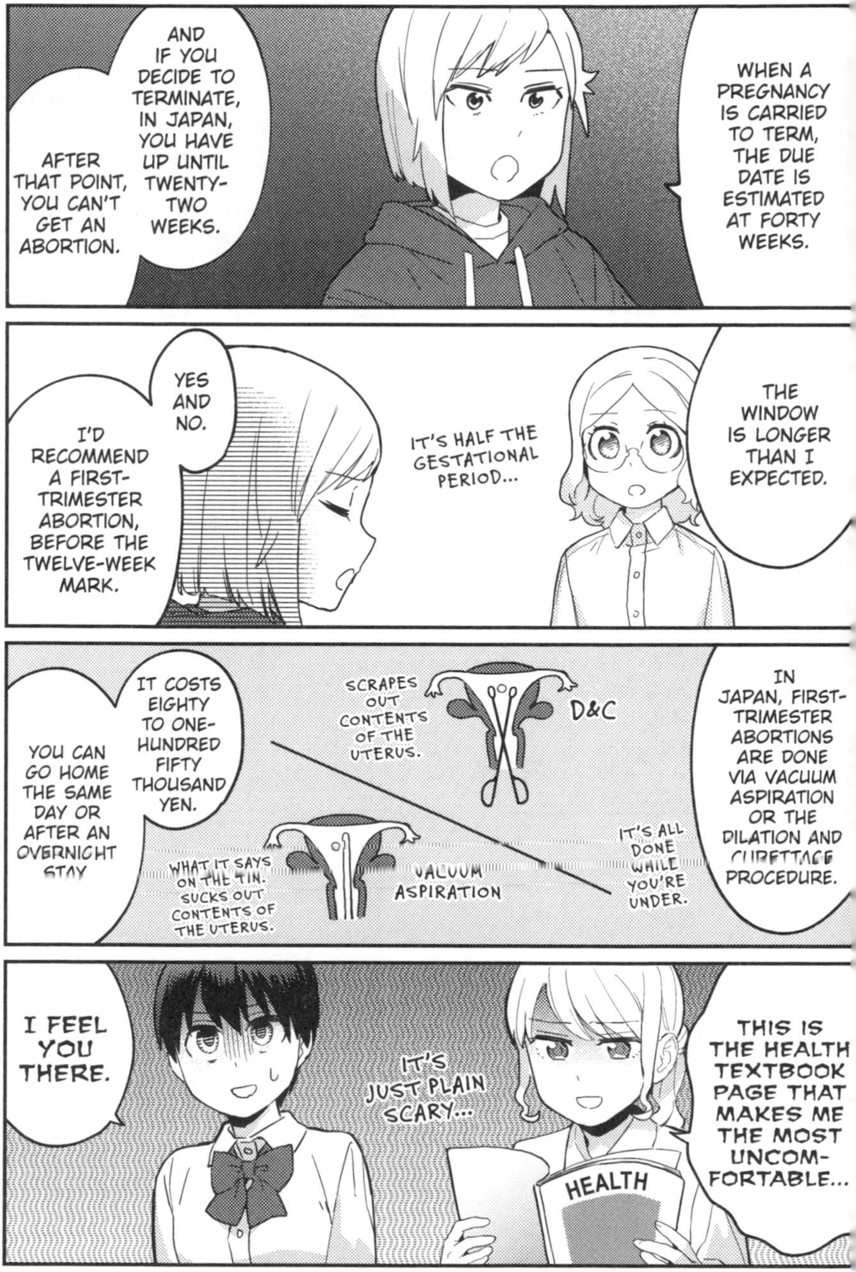
WHEN A PREGNANCY IS CARRIED TO TERM, THE DUE DATE IS ESTIMATED AT FORTY WEEKS.
AND IF YOU DECIDE TO TERMINATE, IN JAPAN, YOU HAVE UP UNTIL TWENTY-TWO WEEKS.
AFTER THAT POINT, YOU CAN'T GET AN ABORTION.
THE WINDOW IS LONGER THAN I EXPECTED.
IT'S HALF THE GESTATIONAL PERIOD...
YES AND NO.
I'D RECOMMEND A FIRST-TRIMESTER ABORTION, BEFORE THE TWELVE-WEEK MARK.
IN JAPAN, FIRST-TRIMESTER ABORTIONS ARE DONE VIA VACUUM ASPIRATION OR THE DILATION AND CURETTAGE PROCEDURE.
IT'S ALL DONE WHILE YOU'RE UNDER.
D&C
SCRAPES OUT CONTENTS OF THE UTERUS.
VACUUM ASPIRATION
WHAT IT SAYS ON THE TIN. SUCKS OUT CONTENTS OF THE UTERUS.
IT COSTS EIGHTY TO ONE-HUNDRED FIFTY THOUSAND YEN.
YOU CAN GO HOME THE SAME DAY OR AFTER AN OVERNIGHT STAY.
THIS IS THE HEALTH TEXTBOOK PAGE THAT MAKES ME THE MOST UNCOMFORTABLE...
HEALTH
IT'S JUST PLAIN SCARY...
I FEEL YOU THERE.

[CONVERSION NOTE: ABOUT 14 OUNCES.]

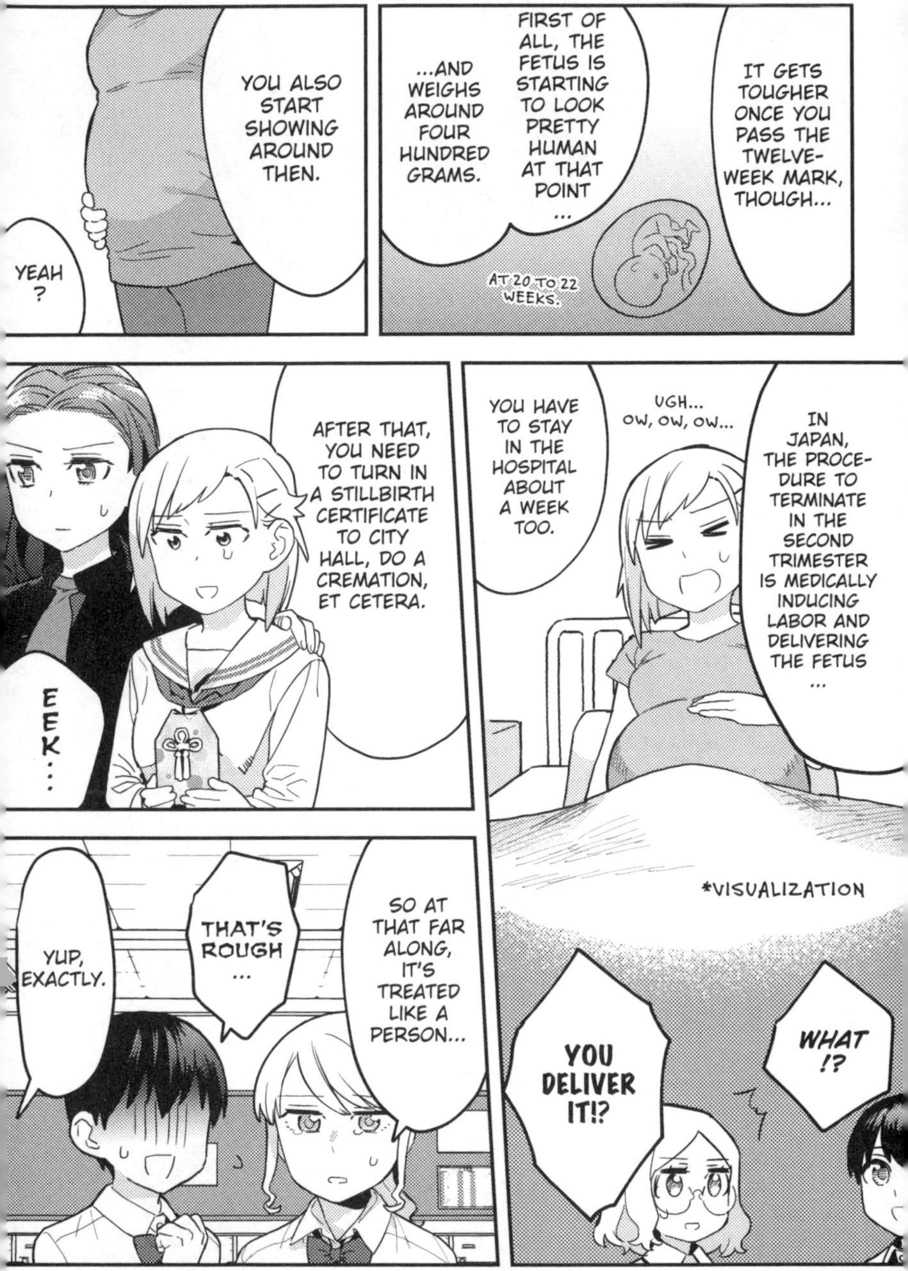
IT GETS TOUGHER ONCE YOU PASS THE TWELVE-WEEK MARK, THOUGH...
FIRST OF ALL, THE FETUS IS STARTING TO LOOK PRETTY HUMAN AT THAT POINT ...
...AND WEIGHS AROUND FOUR HUNDRED GRAMS.
AT 20 TO 22 WEEKS.
YOU ALSO START SHOWING AROUND THEN.
YEAH?
IN JAPAN, THE PROCEDURE TO TERMINATE IN THE SECOND TRIMESTER IS MEDICALLY INDUCING LABOR AND DELIVERING THE FETUS ...
UGH... OW, OW, OW...
YOU HAVE TO STAY IN THE HOSPITAL ABOUT A WEEK TOO.
*VISUALIZATION
WHAT!?
YOU DELIVER IT!?
AFTER THAT, YOU NEED TO TURN IN A STILLBIRTH CERTIFICATE TO CITY HALL, DO A CREMATION, ET CETERA.
EEK...
SO AT THAT FAR ALONG, IT'S TREATED LIKE A PERSON...
THAT'S ROUGH ...
YUP, EXACTLY.

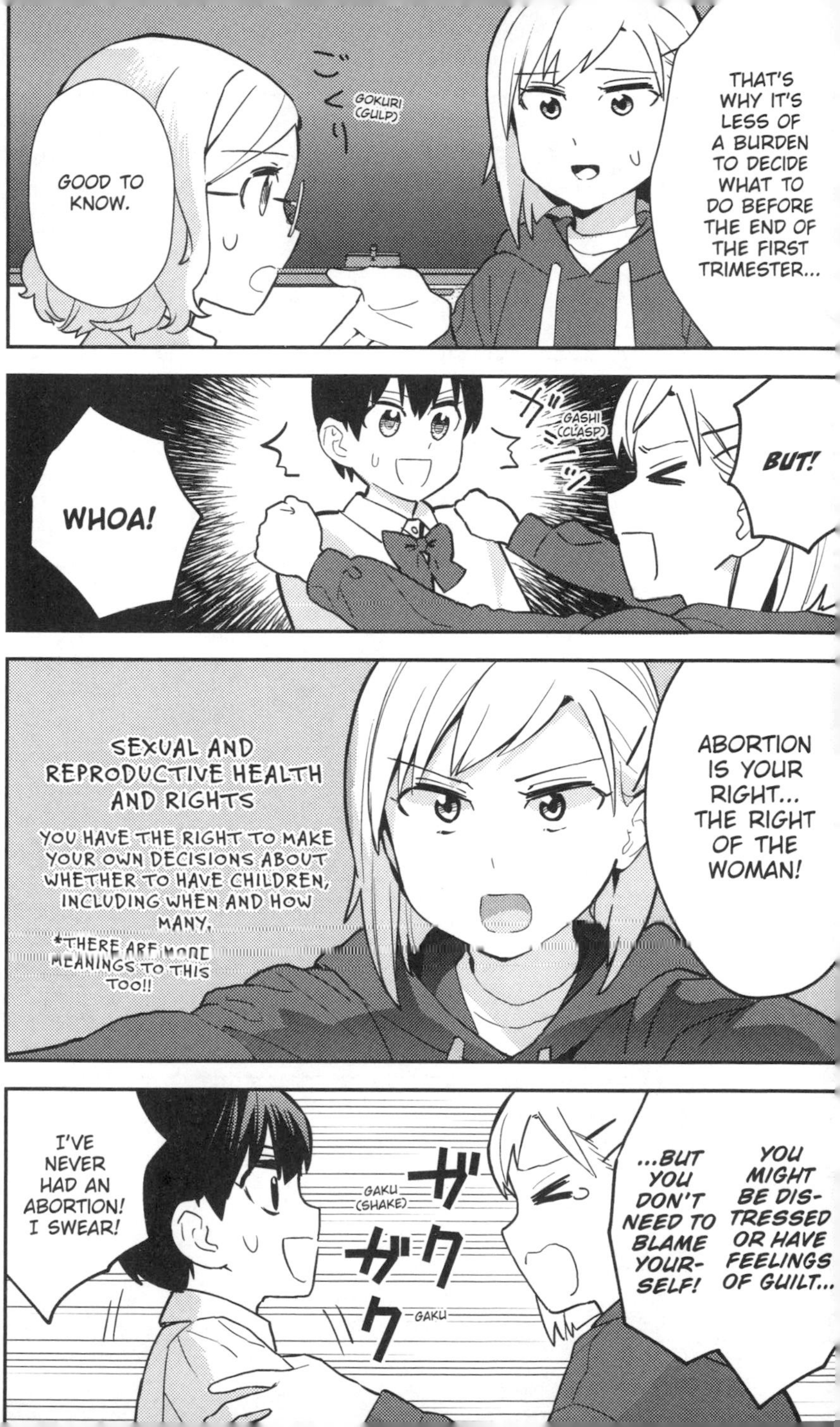

THAT'S WHY IT'S LESS OF A BURDEN TO DECIDE WHAT TO DO BEFORE THE END OF THE FIRST TRIMESTER...
ごくり
GOKURI (GULP)
GOOD TO KNOW.
BUT!
GASHI (CLASP)
WHOA!
ABORTION IS YOUR RIGHT... THE RIGHT OF THE WOMAN!
SEXUAL AND REPRODUCTIVE HEALTH AND RIGHTS
YOU HAVE THE RIGHT TO MAKE YOUR OWN DECISIONS ABOUT WHETHER TO HAVE CHILDREN, INCLUDING WHEN AND HOW MANY.
*THERE ARE MORE MEANINGS TO THIS TOO!!
YOU MIGHT BE DIS-TRESSED OR HAVE FEELINGS OF GUILT...
...BUT YOU DON'T NEED TO BLAME YOUR-SELF!
ガクガク
GAKU (SHAKE)
GAKU
I'VE NEVER HAD AN ABORTION! I SWEAR!

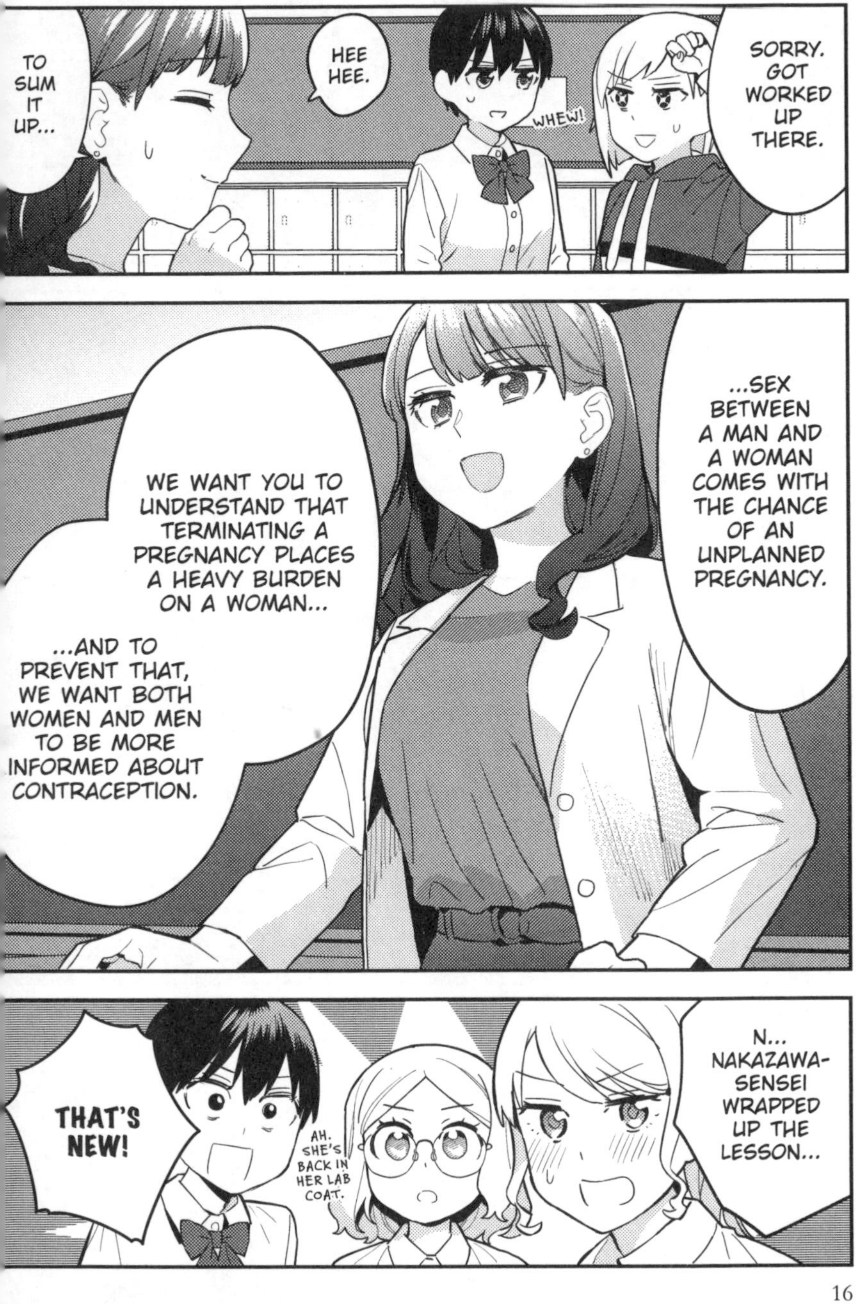
SORRY. GOT WORKED UP THERE.
WHEW!
HEE HEE.
TO SUM IT UP...
...SEX BETWEEN A MAN AND A WOMAN COMES WITH THE CHANCE OF AN UNPLANNED PREGNANCY.
WE WANT YOU TO UNDERSTAND THAT TERMINATING A PREGNANCY PLACES A HEAVY BURDEN ON A WOMAN...
...AND TO PREVENT THAT, WE WANT BOTH WOMEN AND MEN TO BE MORE INFORMED ABOUT CONTRACEPTION.
N... NAKAZAWA-SENSEI WRAPPED UP THE LESSON...
AH. SHE'S BACK IN HER LAB COAT.
THAT'S NEW!

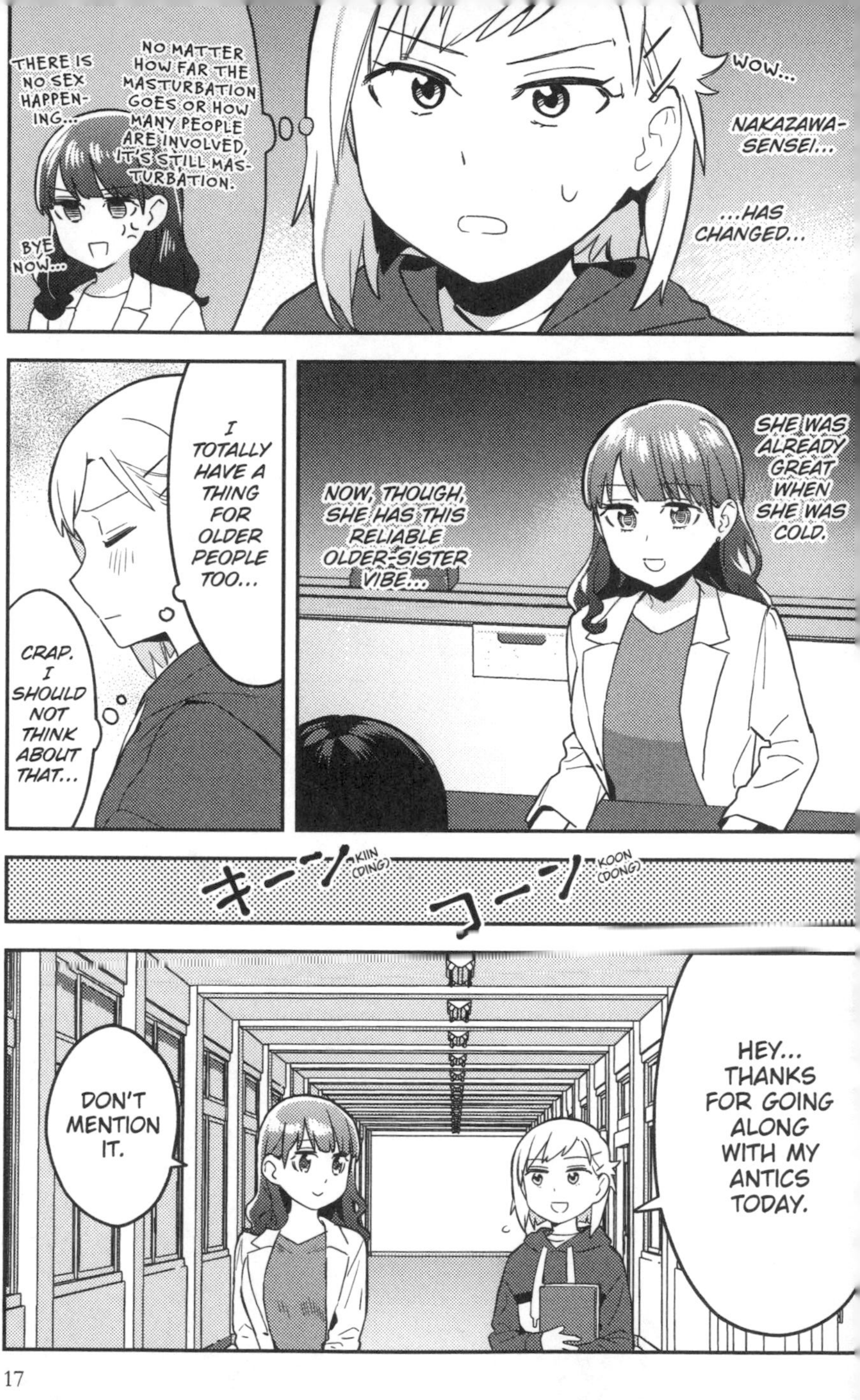
WOW...
NAKAZAWA-SENSEI...
...HAS CHANGED...
NO MATTER HOW FAR THE MASTURBATION GOES OR HOW MANY PEOPLE ARE INVOLVED, IT'S STILL MASTURBATION.
THERE IS NO SEX HAPPENING...
BYE NOW...
SHE WAS ALREADY GREAT WHEN SHE WAS COLD.
NOW, THOUGH, SHE HAS THIS RELIABLE OLDER-SISTER VIBE...
I TOTALLY HAVE A THING FOR OLDER PEOPLE TOO...
CRAP. I SHOULD NOT THINK ABOUT THAT...
キーン
KIIN (DING)
コーン
KOON (DONG)
HEY... THANKS FOR GOING ALONG WITH MY ANTICS TODAY.
DON'T MENTION IT.

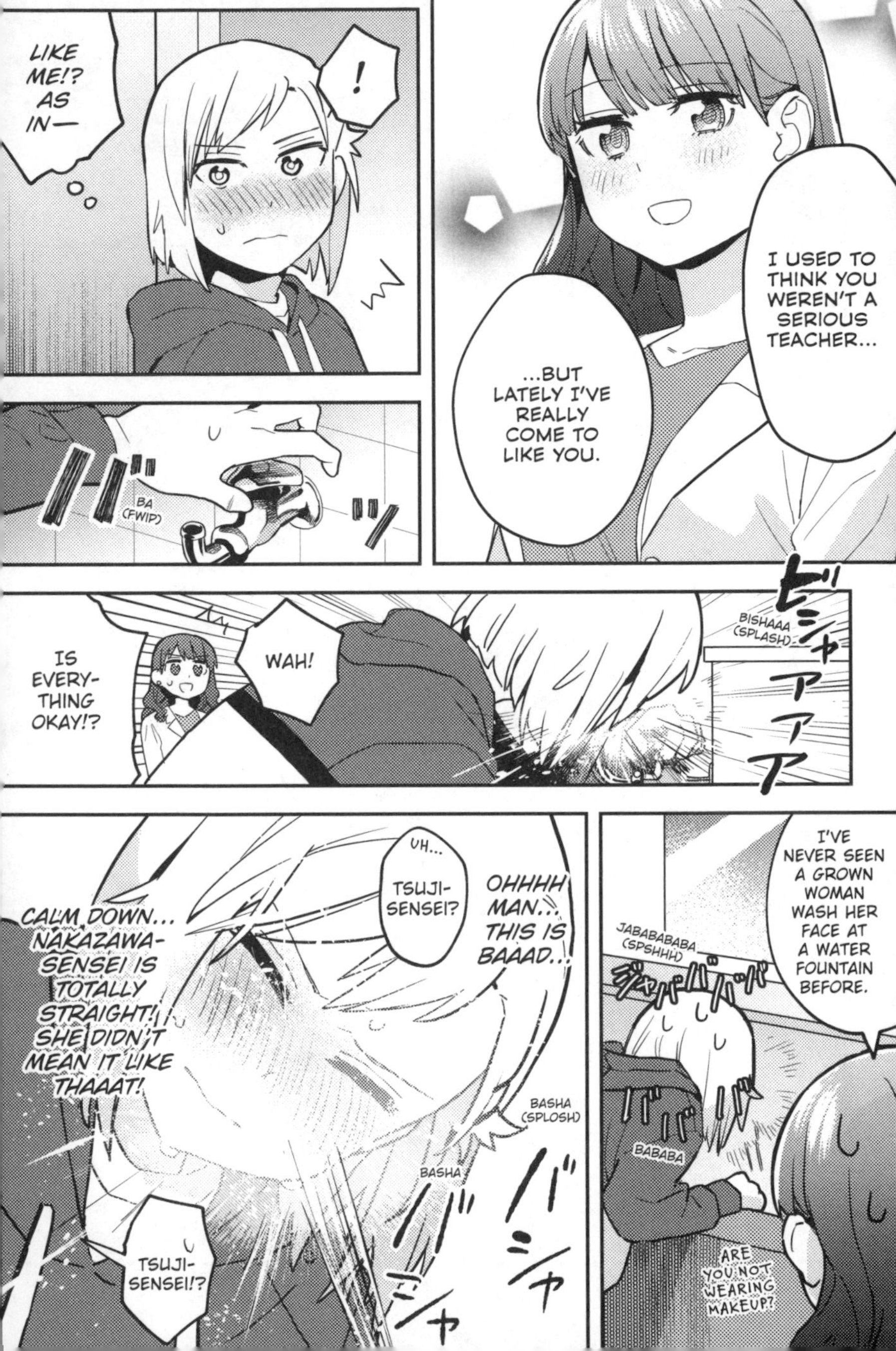
I USED TO THINK YOU WEREN'T A SERIOUS TEACHER...
...BUT LATELY I'VE REALLY COME TO LIKE YOU.
!
LIKE ME!? AS IN—
BA (FWIP)
BISHAAA (SPLASH)
WAH!
IS EVERY-THING OKAY!?
I'VE NEVER SEEN A GROWN WOMAN WASH HER FACE AT A WATER FOUNTAIN BEFORE.
JABABABABA (SPSHHH)
BABABA
ARE YOU NOT WEARING MAKEUP?
UH...
TSUJI-SENSEI?
OHHHH MAN... THIS IS BAAAD...
CALM DOWN... NAKAZAWA-SENSEI IS TOTALLY STRAIGHT! SHE DIDN'T MEAN IT LIKE THAAAT!
BASHA (SPLOSH)
BASHA
TSUJI-SENSEI!?

Class 13 Candid Shot

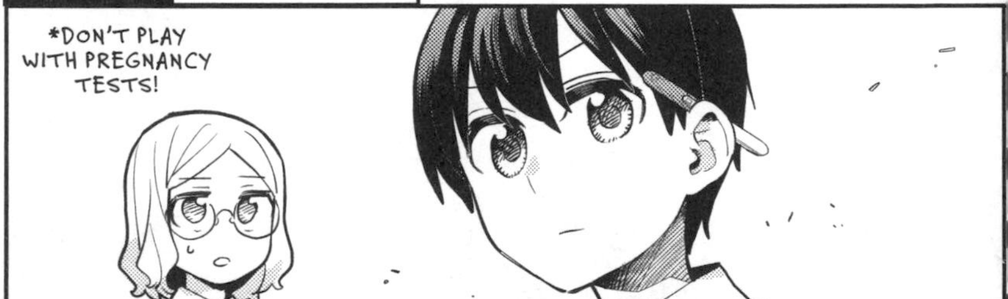
*DON'T PLAY WITH PREGNANCY TESTS!

Knocking Out 12 Sex Concerns! 1

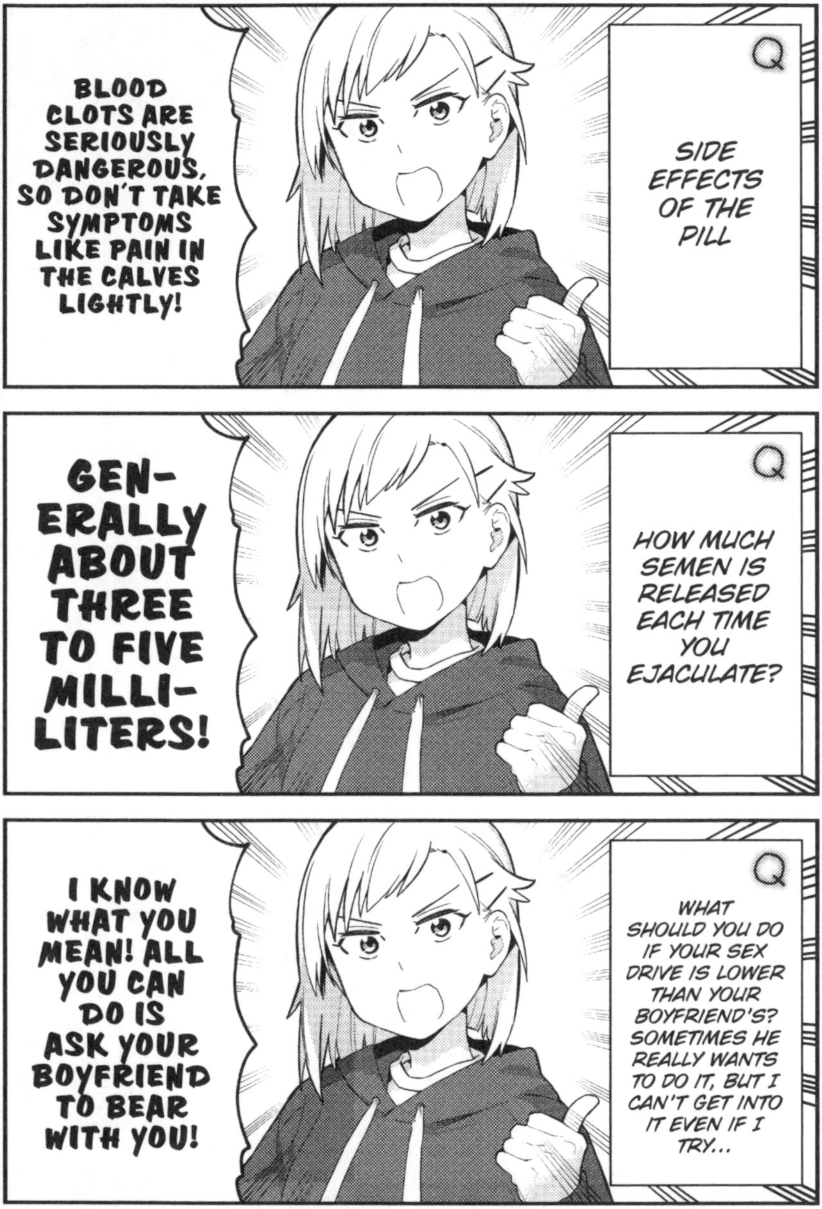
Q
SIDE EFFECTS OF THE PILL
BLOOD CLOTS ARE SERIOUSLY DANGEROUS, SO DON'T TAKE SYMPTOMS LIKE PAIN IN THE CALVES LIGHTLY!
Q
HOW MUCH SEMEN IS RELEASED EACH TIME YOU EJACULATE?
GEN-ERALLY ABOUT THREE TO FIVE MILLI-LITERS!
Q
WHAT SHOULD YOU DO IF YOUR SEX DRIVE IS LOWER THAN YOUR BOYFRIEND'S? SOMETIMES HE REALLY WANTS TO DO IT, BUT I CAN'T GET INTO IT EVEN IF I TRY...
I KNOW WHAT YOU MEAN! ALL YOU CAN DO IS ASK YOUR BOYFRIEND TO BEAR WITH YOU!

[Class 14] **Transgender**

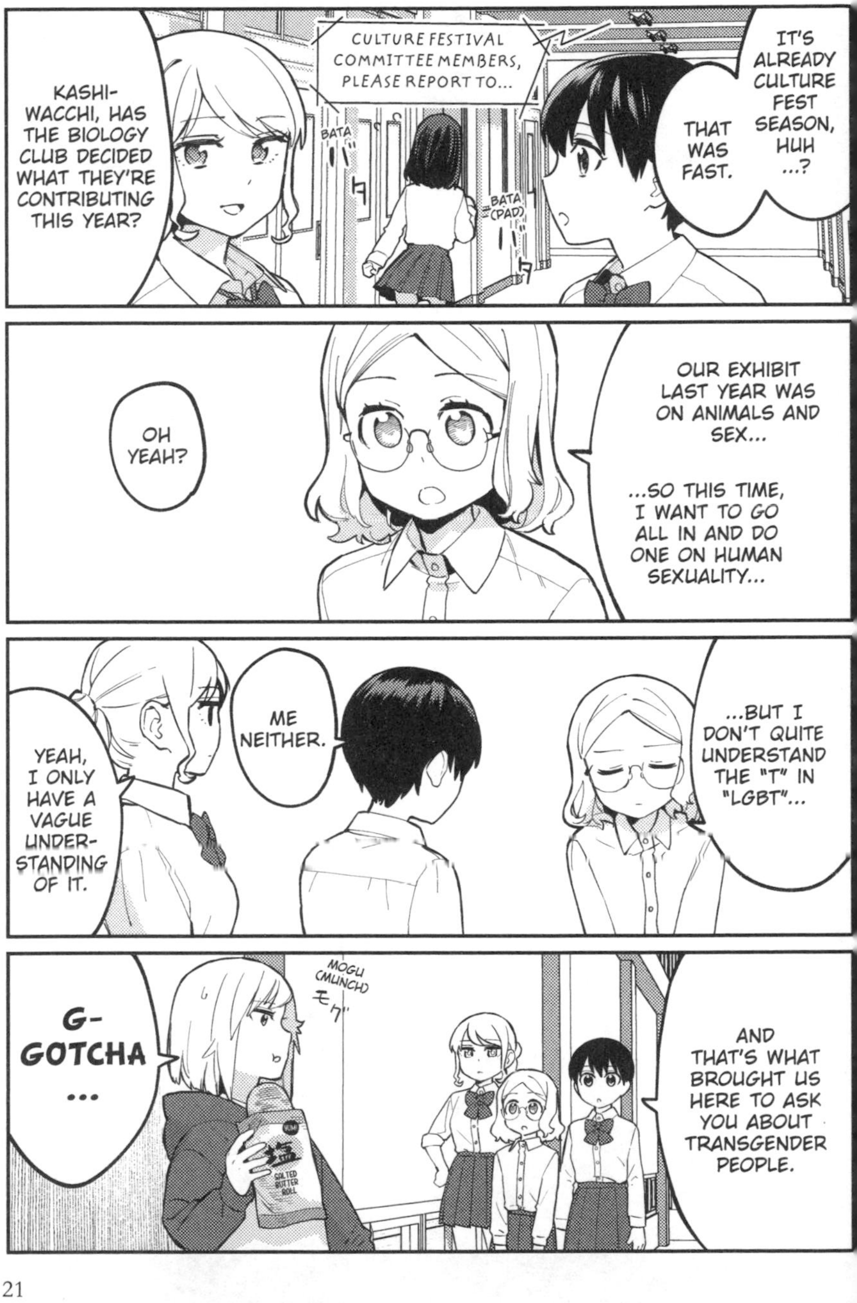
IT'S ALREADY CULTURE FEST SEASON, HUH...?
THAT WAS FAST.
CULTURE FESTIVAL COMMITTEE MEMBERS, PLEASE REPORT TO...
BATA (PAD)
BATA
KASHI-WACCHI, HAS THE BIOLOGY CLUB DECIDED WHAT THEY'RE CONTRIBUTING THIS YEAR?
OUR EXHIBIT LAST YEAR WAS ON ANIMALS AND SEX...
...SO THIS TIME, I WANT TO GO ALL IN AND DO ONE ON HUMAN SEXUALITY...
OH YEAH?
...BUT I DON'T QUITE UNDERSTAND THE "T" IN "LGBT"...
ME NEITHER.
YEAH, I ONLY HAVE A VAGUE UNDER-STANDING OF IT.
AND THAT'S WHAT BROUGHT US HERE TO ASK YOU ABOUT TRANSGENDER PEOPLE.
MOGU (MUNCH)
G-GOTCHA...
SALTED BUTTER ROLL

Class 9
Transgender

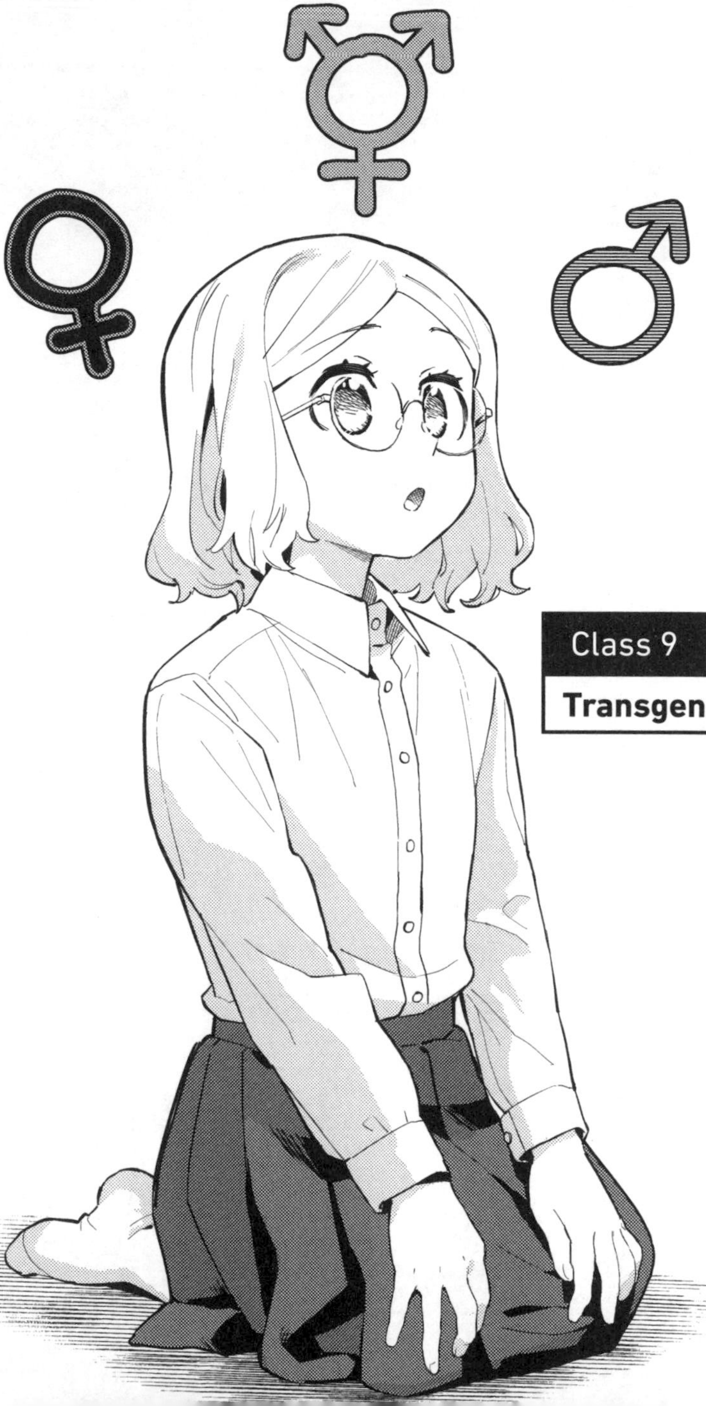

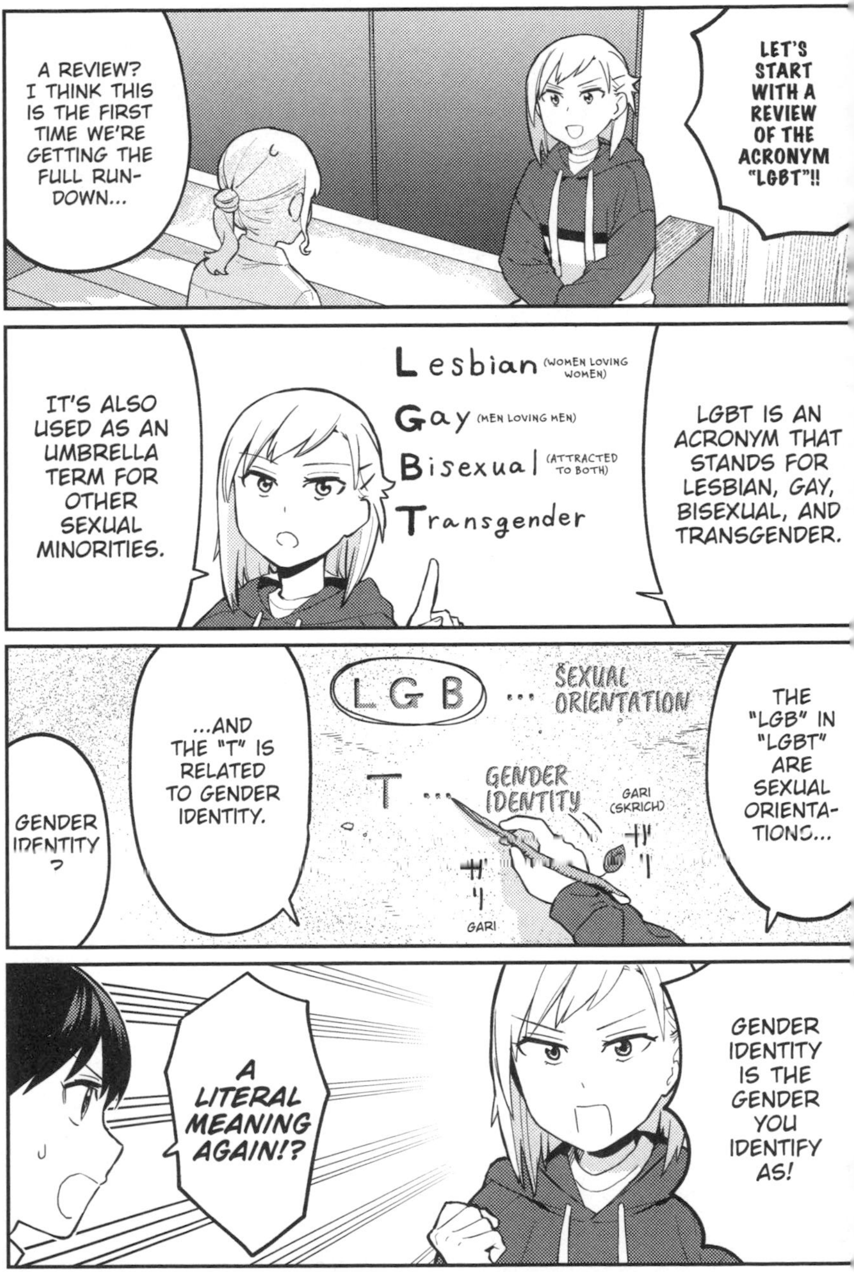
LET'S START WITH A REVIEW OF THE ACRONYM "LGBT"!!
A REVIEW? I THINK THIS IS THE FIRST TIME WE'RE GETTING THE FULL RUN-DOWN...
LGBT IS AN ACRONYM THAT STANDS FOR LESBIAN, GAY, BISEXUAL, AND TRANSGENDER.
Lesbian (WOMEN LOVING WOMEN)
Gay (MEN LOVING MEN)
Bisexual (ATTRACTED TO BOTH)
Transgender
IT'S ALSO USED AS AN UMBRELLA TERM FOR OTHER SEXUAL MINORITIES.
THE "LGB" IN "LGBT" ARE SEXUAL ORIENTATIONS...
LGB ... SEXUAL ORIENTATION
T ... GENDER IDENTITY
GARI (SKRICH)
GARI
...AND THE "T" IS RELATED TO GENDER IDENTITY.
GENDER IDENTITY?
GENDER IDENTITY IS THE GENDER YOU IDENTIFY AS!
A LITERAL MEANING AGAIN!?

Trans and Cis

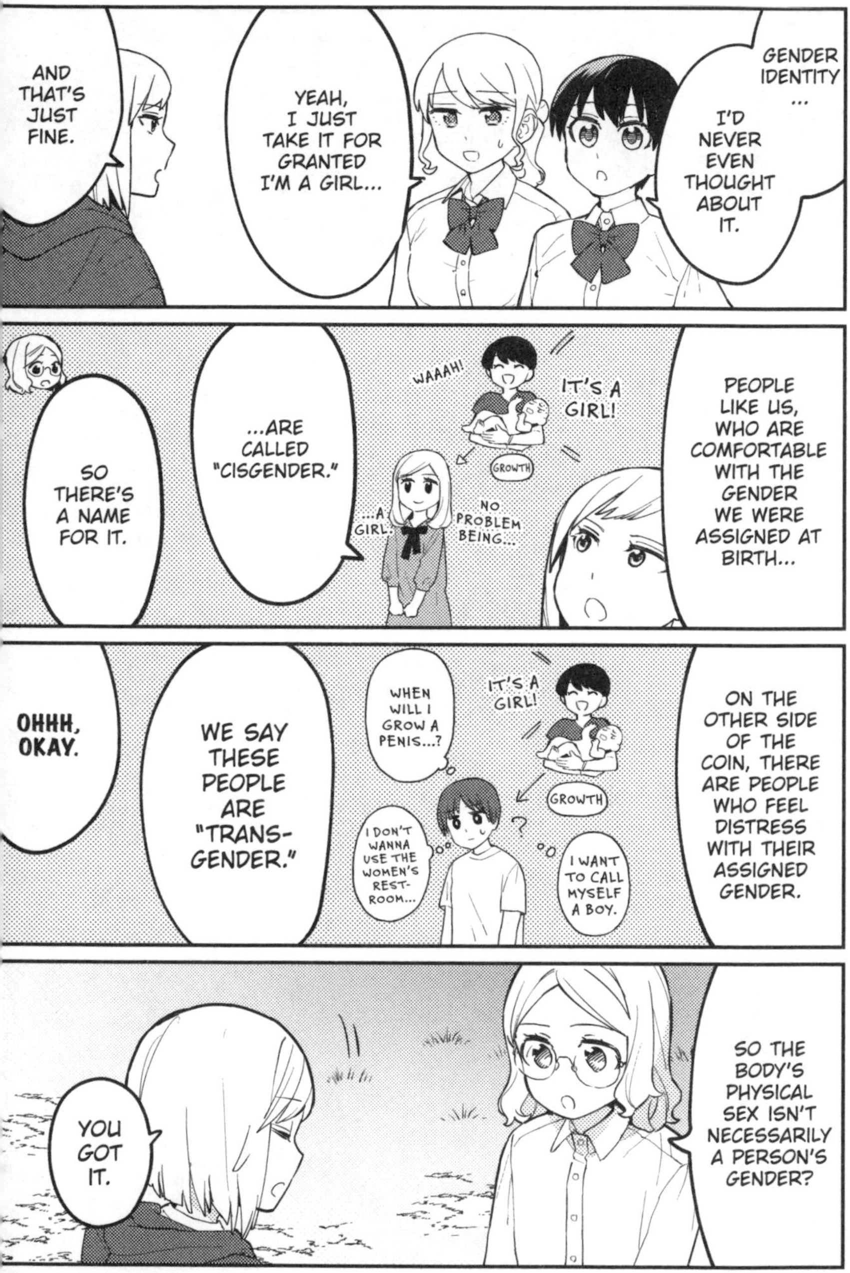
GENDER IDENTITY...
I'D NEVER EVEN THOUGHT ABOUT IT.
YEAH, I JUST TAKE IT FOR GRANTED I'M A GIRL...
AND THAT'S JUST FINE.
PEOPLE LIKE US, WHO ARE COMFORTABLE WITH THE GENDER WE WERE ASSIGNED AT BIRTH...
IT'S A GIRL!
WAAAH!
GROWTH
NO PROBLEM BEING...
...A GIRL.
...ARE CALLED "CISGENDER."
SO THERE'S A NAME FOR IT.
ON THE OTHER SIDE OF THE COIN, THERE ARE PEOPLE WHO FEEL DISTRESS WITH THEIR ASSIGNED GENDER.
IT'S A GIRL!
WHEN WILL I GROW A PENIS...?
GROWTH
I WANT TO CALL MYSELF A BOY.
I DON'T WANNA USE THE WOMEN'S REST-ROOM...
WE SAY THESE PEOPLE ARE "TRANS-GENDER."
OHHH, OKAY.
SO THE BODY'S PHYSICAL SEX ISN'T NECESSARILY A PERSON'S GENDER?
YOU GOT IT.

Different Trans Experiences

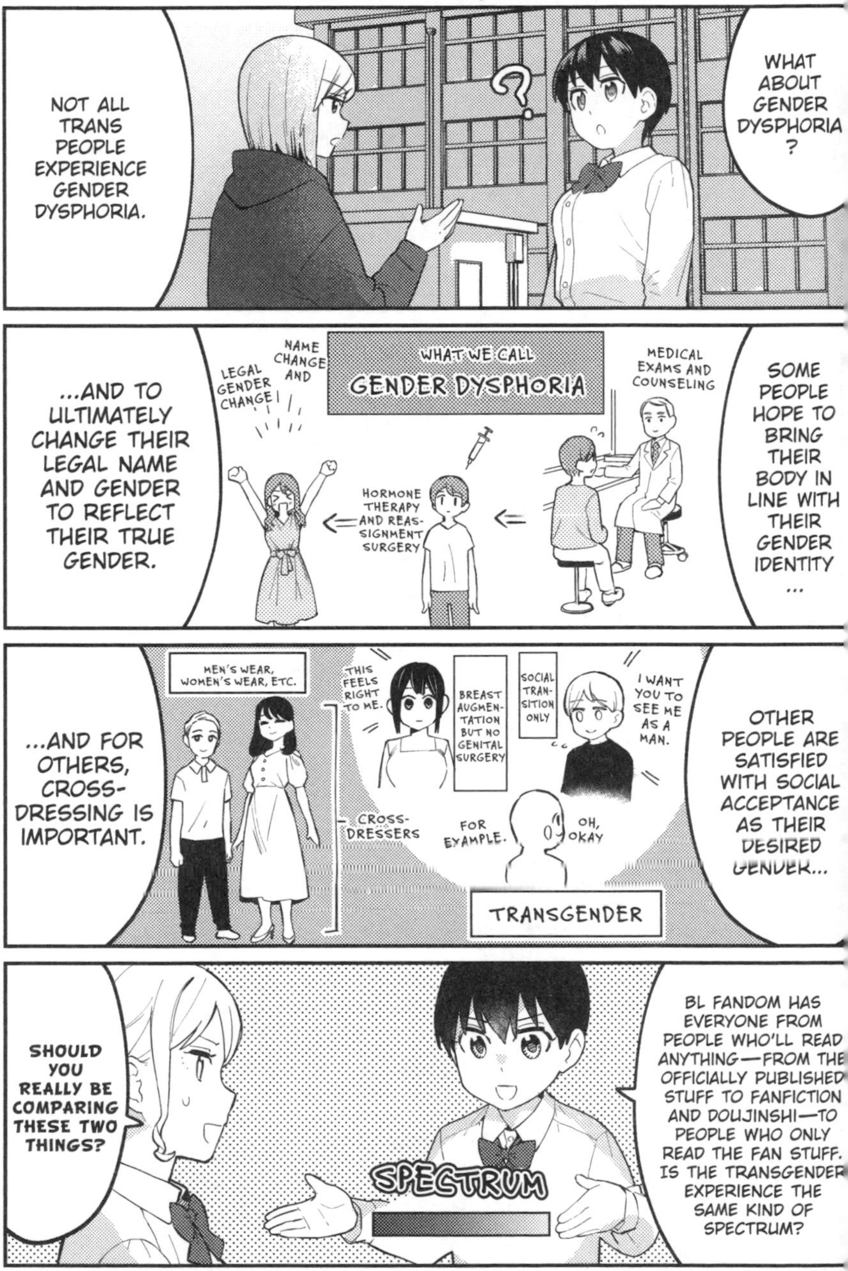
WHAT ABOUT GENDER DYSPHORIA?
NOT ALL TRANS PEOPLE EXPERIENCE GENDER DYSPHORIA.
SOME PEOPLE HOPE TO BRING THEIR BODY IN LINE WITH THEIR GENDER IDENTITY...
MEDICAL EXAMS AND COUNSELING
WHAT WE CALL
GENDER DYSPHORIA
HORMONE THERAPY AND REAS-SIGNMENT SURGERY
NAME CHANGE AND
LEGAL GENDER CHANGE
...AND TO ULTIMATELY CHANGE THEIR LEGAL NAME AND GENDER TO REFLECT THEIR TRUE GENDER.
OTHER PEOPLE ARE SATISFIED WITH SOCIAL ACCEPTANCE AS THEIR DESIRED GENDER...
I WANT YOU TO SEE ME AS A MAN.
SOCIAL TRAN-SITION ONLY
BREAST AUGMEN-TATION BUT NO GENITAL SURGERY
THIS FEELS RIGHT TO ME.
OH, OKAY
FOR EXAMPLE.
TRANSGENDER
MEN'S WEAR, WOMEN'S WEAR, ETC.
CROSS-DRESSERS
...AND FOR OTHERS, CROSS-DRESSING IS IMPORTANT.
BL FANDOM HAS EVERYONE FROM PEOPLE WHO'LL READ ANYTHING—FROM THE OFFICIALLY PUBLISHED STUFF TO FANFICTION AND DOUJINSHI—TO PEOPLE WHO ONLY READ THE FAN STUFF. IS THE TRANSGENDER EXPERIENCE THE SAME KIND OF SPECTRUM?
SPECTRUM
SHOULD YOU REALLY BE COMPARING THESE TWO THINGS?

The Opposite Sex at an All-Girls School

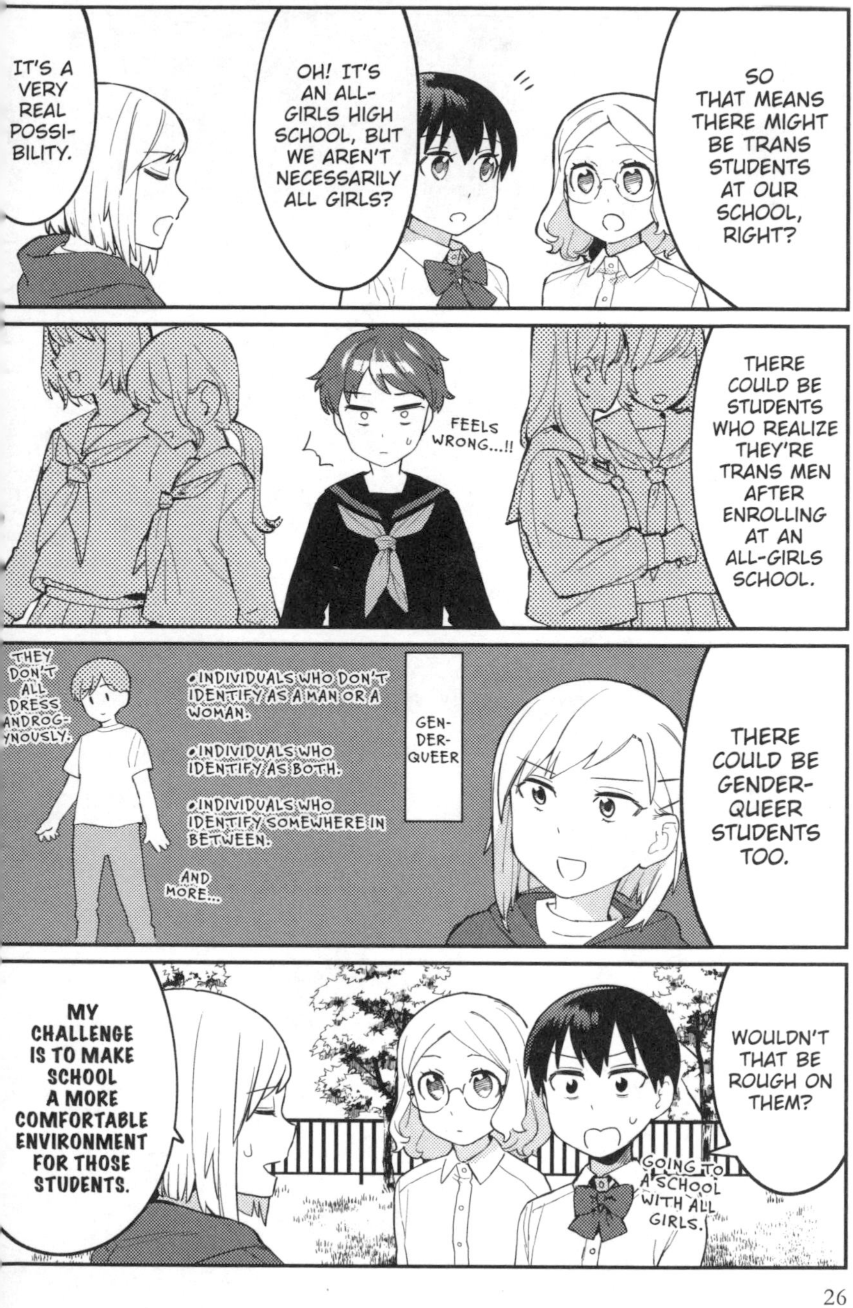

SO THAT MEANS THERE MIGHT BE TRANS STUDENTS AT OUR SCHOOL, RIGHT?
OH! IT'S AN ALL-GIRLS HIGH SCHOOL, BUT WE AREN'T NECESSARILY ALL GIRLS?
IT'S A VERY REAL POSSIBILITY.
THERE COULD BE STUDENTS WHO REALIZE THEY'RE TRANS MEN AFTER ENROLLING AT AN ALL-GIRLS SCHOOL.
FEELS WRONG...!!
THERE COULD BE GENDER-QUEER STUDENTS TOO.
GEN-DER-QUEER
• INDIVIDUALS WHO DON'T IDENTIFY AS A MAN OR A WOMAN.
• INDIVIDUALS WHO IDENTIFY AS BOTH.
• INDIVIDUALS WHO IDENTIFY SOMEWHERE IN BETWEEN.
AND MORE...
THEY DON'T ALL DRESS ANDROG-YNOUSLY.
WOULDN'T THAT BE ROUGH ON THEM?
GOING TO A SCHOOL WITH ALL GIRLS.
MY CHALLENGE IS TO MAKE SCHOOL A MORE COMFORTABLE ENVIRONMENT FOR THOSE STUDENTS.

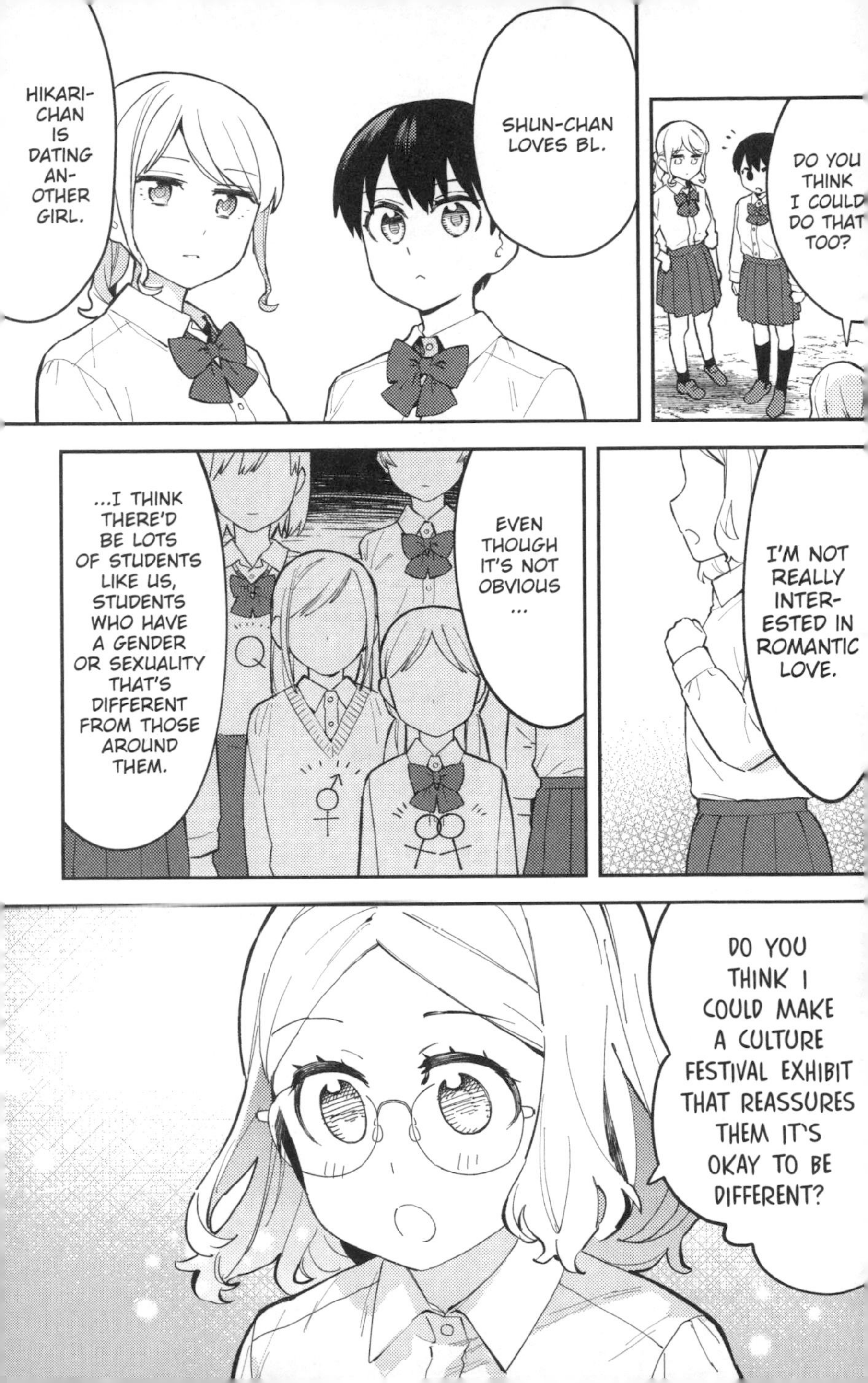
DO YOU THINK I COULD DO THAT TOO?
SHUN-CHAN LOVES BL.
HIKARI-CHAN IS DATING AN-OTHER GIRL.
I'M NOT REALLY INTER-ESTED IN ROMANTIC LOVE.
EVEN THOUGH IT'S NOT OBVIOUS ...
...I THINK THERE'D BE LOTS OF STUDENTS LIKE US, STUDENTS WHO HAVE A GENDER OR SEXUALITY THAT'S DIFFERENT FROM THOSE AROUND THEM.
DO YOU THINK I COULD MAKE A CULTURE FESTIVAL EXHIBIT THAT REASSURES THEM IT'S OKAY TO BE DIFFERENT?

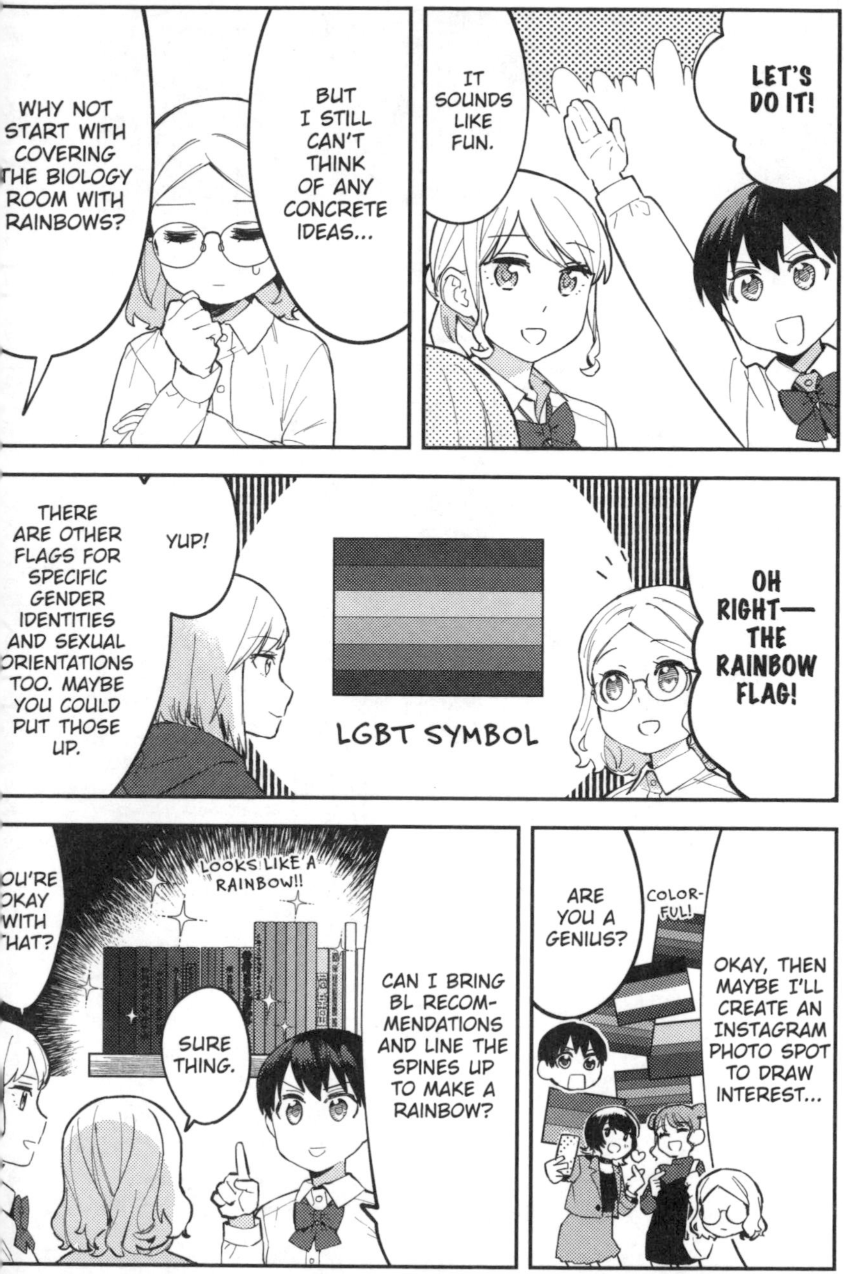
LET'S DO IT!
IT SOUNDS LIKE FUN.
BUT I STILL CAN'T THINK OF ANY CONCRETE IDEAS...
WHY NOT START WITH COVERING THE BIOLOGY ROOM WITH RAINBOWS?
OH RIGHT—THE RAINBOW FLAG!
LGBT SYMBOL
YUP!
THERE ARE OTHER FLAGS FOR SPECIFIC GENDER IDENTITIES AND SEXUAL ORIENTATIONS TOO. MAYBE YOU COULD PUT THOSE UP.
OKAY, THEN MAYBE I'LL CREATE AN INSTAGRAM PHOTO SPOT TO DRAW INTEREST...
COLOR-FUL!
ARE YOU A GENIUS?
CAN I BRING BL RECOM-MENDATIONS AND LINE THE SPINES UP TO MAKE A RAINBOW?
SURE THING.
LOOKS LIKE A RAINBOW!!
OU'RE OKAY WITH HAT?

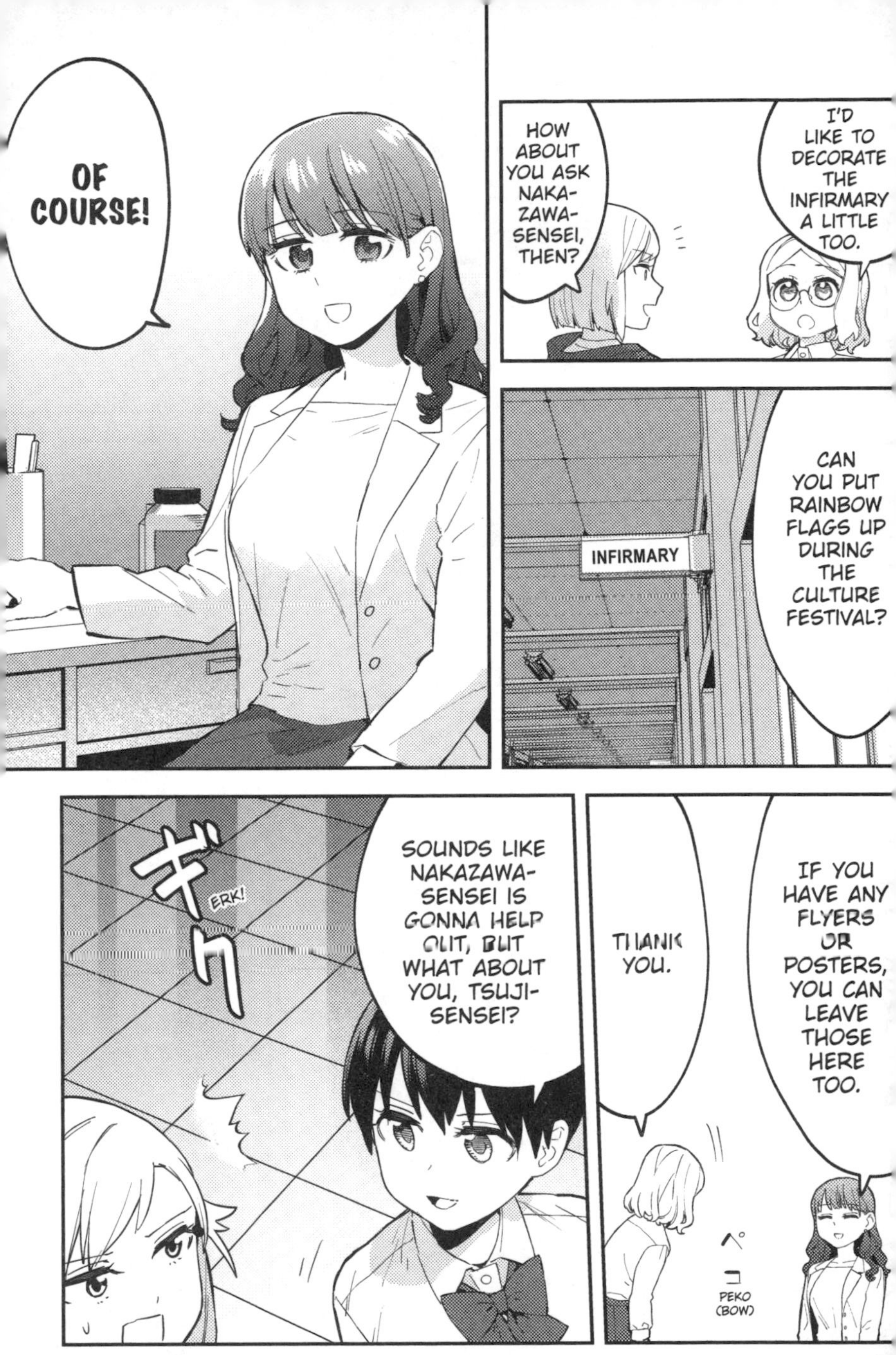
I'D LIKE TO DECORATE THE INFIRMARY A LITTLE TOO.
HOW ABOUT YOU ASK NAKAZAWA-SENSEI, THEN?
CAN YOU PUT RAINBOW FLAGS UP DURING THE CULTURE FESTIVAL?
INFIRMARY
OF COURSE!
IF YOU HAVE ANY FLYERS OR POSTERS, YOU CAN LEAVE THOSE HERE TOO.
THANK YOU.
ペコ
PEKO (BOW)
SOUNDS LIKE NAKAZAWA-SENSEI IS GONNA HELP OUT, BUT WHAT ABOUT YOU, TSUJI-SENSEI?
ギク
ERK!

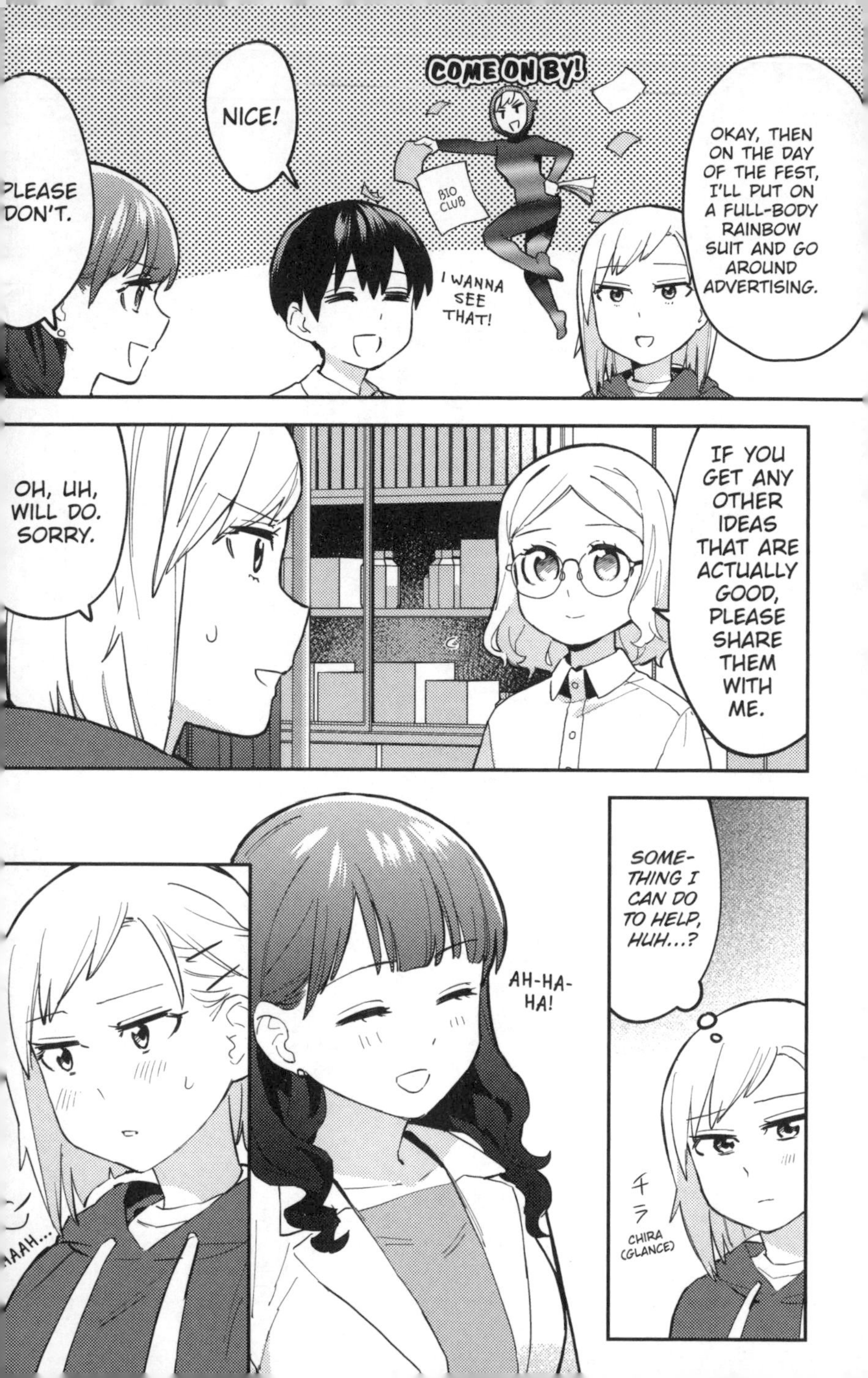
OKAY, THEN ON THE DAY OF THE FEST, I'LL PUT ON A FULL-BODY RAINBOW SUIT AND GO AROUND ADVERTISING.
COME ON BY!
BIO CLUB
I WANNA SEE THAT!
NICE!
PLEASE DON'T.
IF YOU GET ANY OTHER IDEAS THAT ARE ACTUALLY GOOD, PLEASE SHARE THEM WITH ME.
OH, UH, WILL DO. SORRY.
SOME-THING I CAN DO TO HELP, HUH...?
チラ
CHIRA (GLANCE)
AH-HA-HA!
AAAH...

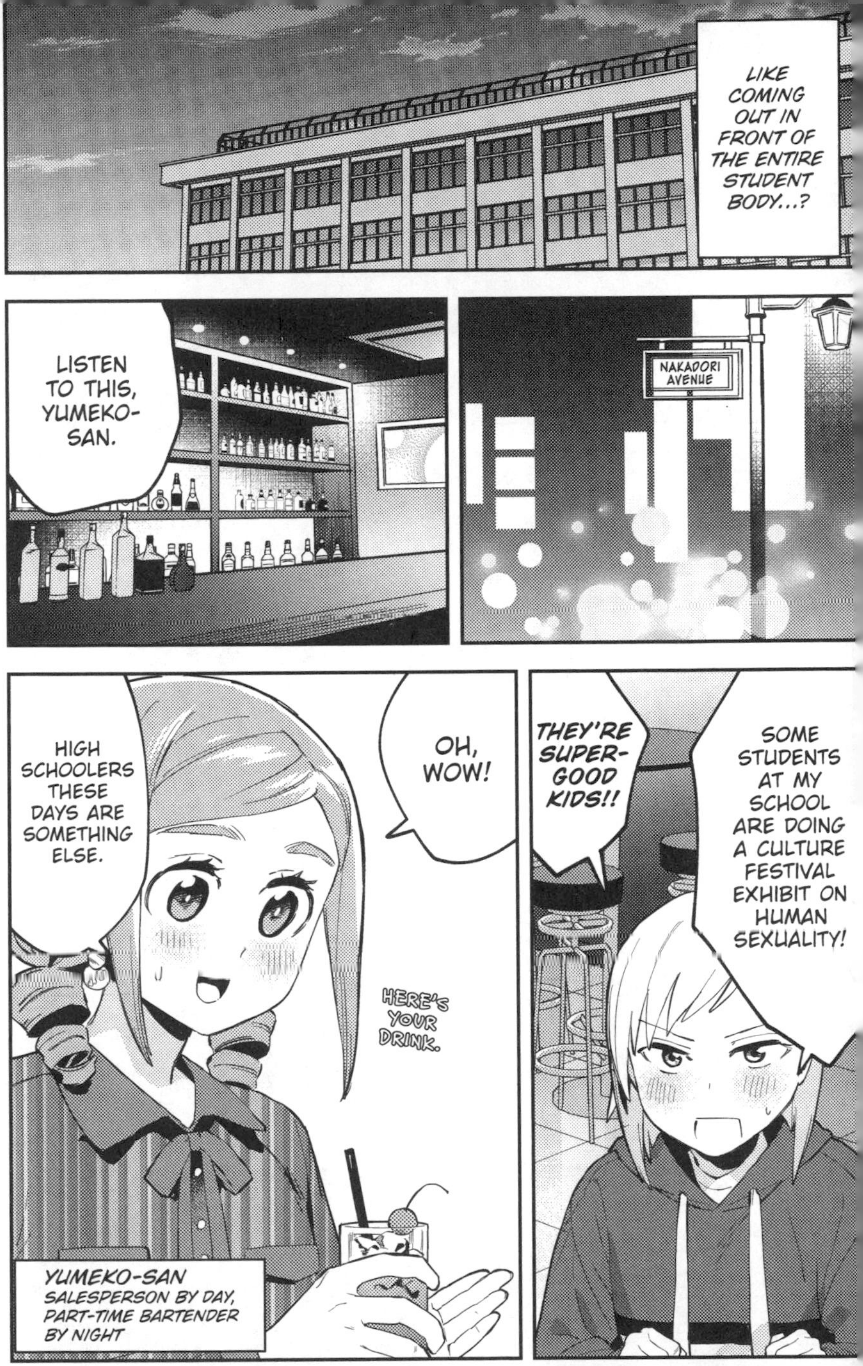
LIKE COMING OUT IN FRONT OF THE ENTIRE STUDENT BODY...?
NAKADORI AVENUE
LISTEN TO THIS, YUMEKO-SAN.
SOME STUDENTS AT MY SCHOOL ARE DOING A CULTURE FESTIVAL EXHIBIT ON HUMAN SEXUALITY!
THEY'RE SUPER-GOOD KIDS!!
OH, WOW!
HIGH SCHOOLERS THESE DAYS ARE SOMETHING ELSE.
HERE'S YOUR DRINK.
YUMEKO-SAN
SALESPERSON BY DAY, PART-TIME BARTENDER BY NIGHT

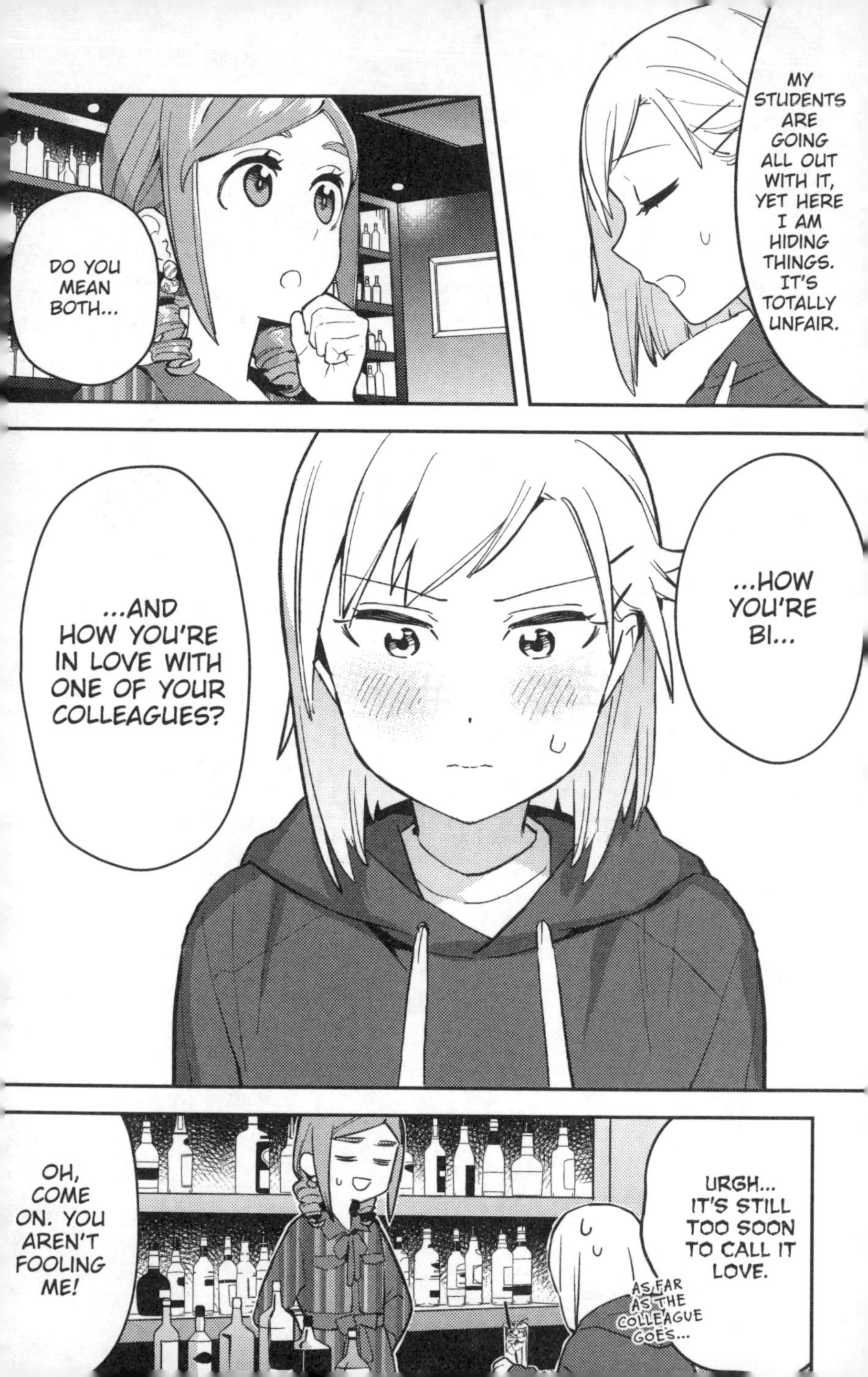
MY STUDENTS ARE GOING ALL OUT WITH IT, YET HERE I AM HIDING THINGS. IT'S TOTALLY UNFAIR.
DO YOU MEAN BOTH...
...HOW YOU'RE BI...
...AND HOW YOU'RE IN LOVE WITH ONE OF YOUR COLLEAGUES?
URGH... IT'S STILL TOO SOON TO CALL IT LOVE.
AS FAR AS THE COLLEAGUE GOES...
OH, COME ON. YOU AREN'T FOOLING ME!

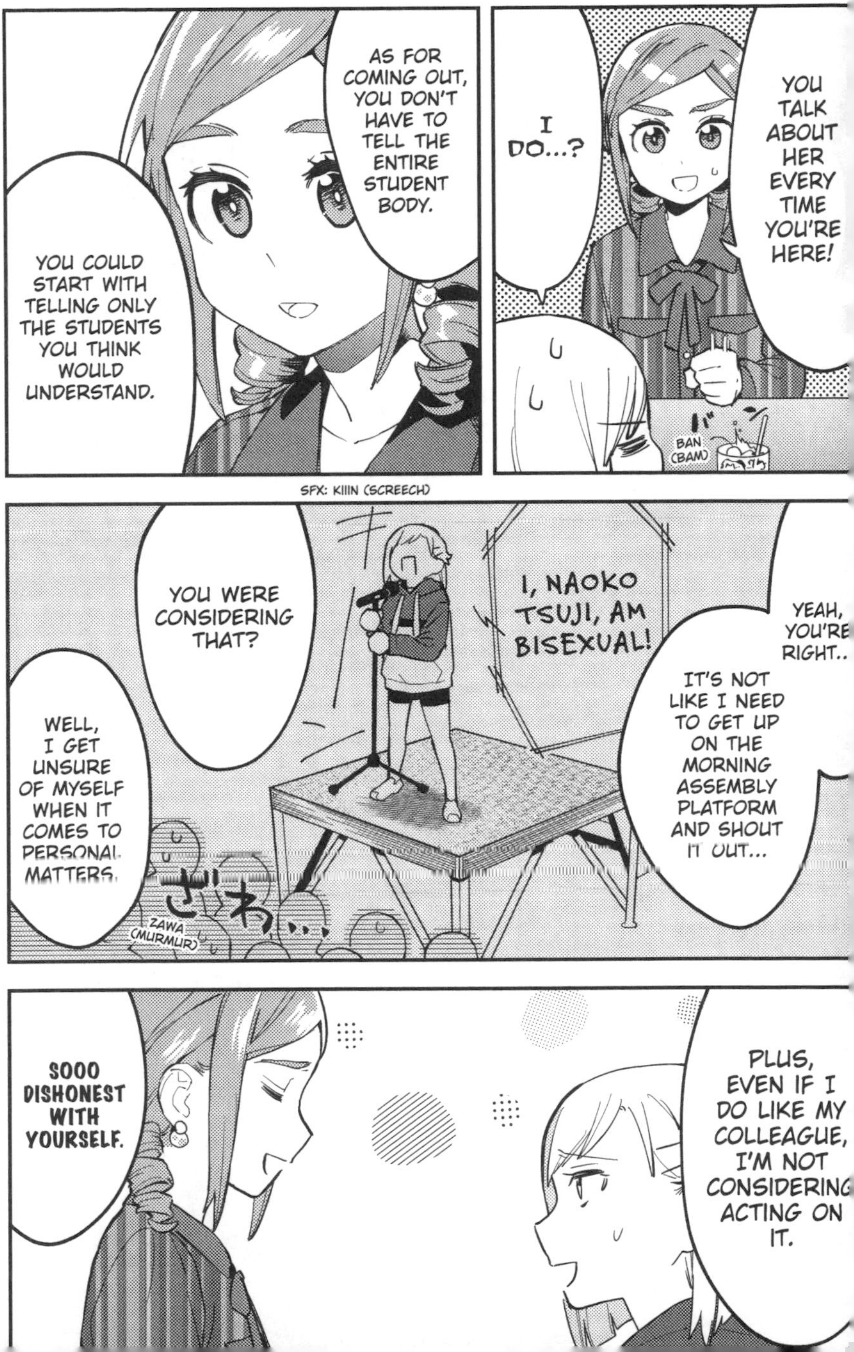
YOU TALK ABOUT HER EVERY TIME YOU'RE HERE!
I DO...?
BAN (BAM)
AS FOR COMING OUT, YOU DON'T HAVE TO TELL THE ENTIRE STUDENT BODY.
YOU COULD START WITH TELLING ONLY THE STUDENTS YOU THINK WOULD UNDERSTAND.
SFX: KIIIN (SCREECH)
YEAH, YOU'RE RIGHT..
IT'S NOT LIKE I NEED TO GET UP ON THE MORNING ASSEMBLY PLATFORM AND SHOUT IT OUT...
I, NAOKO TSUJI, AM BISEXUAL!
YOU WERE CONSIDERING THAT?
WELL, I GET UNSURE OF MYSELF WHEN IT COMES TO PERSONAL MATTERS.
ZAWA (MURMUR)
PLUS, EVEN IF I DO LIKE MY COLLEAGUE, I'M NOT CONSIDERING ACTING ON IT.
SOOO DISHONEST WITH YOURSELF.

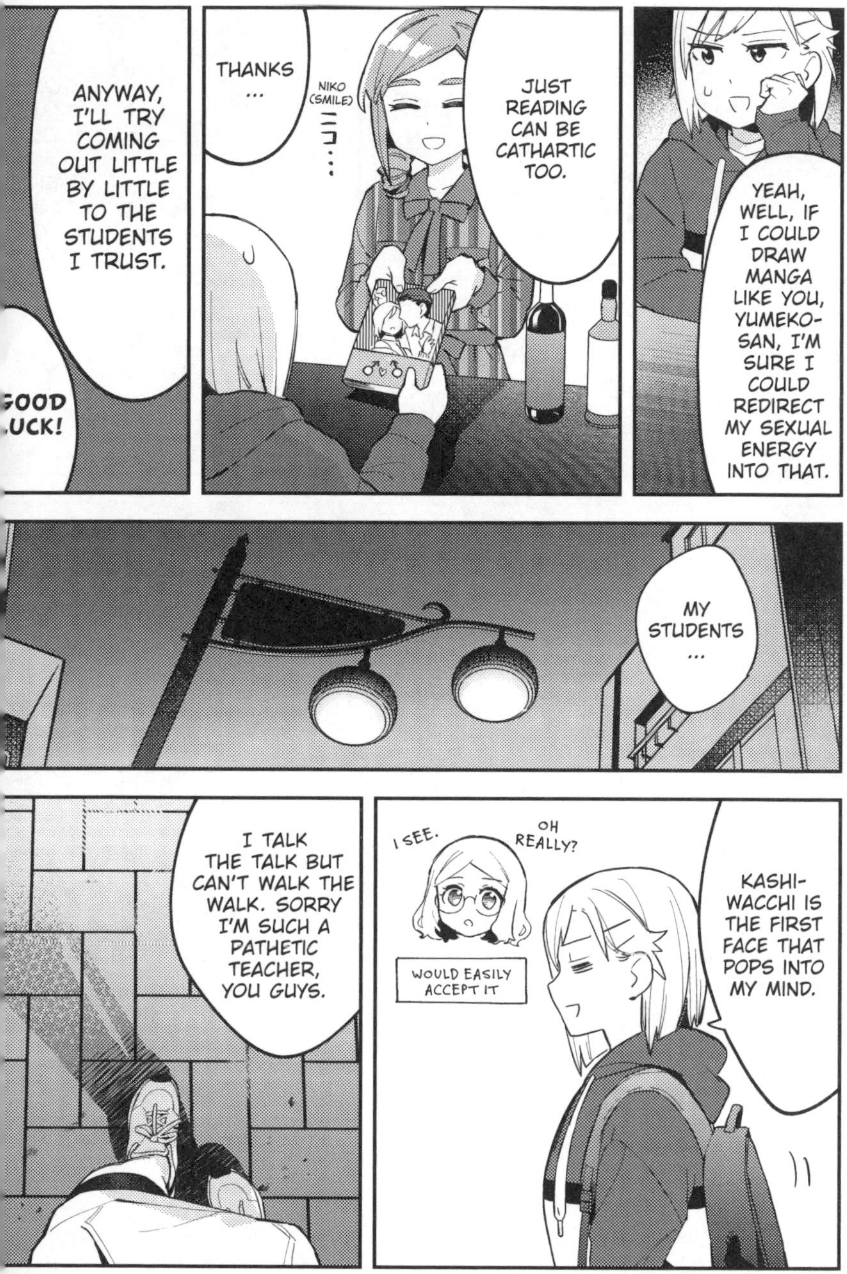
YEAH, WELL, IF I COULD DRAW MANGA LIKE YOU, YUMEKO-SAN, I'M SURE I COULD REDIRECT MY SEXUAL ENERGY INTO THAT.
JUST READING CAN BE CATHARTIC TOO.
NIKO (SMILE)
ニコ…
THANKS ...
ANYWAY, I'LL TRY COMING OUT LITTLE BY LITTLE TO THE STUDENTS I TRUST.
OOD UCK!
MY STUDENTS ...
KASHI-WACCHI IS THE FIRST FACE THAT POPS INTO MY MIND.
OH REALLY?
I SEE.
WOULD EASILY ACCEPT IT
I TALK THE TALK BUT CAN'T WALK THE WALK. SORRY I'M SUCH A PATHETIC TEACHER, YOU GUYS.

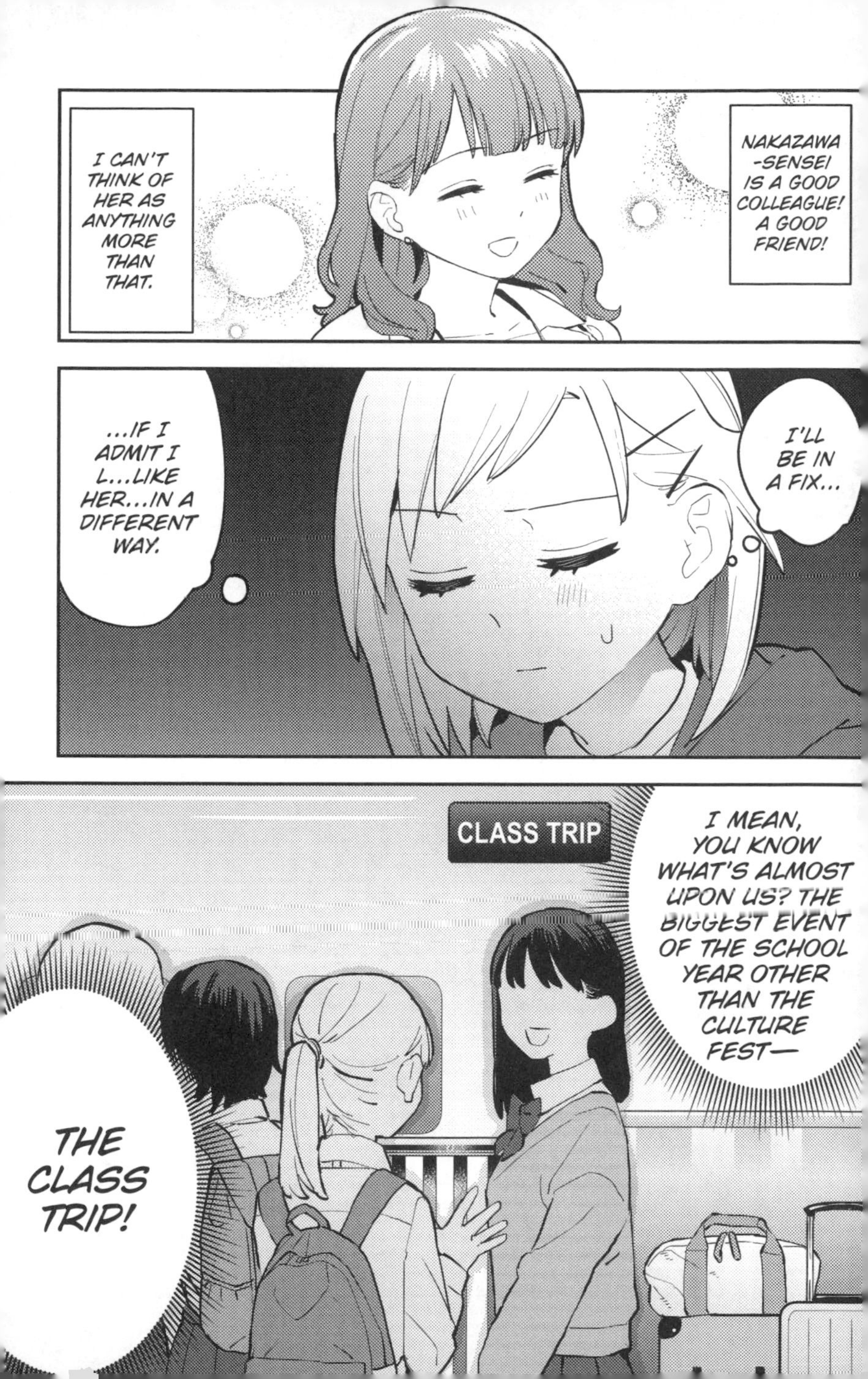
NAKAZAWA-SENSEI IS A GOOD COLLEAGUE! A GOOD FRIEND!
I CAN'T THINK OF HER AS ANYTHING MORE THAN THAT.
I'LL BE IN A FIX...
...IF I ADMIT I L...LIKE HER...IN A DIFFERENT WAY.
I MEAN, YOU KNOW WHAT'S ALMOST UPON US? THE BIGGEST EVENT OF THE SCHOOL YEAR OTHER THAN THE CULTURE FEST—
CLASS TRIP
THE CLASS TRIP!

ROOM
ASSIGNMENTS

ROOM 302	ROOM 303
TSUJI-SENSEI	SAITOU-SENSEI
NAKAZAWA-SENSEI	TANAKA-SENSEI

OH CRAP!

NAKAZAWA-SENSEI WEARING HOTEL ROOMWEAR

...AND SOMEHOW, I WOUND UP ASSIGNED AS HER ROOMMATE ON IT!

THERE'S NOTHING AWKWARD ABOUT THAT!

PLUS, ANY SICK STUDENTS WILL COME TO OUR ROOM.

NO, COME ON. WE'LL HAVE PATROL. AND MEETINGS UNTIL LATE AT NIGHT. AND WE'LL HAVE TO GET UP AT FIVE IN THE MORNING.

NEXT TIME: THE CLASS TRIP!

OOPS, I GAVE MYSELF A TUMMY ACHE!

A TERRIBLE THOUGHT FOR A TEACHER

SOMEBODY COME BY! MATSUDA, GET SICK AND COME TO SEE THE NURSE!

Class 14 Candid Shot

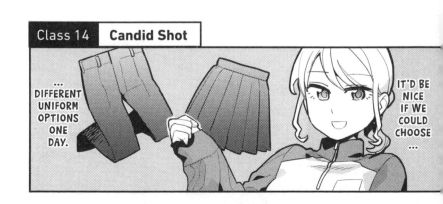

IT'D BE NICE IF WE COULD CHOOSE ...
... DIFFERENT UNIFORM OPTIONS ONE DAY.

Knocking Out 12 Sex Concerns! 2

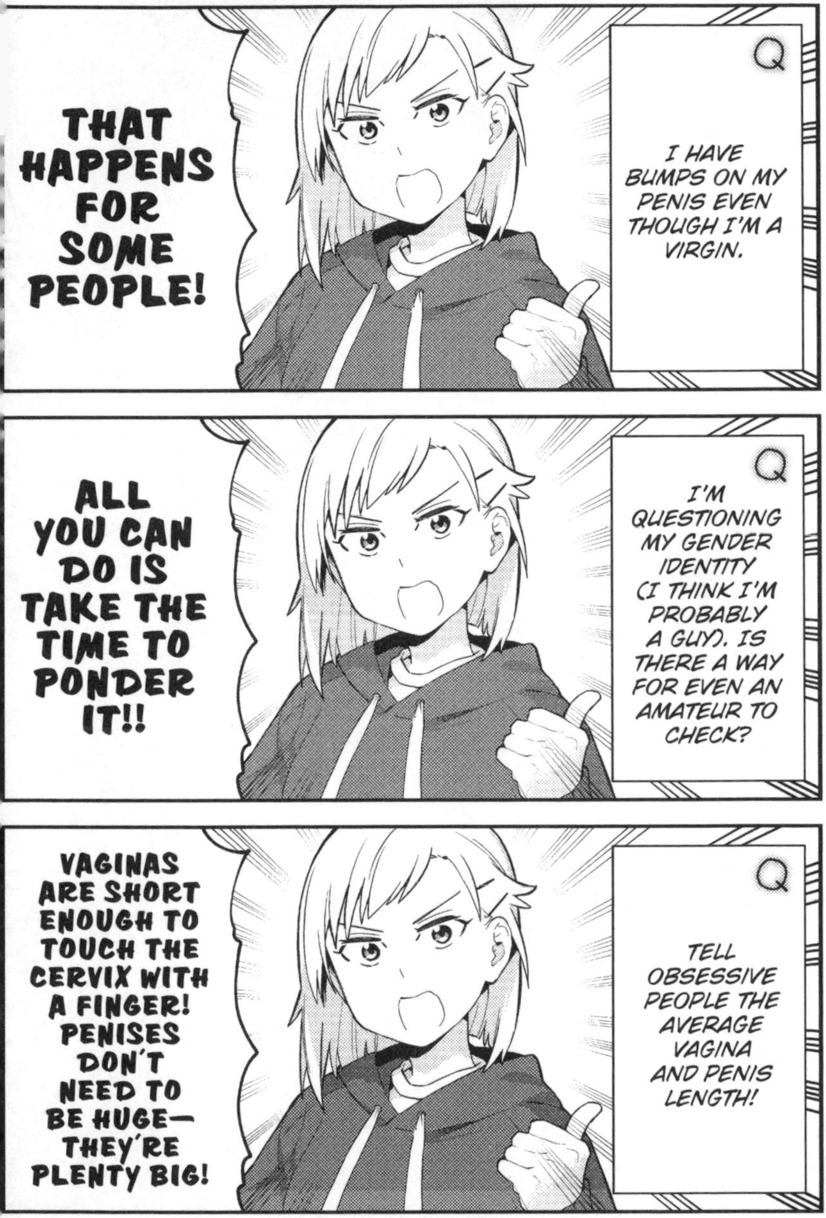
Q
I HAVE BUMPS ON MY PENIS EVEN THOUGH I'M A VIRGIN.
THAT HAPPENS FOR SOME PEOPLE!
Q
I'M QUESTIONING MY GENDER IDENTITY (I THINK I'M PROBABLY A GUY). IS THERE A WAY FOR EVEN AN AMATEUR TO CHECK?
ALL YOU CAN DO IS TAKE THE TIME TO PONDER IT!!
Q
TELL OBSESSIVE PEOPLE THE AVERAGE VAGINA AND PENIS LENGTH!
VAGINAS ARE SHORT ENOUGH TO TOUCH THE CERVIX WITH A FINGER! PENISES DON'T NEED TO BE HUGE—THEY'RE PLENTY BIG!

[Class 15] **LGBT History**

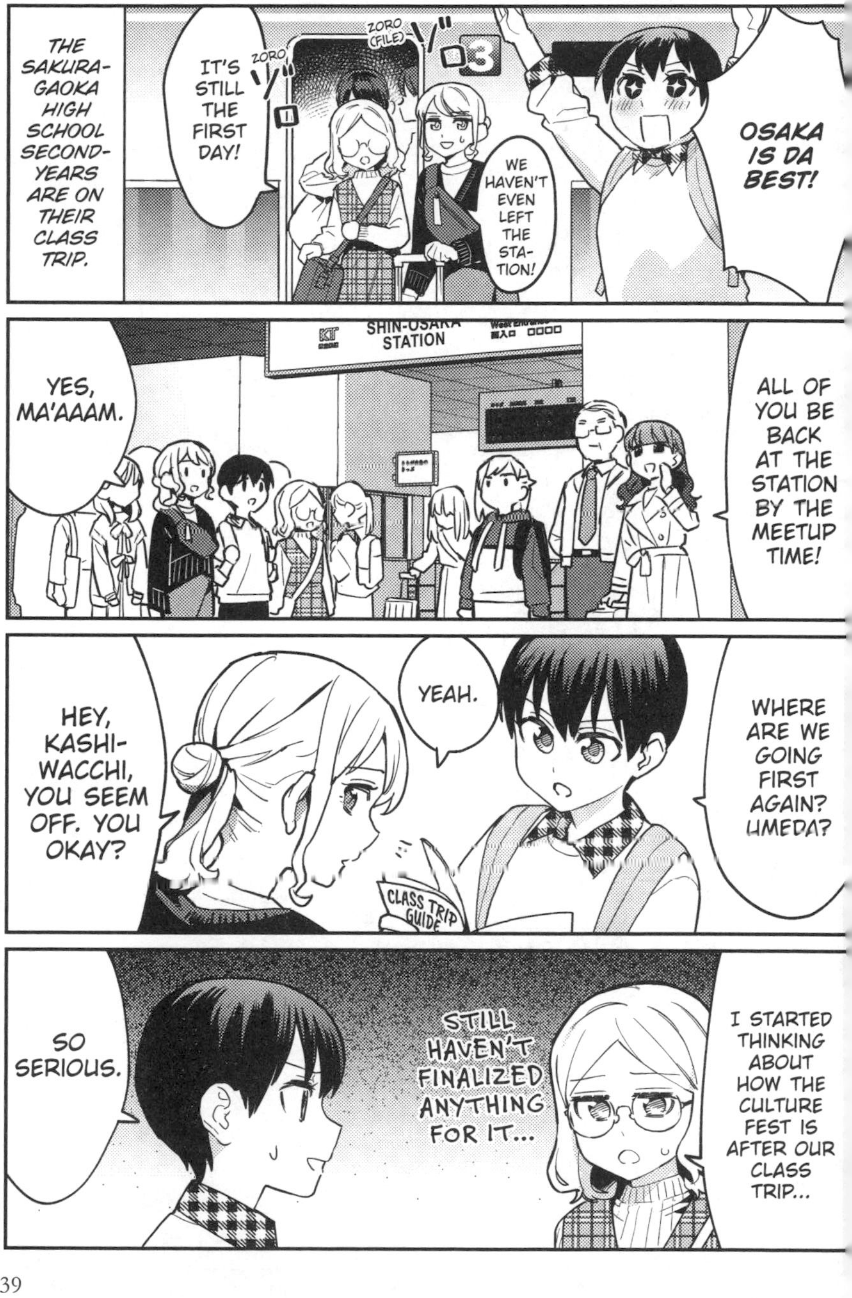
OSAKA IS DA BEST!
ZORO (FILE)
WE HAVEN'T EVEN LEFT THE STATION!
ZORO
IT'S STILL THE FIRST DAY!
THE SAKURA-GAOKA HIGH SCHOOL SECOND-YEARS ARE ON THEIR CLASS TRIP.
SHIN-OSAKA STATION
West Entrance
ALL OF YOU BE BACK AT THE STATION BY THE MEETUP TIME!
YES, MA'AAAM.
WHERE ARE WE GOING FIRST AGAIN? UMEDA?
YEAH.
HEY, KASHI-WACCHI, YOU SEEM OFF. YOU OKAY?
CLASS TRIP GUIDE
I STARTED THINKING ABOUT HOW THE CULTURE FEST IS AFTER OUR CLASS TRIP...
STILL HAVEN'T FINALIZED ANYTHING FOR IT...
SO SERIOUS.

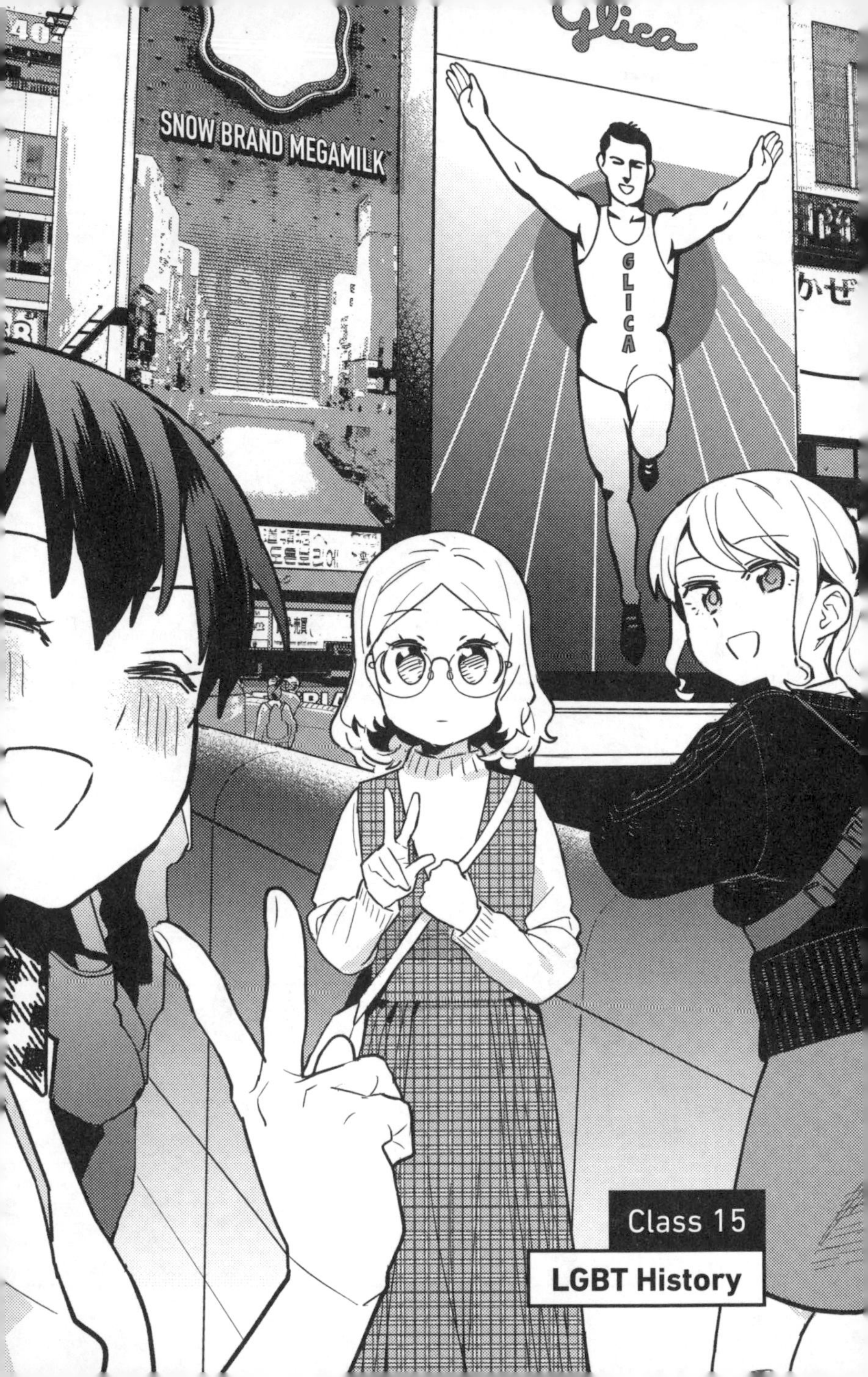
Glica
SNOW BRAND MEGAMILK
GLICA

Class 15

LGBT History

Adult Tourist Destination

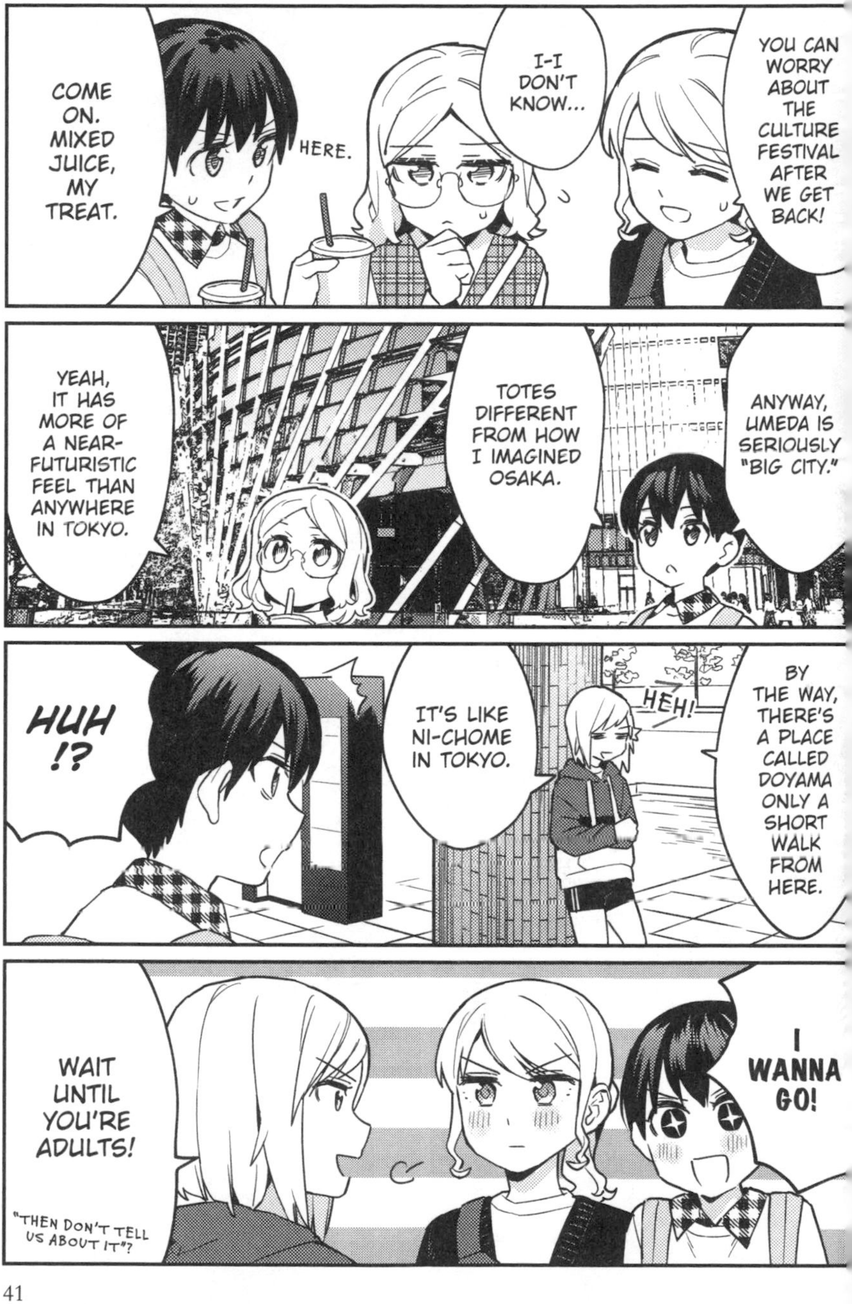
YOU CAN WORRY ABOUT THE CULTURE FESTIVAL AFTER WE GET BACK!
I-I DON'T KNOW...
HERE.
COME ON. MIXED JUICE, MY TREAT.
ANYWAY, UMEDA IS SERIOUSLY "BIG CITY."
TOTES DIFFERENT FROM HOW I IMAGINED OSAKA.
YEAH, IT HAS MORE OF A NEAR-FUTURISTIC FEEL THAN ANYWHERE IN TOKYO.
BY THE WAY, THERE'S A PLACE CALLED DOYAMA ONLY A SHORT WALK FROM HERE.
HEH!
IT'S LIKE NI-CHOME IN TOKYO.
HUH!?
I WANNA GO!
WAIT UNTIL YOU'RE ADULTS!
"THEN DON'T TELL US ABOUT IT"?

Only There?

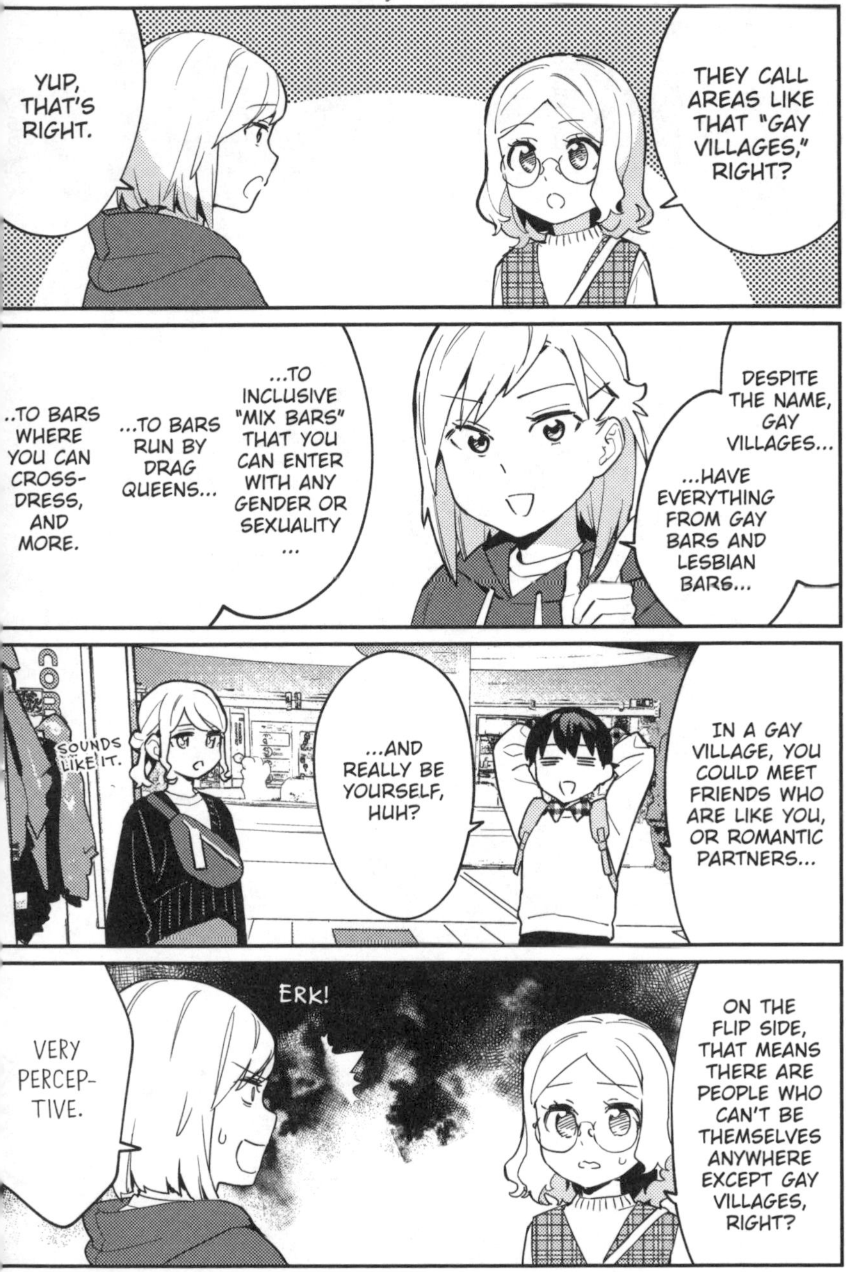

THEY CALL AREAS LIKE THAT "GAY VILLAGES," RIGHT?
YUP, THAT'S RIGHT.
DESPITE THE NAME, GAY VILLAGES...
...HAVE EVERYTHING FROM GAY BARS AND LESBIAN BARS...
...TO INCLUSIVE "MIX BARS" THAT YOU CAN ENTER WITH ANY GENDER OR SEXUALITY ...
...TO BARS RUN BY DRAG QUEENS...
..TO BARS WHERE YOU CAN CROSS-DRESS, AND MORE.
IN A GAY VILLAGE, YOU COULD MEET FRIENDS WHO ARE LIKE YOU, OR ROMANTIC PARTNERS...
...AND REALLY BE YOURSELF, HUH?
SOUNDS LIKE IT.
ON THE FLIP SIDE, THAT MEANS THERE ARE PEOPLE WHO CAN'T BE THEMSELVES ANYWHERE EXCEPT GAY VILLAGES, RIGHT?
ERK!
VERY PERCEPTIVE.

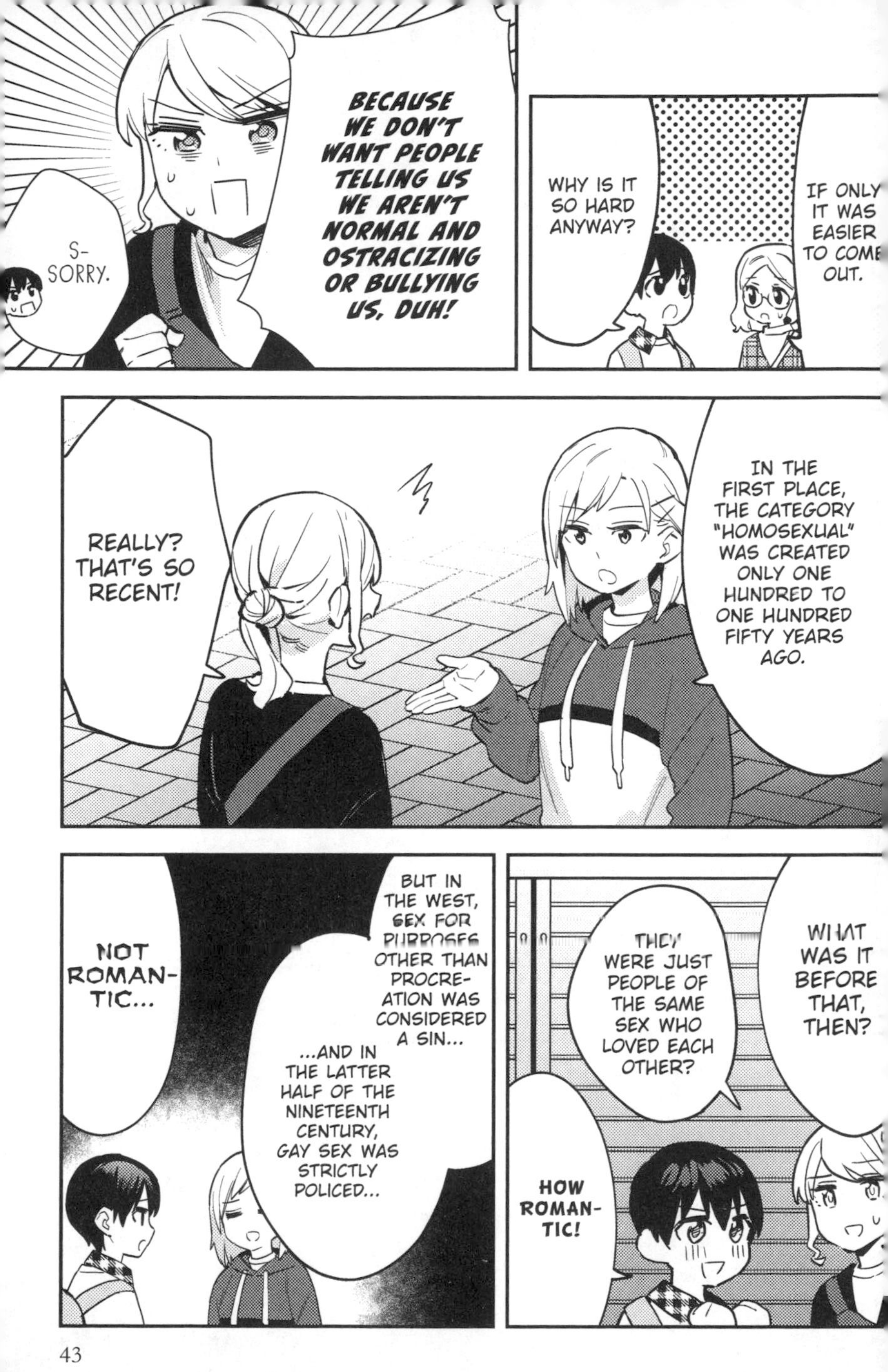
IF ONLY IT WAS EASIER TO COME OUT.
WHY IS IT SO HARD ANYWAY?
BECAUSE WE DON'T WANT PEOPLE TELLING US WE AREN'T NORMAL AND OSTRACIZING OR BULLYING US, DUH!
S-SORRY.
IN THE FIRST PLACE, THE CATEGORY "HOMOSEXUAL" WAS CREATED ONLY ONE HUNDRED TO ONE HUNDRED FIFTY YEARS AGO.
REALLY? THAT'S SO RECENT!
WHAT WAS IT BEFORE THAT, THEN?
THEY WERE JUST PEOPLE OF THE SAME SEX WHO LOVED EACH OTHER?
HOW ROMANTIC!
BUT IN THE WEST, SEX FOR PURPOSES OTHER THAN PROCREATION WAS CONSIDERED A SIN...
...AND IN THE LATTER HALF OF THE NINETEENTH CENTURY, GAY SEX WAS STRICTLY POLICED...
NOT ROMANTIC...

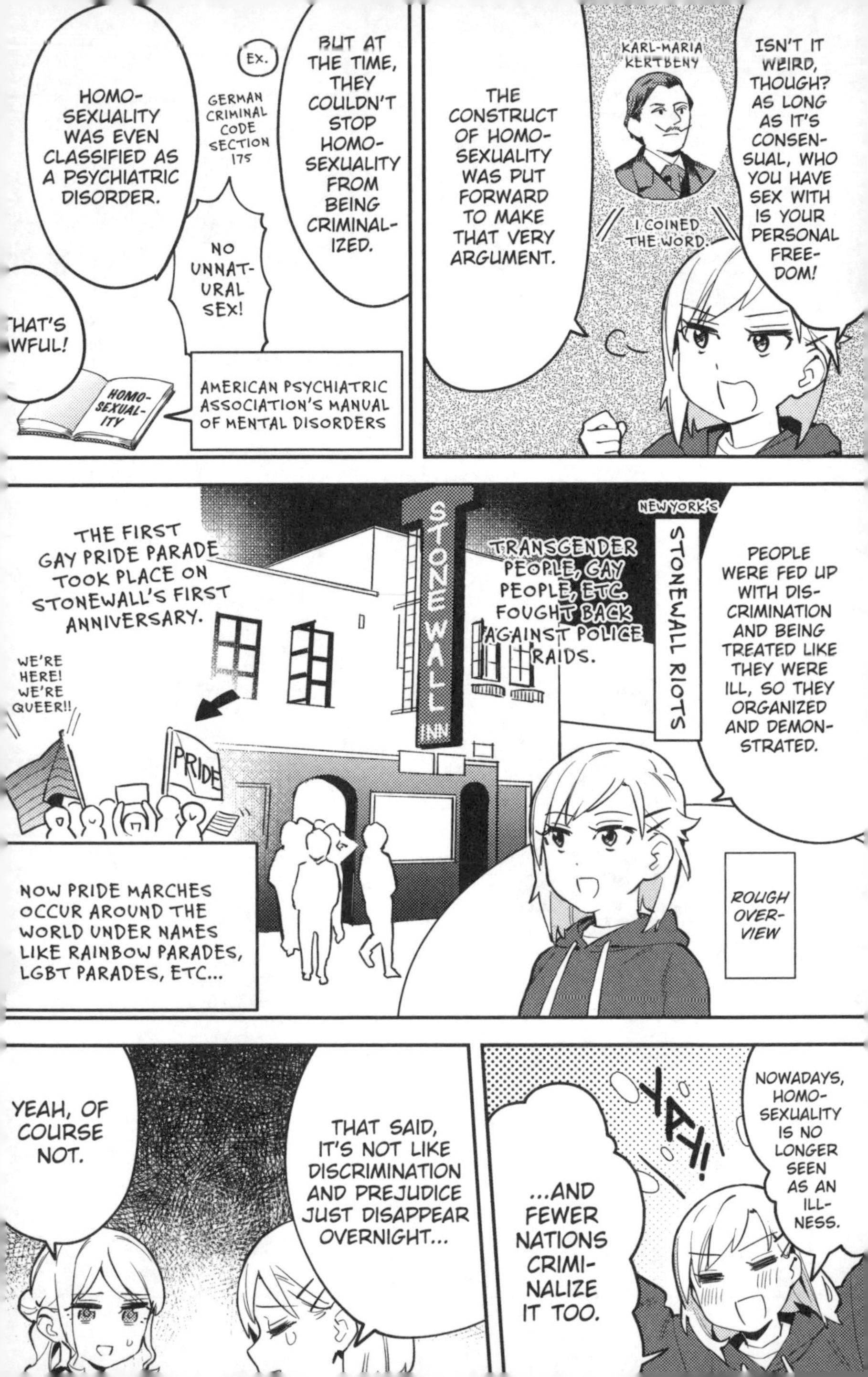
ISN'T IT WEIRD, THOUGH? AS LONG AS IT'S CONSENSUAL, WHO YOU HAVE SEX WITH IS YOUR PERSONAL FREEDOM!
KARL-MARIA KERTBENY
I COINED THE WORD.
THE CONSTRUCT OF HOMOSEXUALITY WAS PUT FORWARD TO MAKE THAT VERY ARGUMENT.
BUT AT THE TIME, THEY COULDN'T STOP HOMOSEXUALITY FROM BEING CRIMINALIZED.
EX.
GERMAN CRIMINAL CODE SECTION 175
NO UNNATURAL SEX!
HOMOSEXUALITY WAS EVEN CLASSIFIED AS A PSYCHIATRIC DISORDER.
HOMOSEXUALITY
AMERICAN PSYCHIATRIC ASSOCIATION'S MANUAL OF MENTAL DISORDERS
HAT'S WFUL!
PEOPLE WERE FED UP WITH DISCRIMINATION AND BEING TREATED LIKE THEY WERE ILL, SO THEY ORGANIZED AND DEMONSTRATED.
NEW YORK'S
STONEWALL RIOTS
TRANSGENDER PEOPLE, GAY PEOPLE, ETC. FOUGHT BACK AGAINST POLICE RAIDS.
STONEWALL INN
THE FIRST GAY PRIDE PARADE TOOK PLACE ON STONEWALL'S FIRST ANNIVERSARY.
WE'RE HERE! WE'RE QUEER!!
PRIDE
NOW PRIDE MARCHES OCCUR AROUND THE WORLD UNDER NAMES LIKE RAINBOW PARADES, LGBT PARADES, ETC...
ROUGH OVERVIEW
NOWADAYS, HOMOSEXUALITY IS NO LONGER SEEN AS AN ILLNESS.
YAY!
...AND FEWER NATIONS CRIMINALIZE IT TOO.
THAT SAID, IT'S NOT LIKE DISCRIMINATION AND PREJUDICE JUST DISAPPEAR OVERNIGHT...
YEAH, OF COURSE NOT.

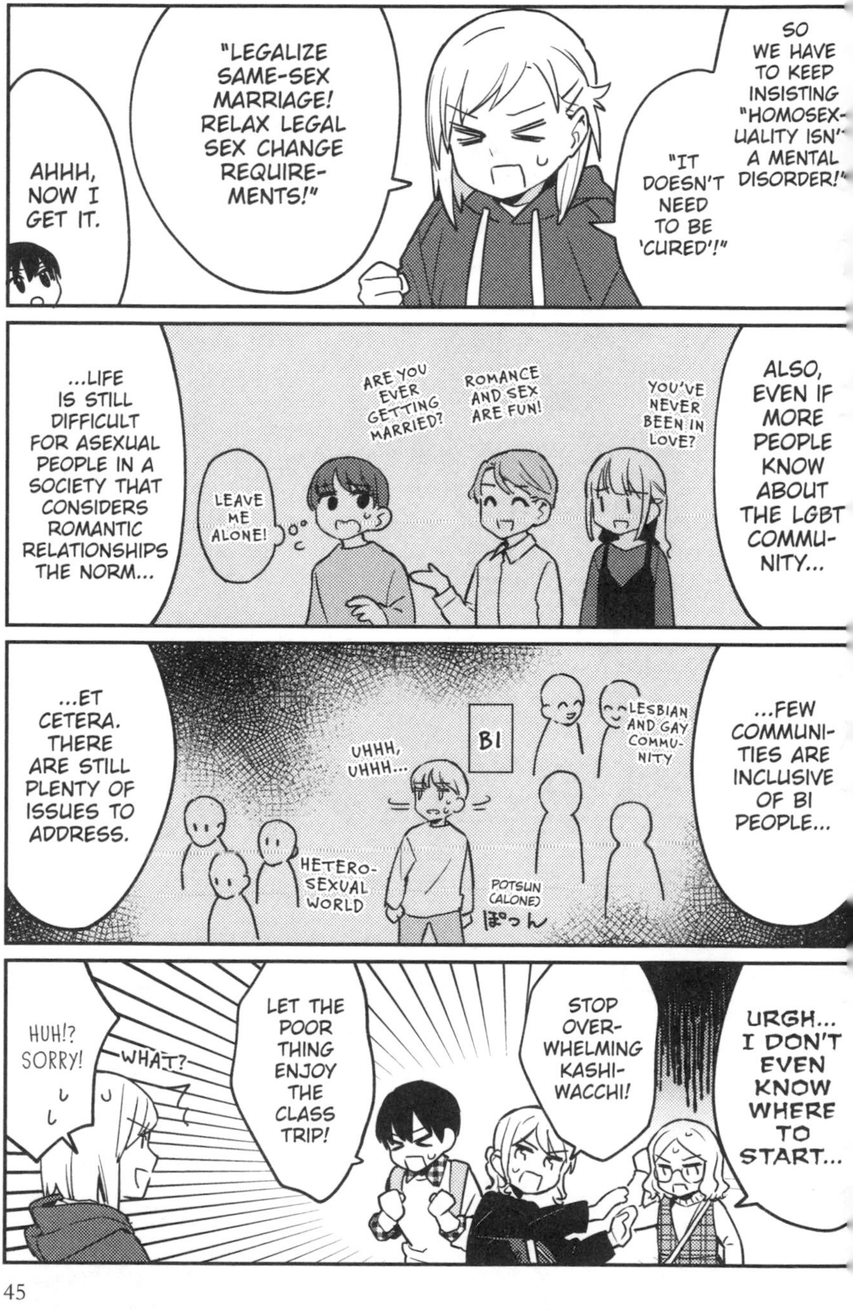
SO WE HAVE TO KEEP INSISTING "HOMOSEXUALITY ISN' A MENTAL DISORDER!"
"IT DOESN'T NEED TO BE 'CURED'!"
"LEGALIZE SAME-SEX MARRIAGE! RELAX LEGAL SEX CHANGE REQUIREMENTS!"
AHHH, NOW I GET IT.
ALSO, EVEN IF MORE PEOPLE KNOW ABOUT THE LGBT COMMUNITY...
YOU'VE NEVER BEEN IN LOVE?
ROMANCE AND SEX ARE FUN!
ARE YOU EVER GETTING MARRIED?
LEAVE ME ALONE!
...LIFE IS STILL DIFFICULT FOR ASEXUAL PEOPLE IN A SOCIETY THAT CONSIDERS ROMANTIC RELATIONSHIPS THE NORM...
...FEW COMMUNITIES ARE INCLUSIVE OF BI PEOPLE...
LESBIAN AND GAY COMMUNITY
BI
UHHH, UHHH...
POTSUN (ALONE)
ぽつん
HETERO-SEXUAL WORLD
...ET CETERA. THERE ARE STILL PLENTY OF ISSUES TO ADDRESS.
URGH... I DON'T EVEN KNOW WHERE TO START...
STOP OVERWHELMING KASHIWACCHI!
LET THE POOR THING ENJOY THE CLASS TRIP!
WHAT?
HUH!? SORRY!

Settled

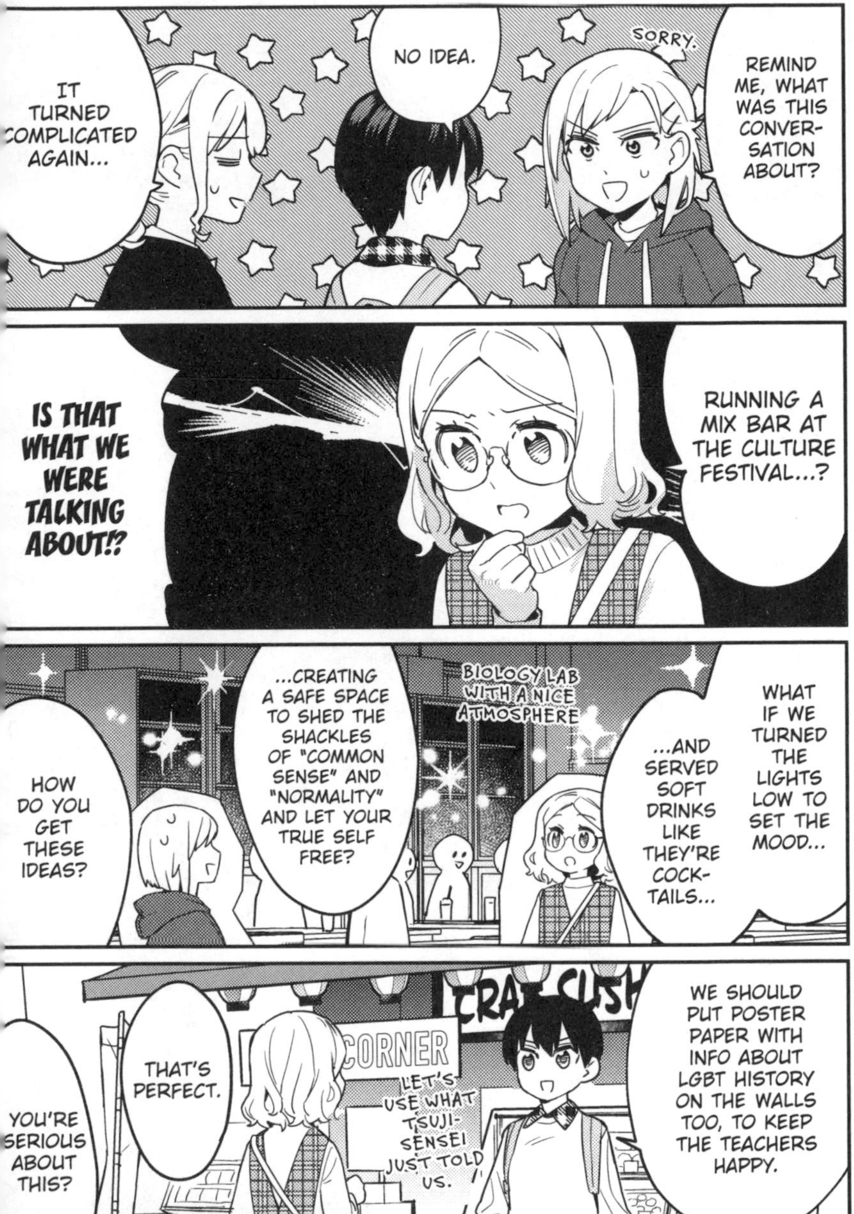
REMIND ME, WHAT WAS THIS CONVERSATION ABOUT?
SORRY.
NO IDEA.
IT TURNED COMPLICATED AGAIN...
RUNNING A MIX BAR AT THE CULTURE FESTIVAL...?
IS THAT WHAT WE WERE TALKING ABOUT!?
WHAT IF WE TURNED THE LIGHTS LOW TO SET THE MOOD...
...AND SERVED SOFT DRINKS LIKE THEY'RE COCKTAILS...
BIOLOGY LAB WITH A NICE ATMOSPHERE
...CREATING A SAFE SPACE TO SHED THE SHACKLES OF "COMMON SENSE" AND "NORMALITY" AND LET YOUR TRUE SELF FREE?
HOW DO YOU GET THESE IDEAS?
WE SHOULD PUT POSTER PAPER WITH INFO ABOUT LGBT HISTORY ON THE WALLS TOO, TO KEEP THE TEACHERS HAPPY.
CORNER
LET'S USE WHAT TSUJI-SENSEI JUST TOLD US.
THAT'S PERFECT.
YOU'RE SERIOUS ABOUT THIS?

Fit Right In

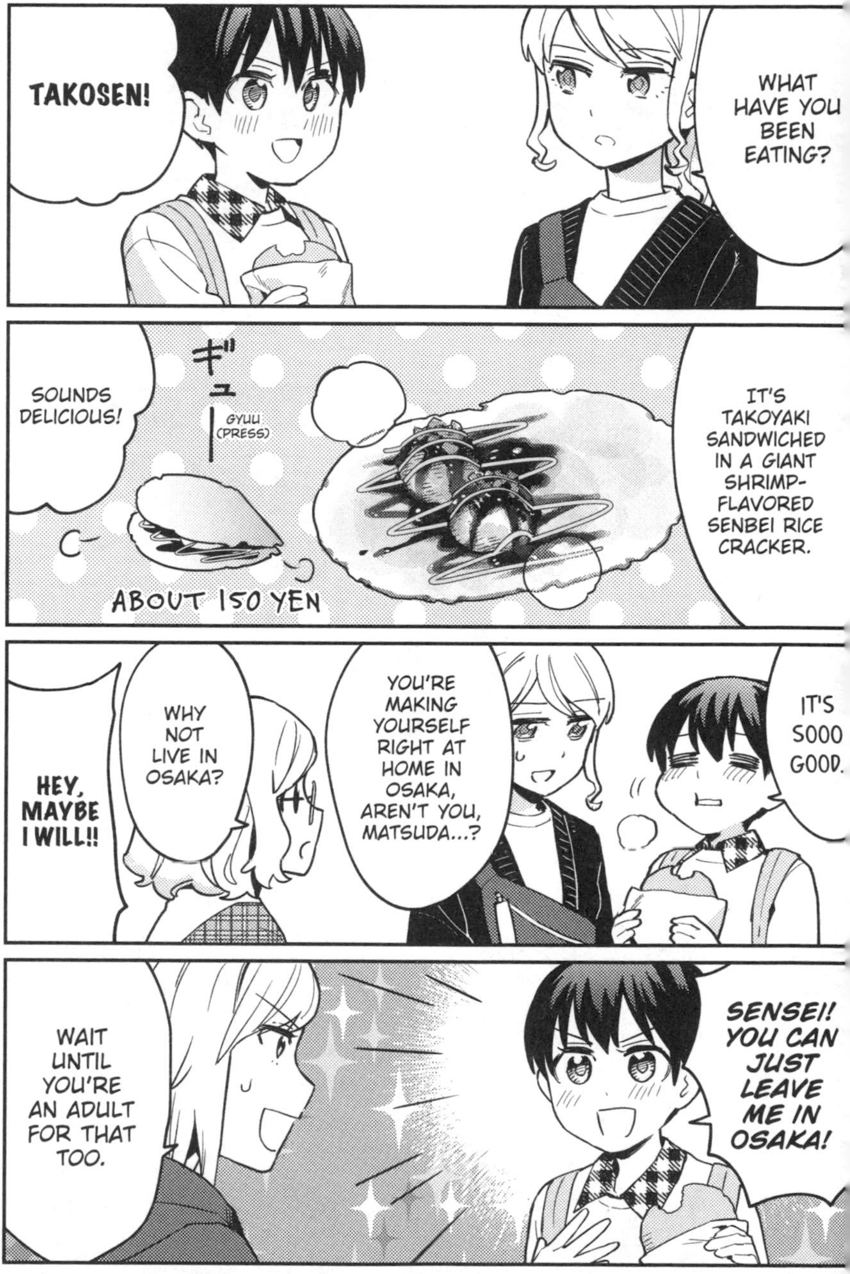
WHAT HAVE YOU BEEN EATING?
TAKOSEN!
IT'S TAKOYAKI SANDWICHED IN A GIANT SHRIMP-FLAVORED SENBEI RICE CRACKER.
ギュ
GYUU (PRESS)
SOUNDS DELICIOUS!
ABOUT 150 YEN
IT'S SOOO GOOD.
YOU'RE MAKING YOURSELF RIGHT AT HOME IN OSAKA, AREN'T YOU, MATSUDA...?
WHY NOT LIVE IN OSAKA?
HEY, MAYBE I WILL!!
SENSEI! YOU CAN JUST LEAVE ME IN OSAKA!
WAIT UNTIL YOU'RE AN ADULT FOR THAT TOO.

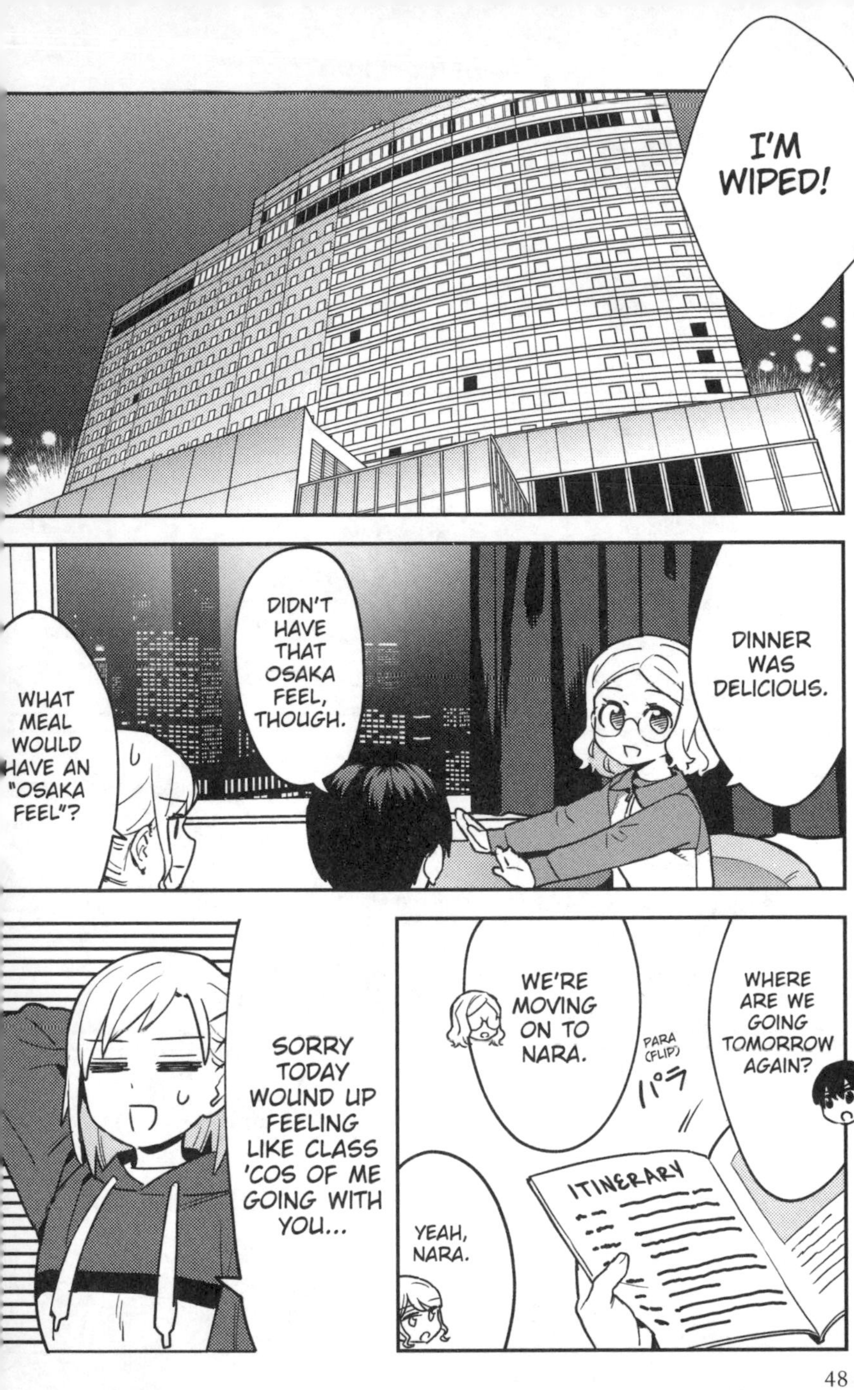
I'M WIPED!
DINNER WAS DELICIOUS.
DIDN'T HAVE THAT OSAKA FEEL, THOUGH.
WHAT MEAL WOULD HAVE AN "OSAKA FEEL"?
WHERE ARE WE GOING TOMORROW AGAIN?
PARA (FLIP)
パラ
WE'RE MOVING ON TO NARA.
ITINERARY
YEAH, NARA.
SORRY TODAY WOUND UP FEELING LIKE CLASS 'COS OF ME GOING WITH YOU...

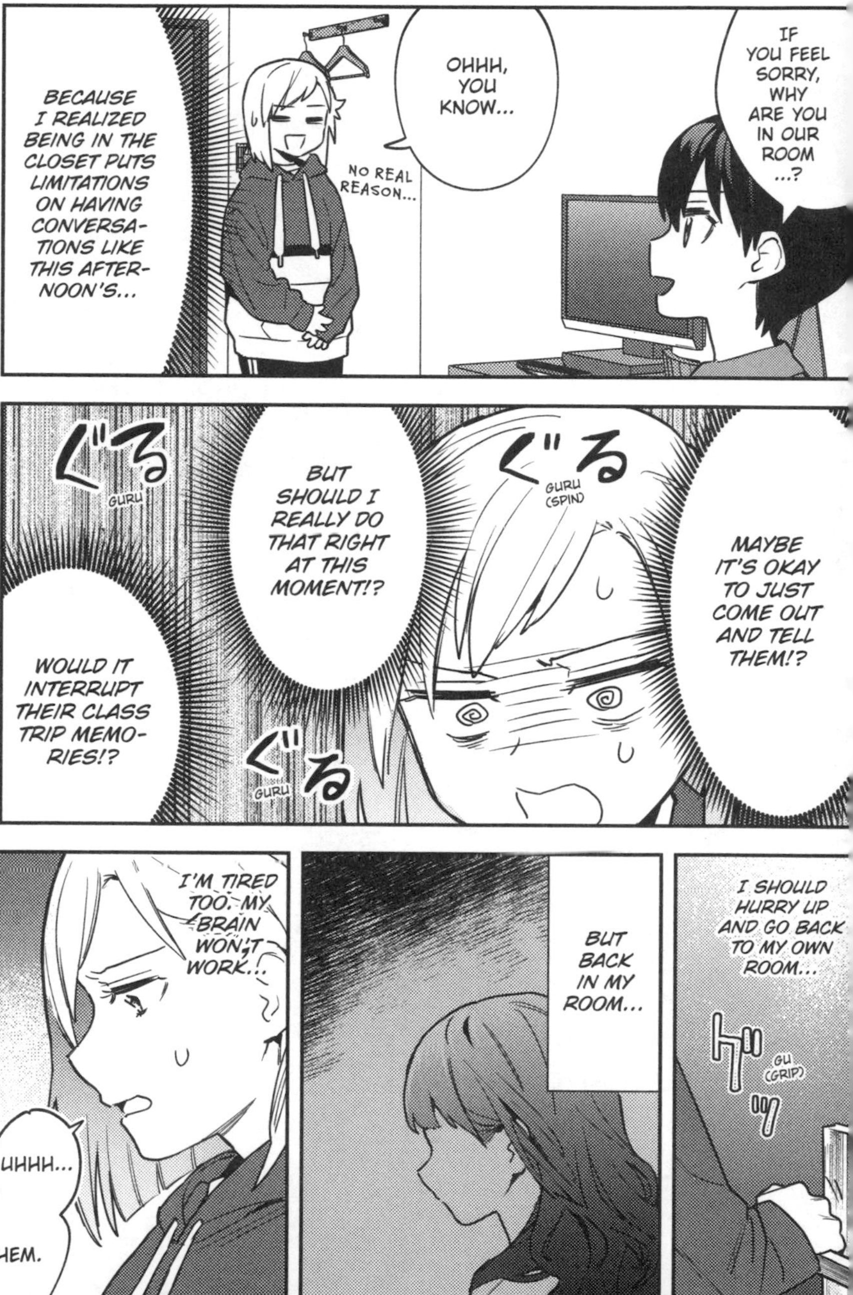
IF YOU FEEL SORRY, WHY ARE YOU IN OUR ROOM ...?
OHHH, YOU KNOW...
NO REAL REASON...
BECAUSE I REALIZED BEING IN THE CLOSET PUTS LIMITATIONS ON HAVING CONVERSA-TIONS LIKE THIS AFTER-NOON'S...
MAYBE IT'S OKAY TO JUST COME OUT AND TELL THEM!?
ぐる
GURU (SPIN)
BUT SHOULD I REALLY DO THAT RIGHT AT THIS MOMENT!?
ぐる
GURU
WOULD IT INTERRUPT THEIR CLASS TRIP MEMO-RIES!?
ぐる
GURU
I SHOULD HURRY UP AND GO BACK TO MY OWN ROOM...
ぐッ
GU (GRIP)
BUT BACK IN MY ROOM...
I'M TIRED TOO. MY BRAIN WON'T WORK...
UHHH...
AHEM.

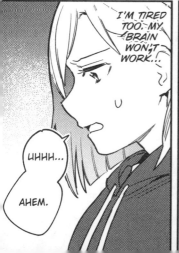

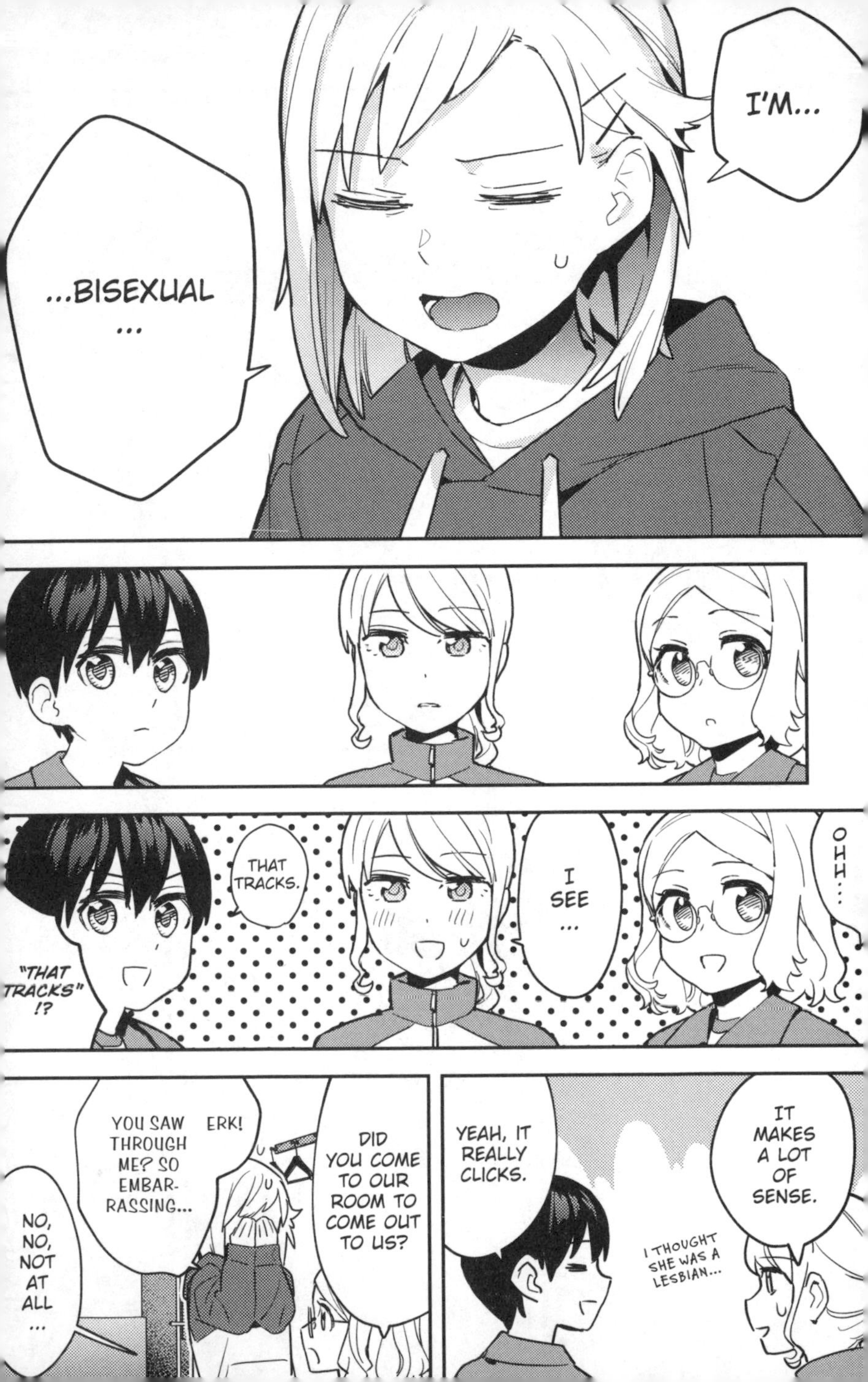
I'M...
...BISEXUAL ...
OHH...
I SEE ...
THAT TRACKS.
"THAT TRACKS" !?
IT MAKES A LOT OF SENSE.
I THOUGHT SHE WAS A LESBIAN...
YEAH, IT REALLY CLICKS.
DID YOU COME TO OUR ROOM TO COME OUT TO US?
ERK!
YOU SAW THROUGH ME? SO EMBAR-RASSING...
NO, NO, NOT AT ALL ...

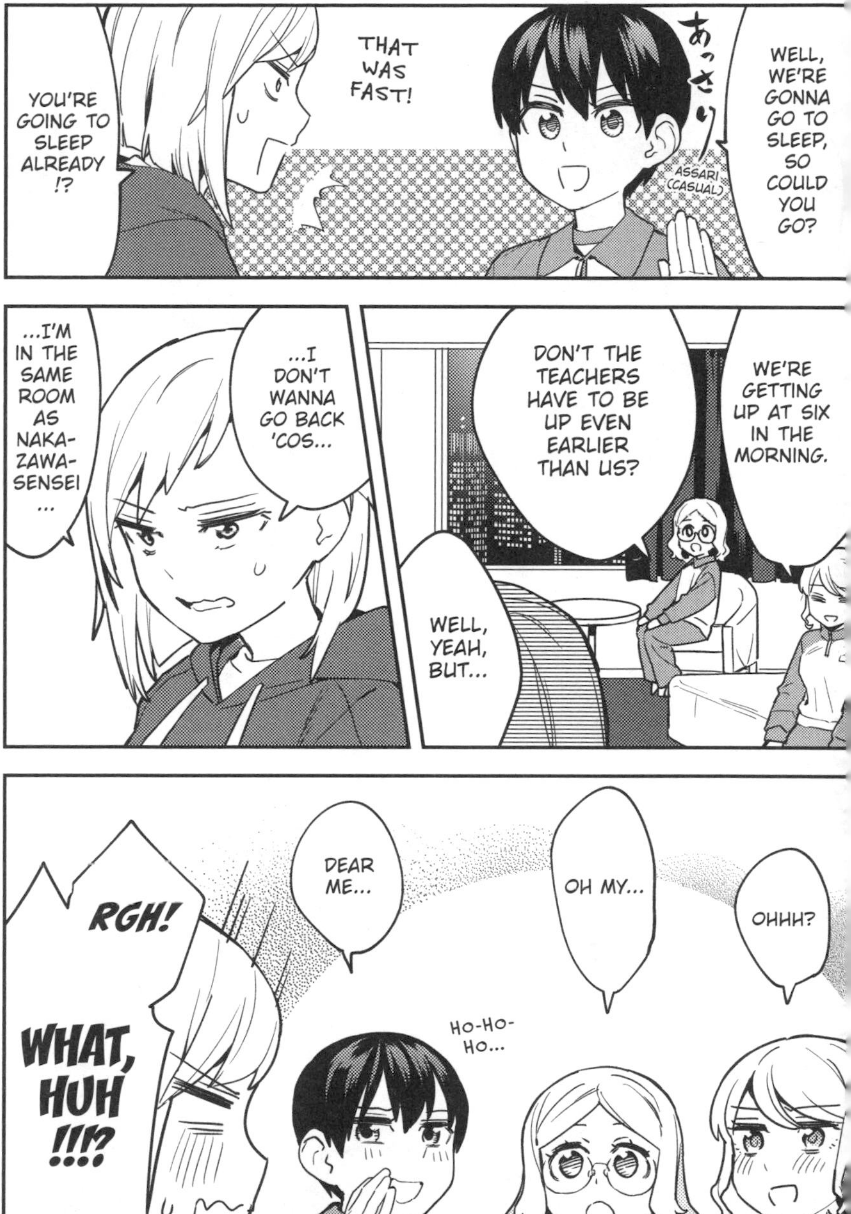
WELL, WE'RE GONNA GO TO SLEEP, SO COULD YOU GO?
あっさり
ASSARI (CASUAL)
THAT WAS FAST!
YOU'RE GOING TO SLEEP ALREADY!?
WE'RE GETTING UP AT SIX IN THE MORNING.
DON'T THE TEACHERS HAVE TO BE UP EVEN EARLIER THAN US?
WELL, YEAH, BUT...
...I DON'T WANNA GO BACK 'COS...
...I'M IN THE SAME ROOM AS NAKA-ZAWA-SENSEI...
OHHH?
OH MY...
DEAR ME...
HO-HO-HO...
RGH!
WHAT, HUH!!!?

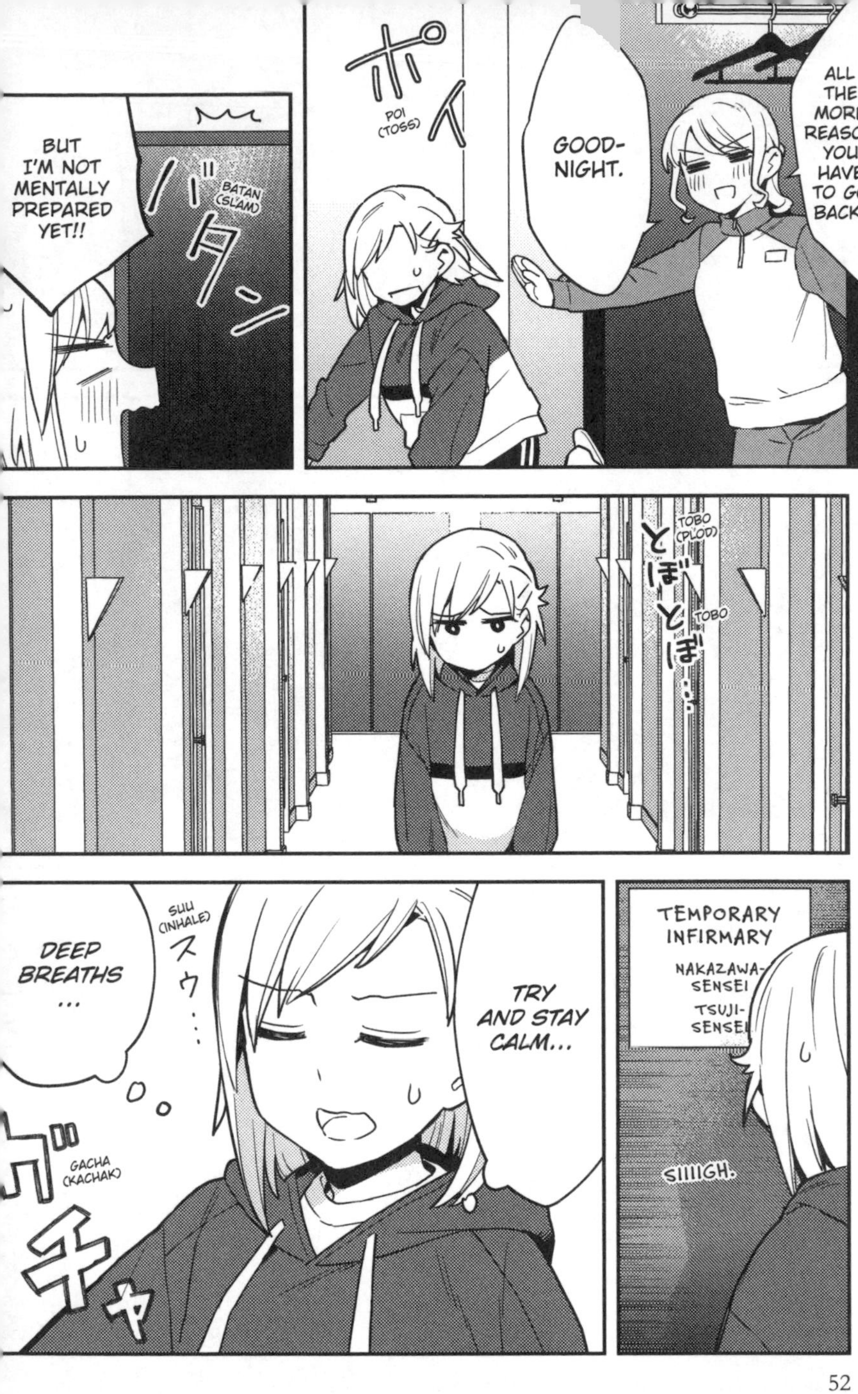
ALL THE MORE REASON YOU HAVE TO GO BACK!
GOOD-NIGHT.
ポイ
POI (TOSS)
BUT I'M NOT MENTALLY PREPARED YET!!
バターン
BATAN (SLAM)
とぼとぼ…
TOBO (PLOD) TOBO
TEMPORARY INFIRMARY
NAKAZAWA-SENSEI
TSUJI-SENSEI
SIIIIGH.
TRY AND STAY CALM…
スウ…
SUU (INHALE)
DEEP BREATHS…
ガチャ
GACHA (KACHAK)

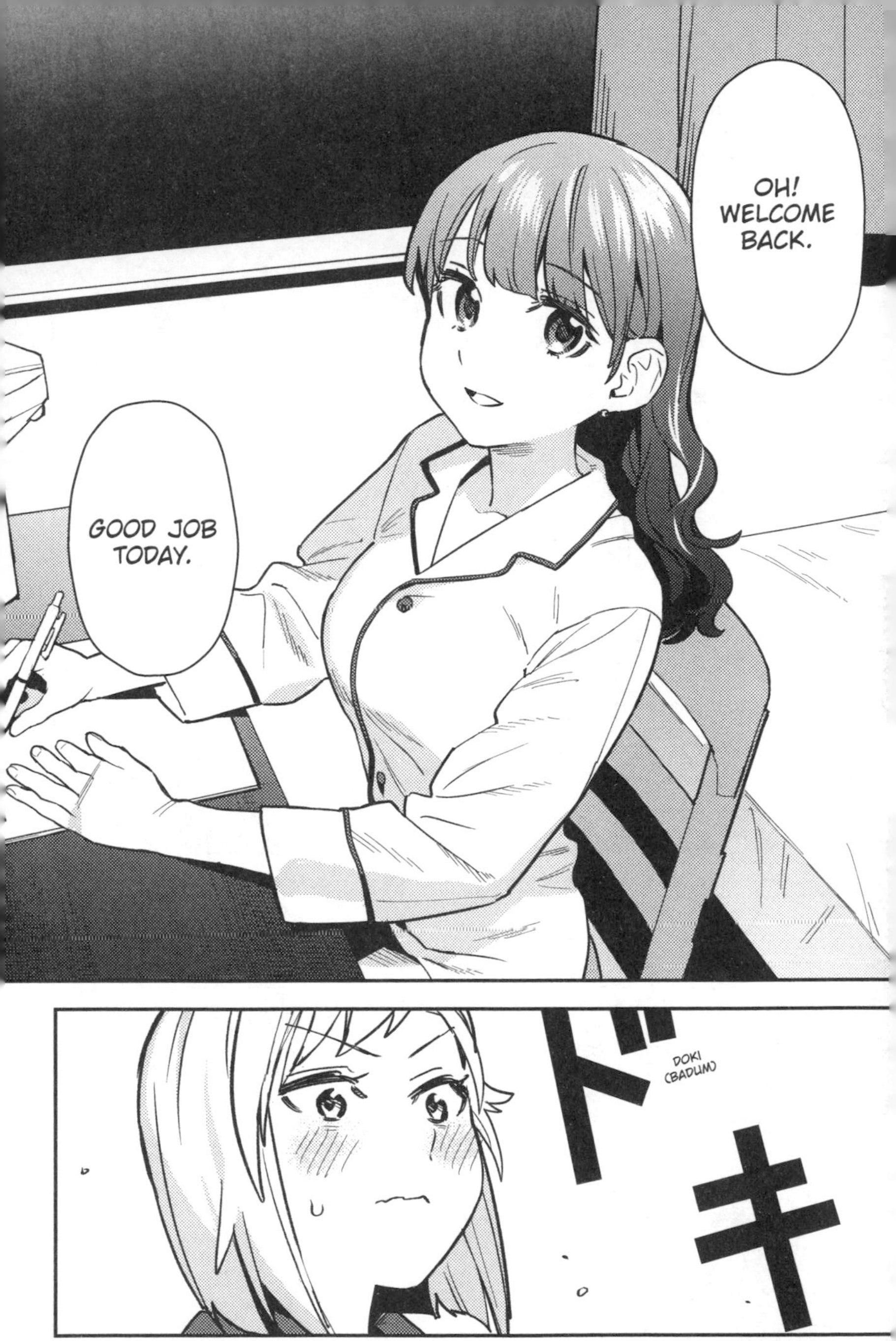
OH! WELCOME BACK.
GOOD JOB TODAY.
DOKI (BADUM)

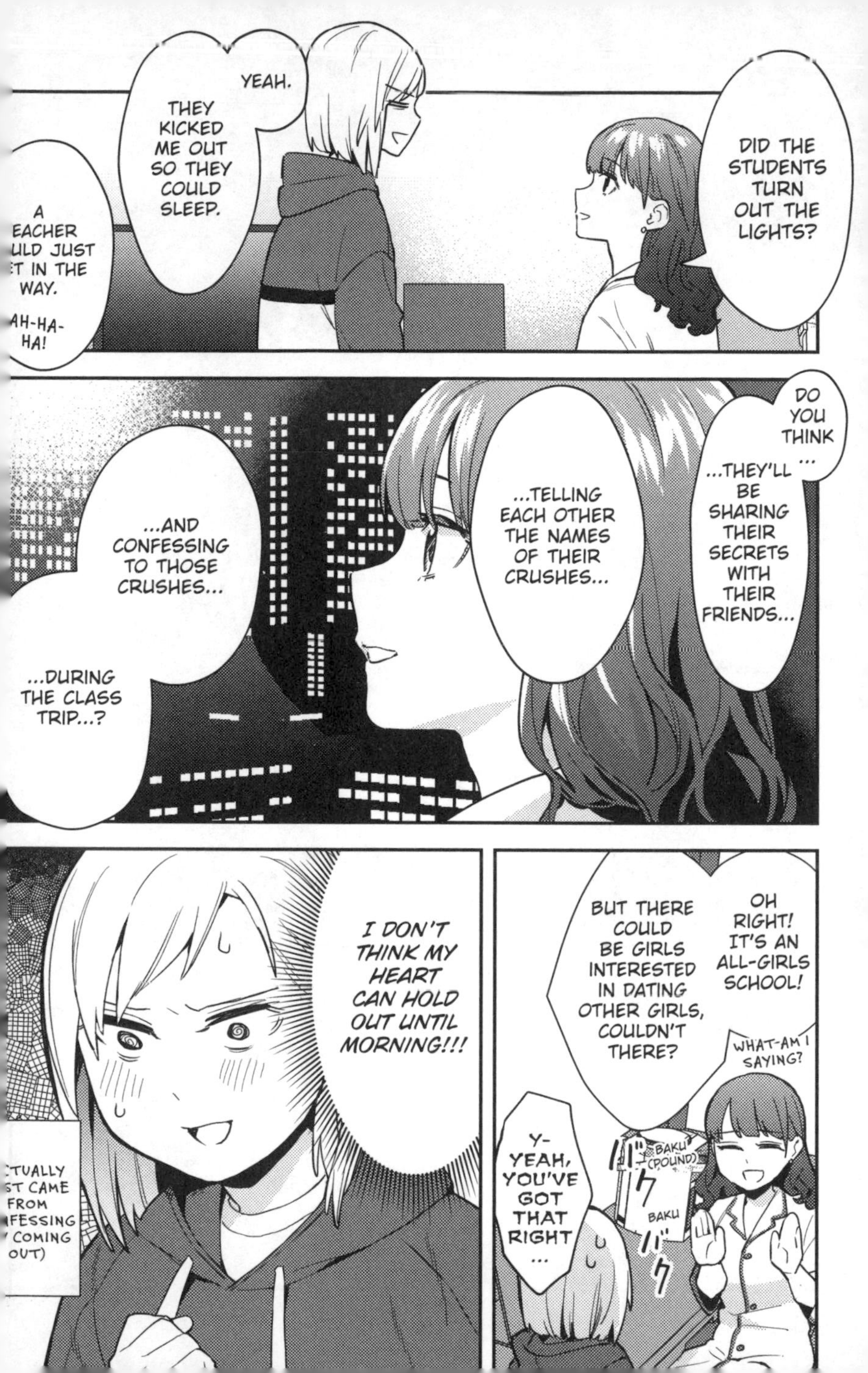

DID THE STUDENTS TURN OUT THE LIGHTS?
YEAH.
THEY KICKED ME OUT SO THEY COULD SLEEP.
A EACHER ULD JUST T IN THE WAY.
AH-HA-HA!
DO YOU THINK...
...THEY'LL BE SHARING THEIR SECRETS WITH THEIR FRIENDS...
...TELLING EACH OTHER THE NAMES OF THEIR CRUSHES...
...AND CONFESSING TO THOSE CRUSHES...
...DURING THE CLASS TRIP...?
OH RIGHT! IT'S AN ALL-GIRLS SCHOOL!
BUT THERE COULD BE GIRLS INTERESTED IN DATING OTHER GIRLS, COULDN'T THERE?
WHAT AM I SAYING?
BAKU (POUND)
BAKU
Y-YEAH, YOU'VE GOT THAT RIGHT...
I DON'T THINK MY HEART CAN HOLD OUT UNTIL MORNING!!!
CTUALLY ST CAME FROM FESSING COMING OUT)

Class 15 **Candid Shot**

ACK!
MY OCTO-PUS...
BOTO (PLOP)

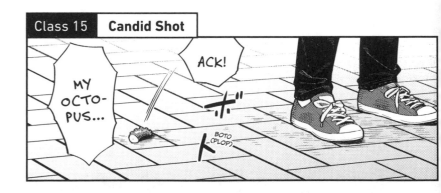

Knocking Out 12 Sex Concerns! 3

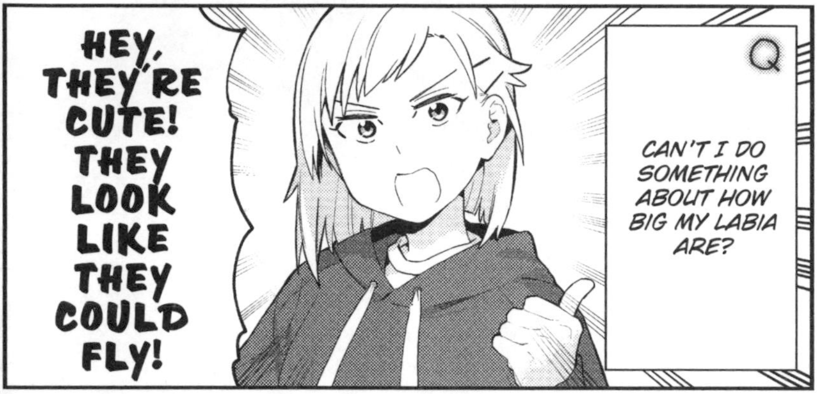
Q
CAN'T I DO SOMETHING ABOUT HOW BIG MY LABIA ARE?
HEY, THEY'RE CUTE! THEY LOOK LIKE THEY COULD FLY!

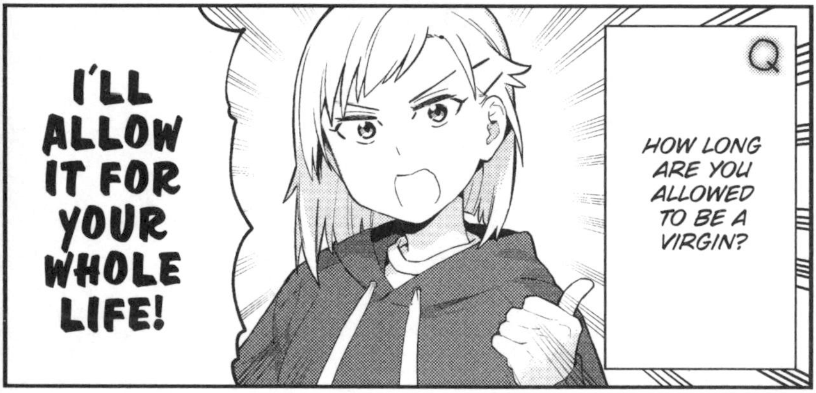
Q
HOW LONG ARE YOU ALLOWED TO BE A VIRGIN?
I'LL ALLOW IT FOR YOUR WHOLE LIFE!

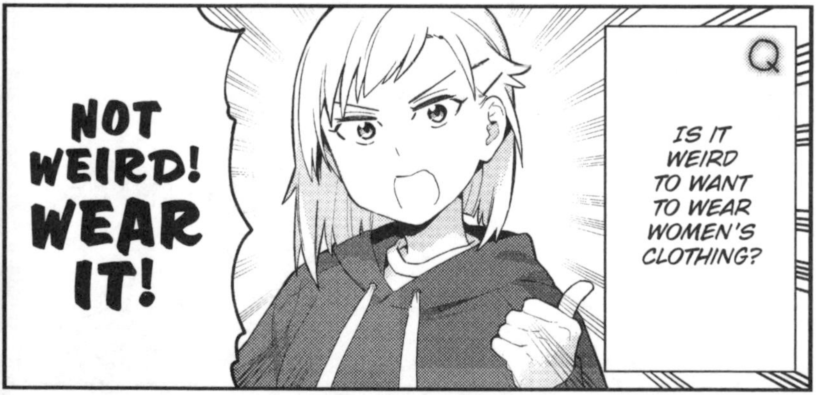
Q
IS IT WEIRD TO WANT TO WEAR WOMEN'S CLOTHING?
NOT WEIRD! WEAR IT!

[Class 16] **Bisexual**

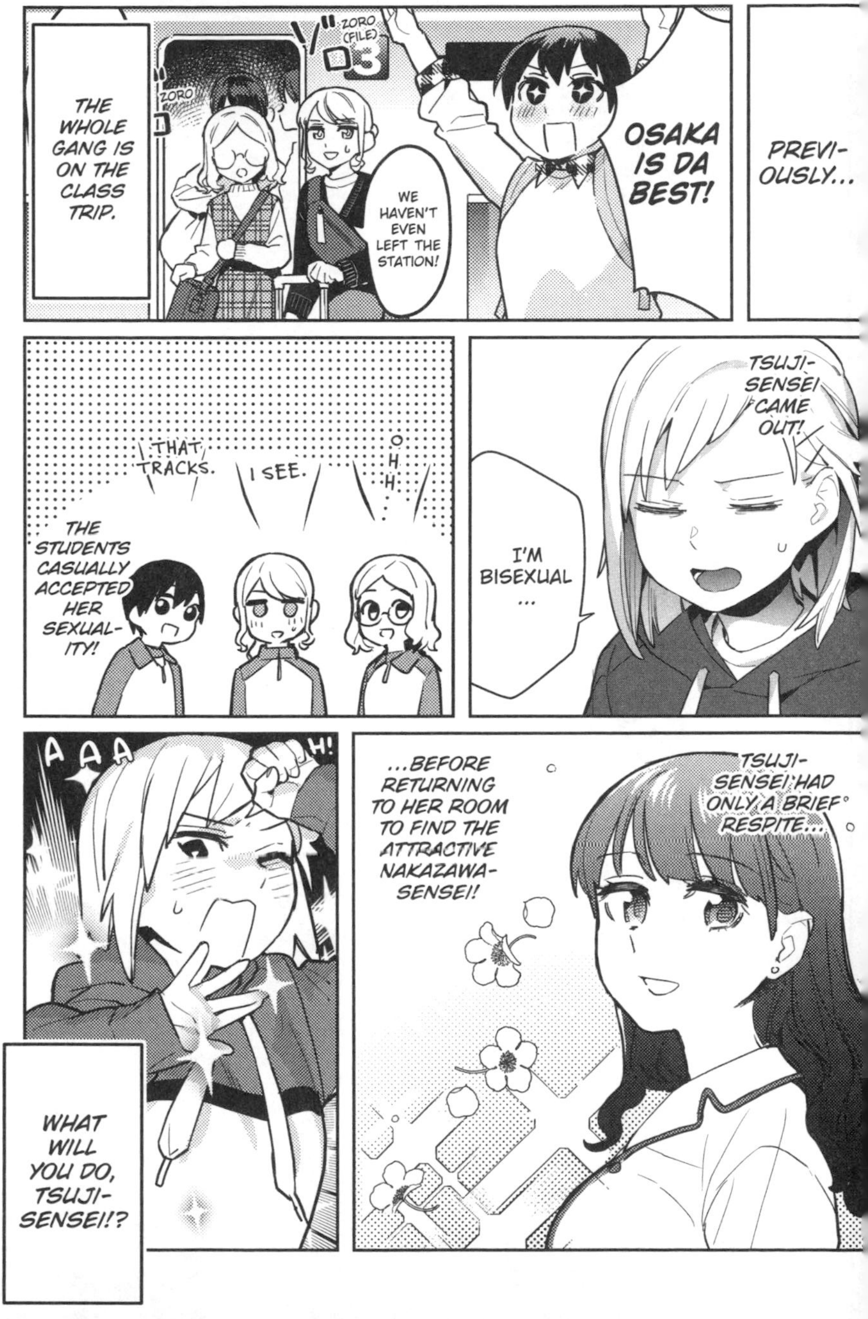
PREVIOUSLY...
OSAKA IS DA BEST!
ZORO (FILE)
WE HAVEN'T EVEN LEFT THE STATION!
ZORO
THE WHOLE GANG IS ON THE CLASS TRIP.
TSUJI-SENSEI CAME OUT!
I'M BISEXUAL ...
OHH
I SEE.
THAT TRACKS.
THE STUDENTS CASUALLY ACCEPTED HER SEXUALITY!
TSUJI-SENSEI HAD ONLY A BRIEF RESPITE...
...BEFORE RETURNING TO HER ROOM TO FIND THE ATTRACTIVE NAKAZAWA-SENSEI!
AAAH!
WHAT WILL YOU DO, TSUJI-SENSEI!?

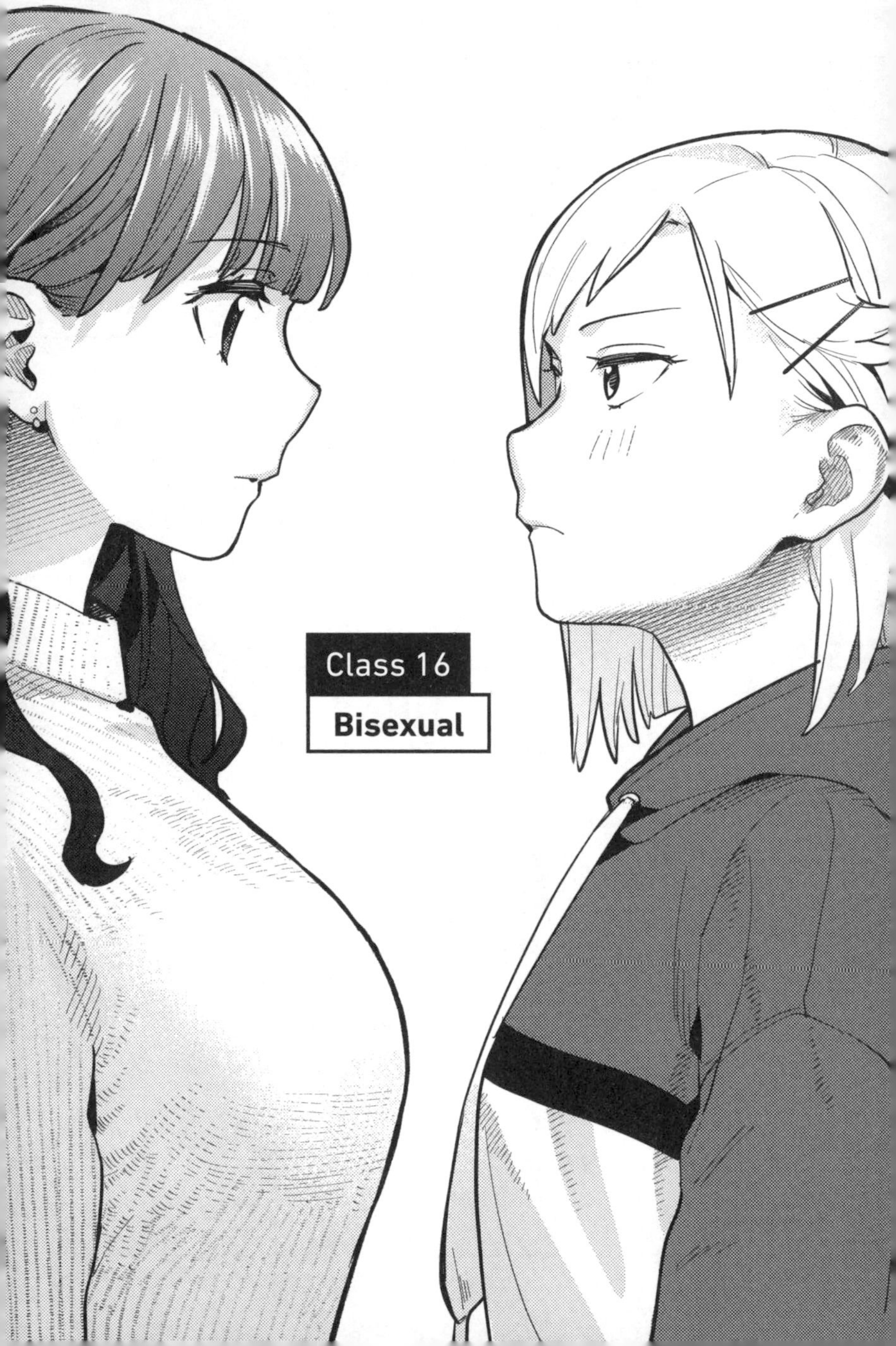
Class 16
Bisexual

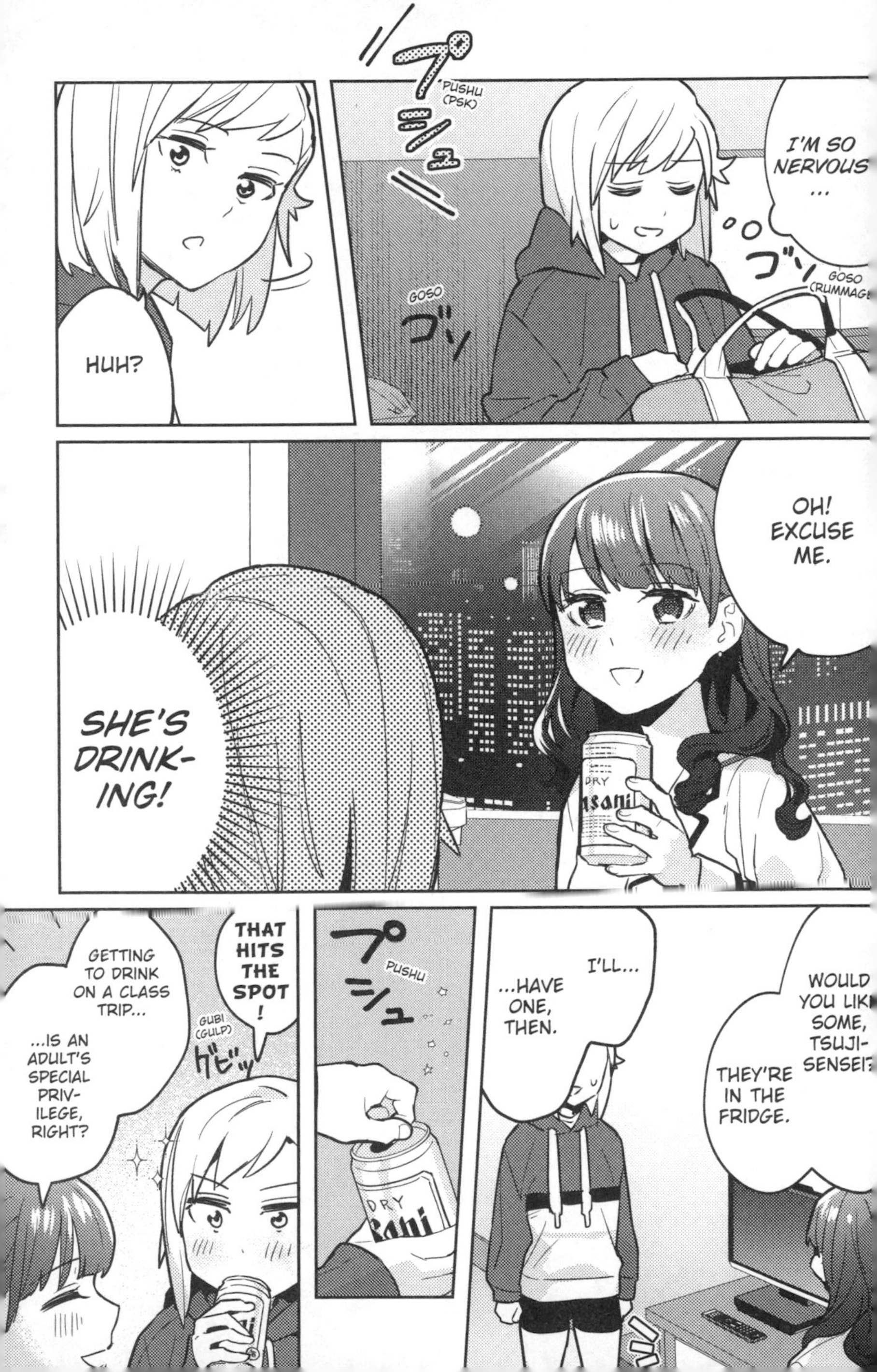
PUSHU (PSK)
I'M SO NERVOUS...
GOSO (RUMMAGE)
GOSO
HUH?
OH! EXCUSE ME.
SHE'S DRINKING!
WOULD YOU LIKE SOME, TSUJI-SENSEI?
THEY'RE IN THE FRIDGE.
I'LL...
...HAVE ONE, THEN.
PUSHU
THAT HITS THE SPOT!
GUBI (GULP)
GETTING TO DRINK ON A CLASS TRIP...
...IS AN ADULT'S SPECIAL PRIVILEGE, RIGHT?

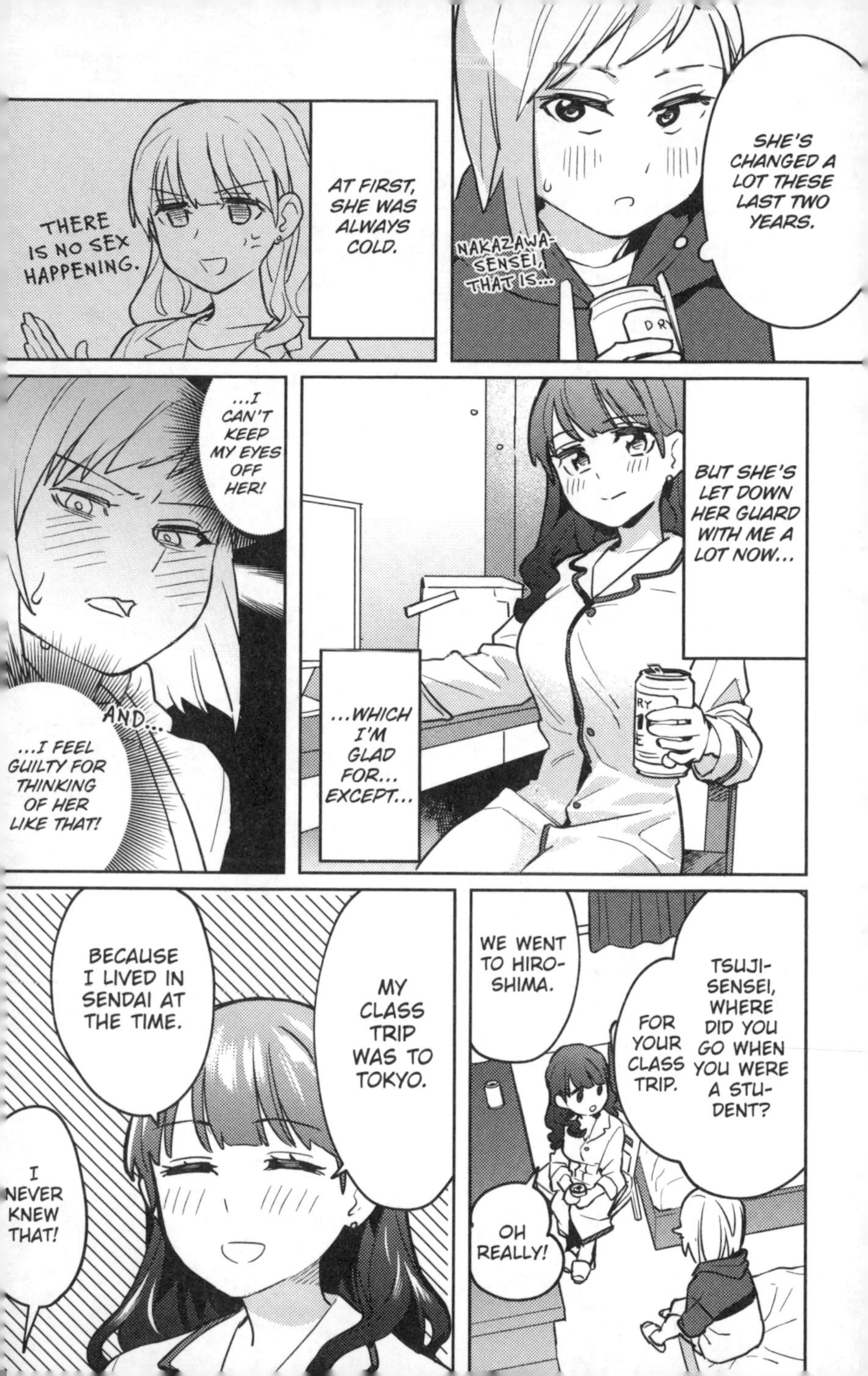
SHE'S CHANGED A LOT THESE LAST TWO YEARS.
NAKAZAWA-SENSEI, THAT IS...
AT FIRST, SHE WAS ALWAYS COLD.
THERE IS NO SEX HAPPENING.
BUT SHE'S LET DOWN HER GUARD WITH ME A LOT NOW...
...WHICH I'M GLAD FOR... EXCEPT...
...I CAN'T KEEP MY EYES OFF HER!
AND...
...I FEEL GUILTY FOR THINKING OF HER LIKE THAT!
TSUJI-SENSEI, WHERE DID YOU GO WHEN YOU WERE A STUDENT?
FOR YOUR CLASS TRIP.
WE WENT TO HIROSHIMA.
OH REALLY!
MY CLASS TRIP WAS TO TOKYO.
BECAUSE I LIVED IN SENDAI AT THE TIME.
I NEVER KNEW THAT!

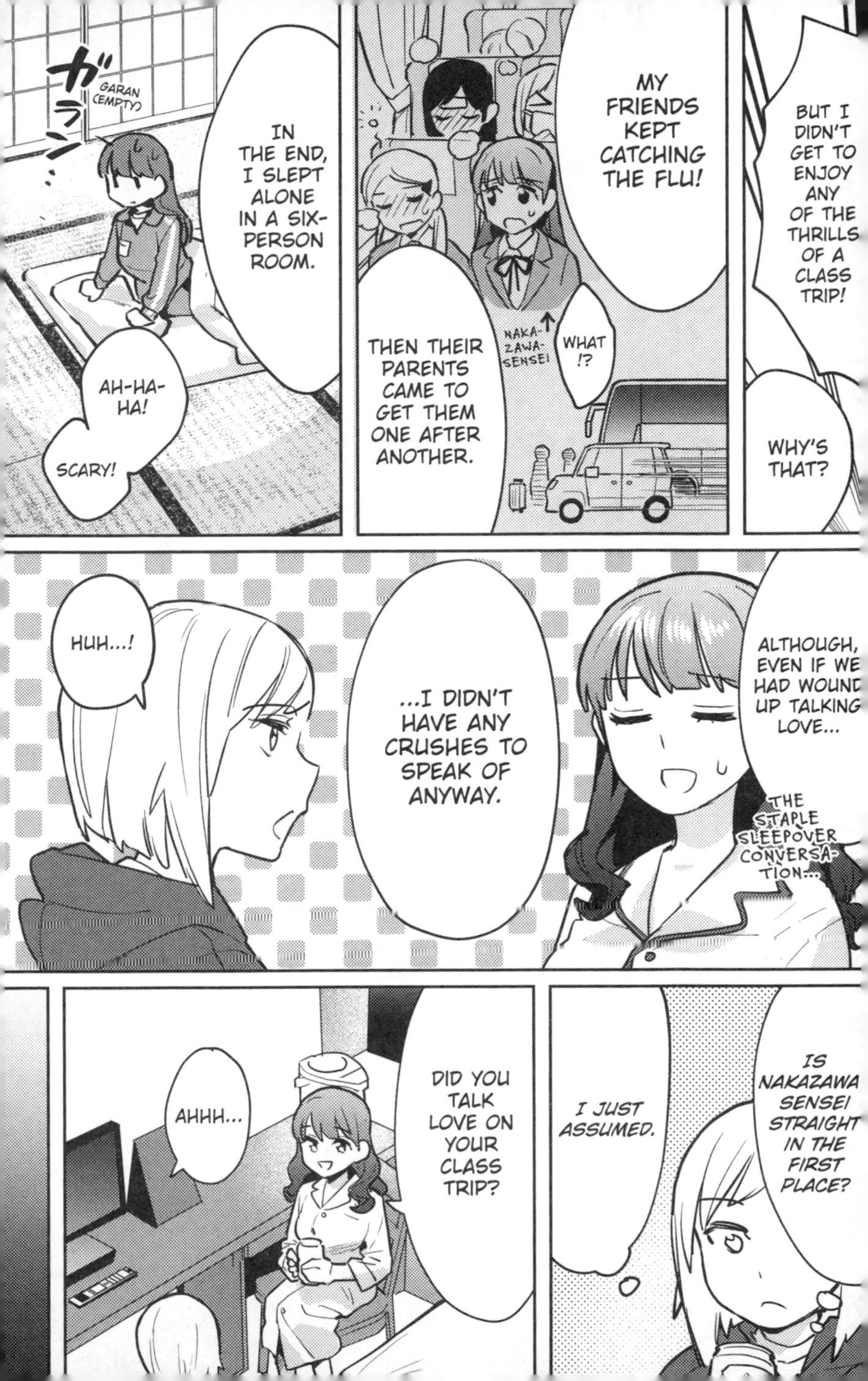
BUT I DIDN'T GET TO ENJOY ANY OF THE THRILLS OF A CLASS TRIP!
WHY'S THAT?
MY FRIENDS KEPT CATCHING THE FLU!
WHAT!?
NAKA-ZAWA-SENSEI
THEN THEIR PARENTS CAME TO GET THEM ONE AFTER ANOTHER.
IN THE END, I SLEPT ALONE IN A SIX-PERSON ROOM.
ガラン
GARAN (EMPTY)
AH-HA-HA!
SCARY!
ALTHOUGH, EVEN IF WE HAD WOUND UP TALKING LOVE...
THE STAPLE SLEEPOVER CONVERSA-TION...
...I DIDN'T HAVE ANY CRUSHES TO SPEAK OF ANYWAY.
HUH...!
IS NAKAZAWA SENSEI STRAIGHT IN THE FIRST PLACE?
I JUST ASSUMED.
DID YOU TALK LOVE ON YOUR CLASS TRIP?
AHHH...

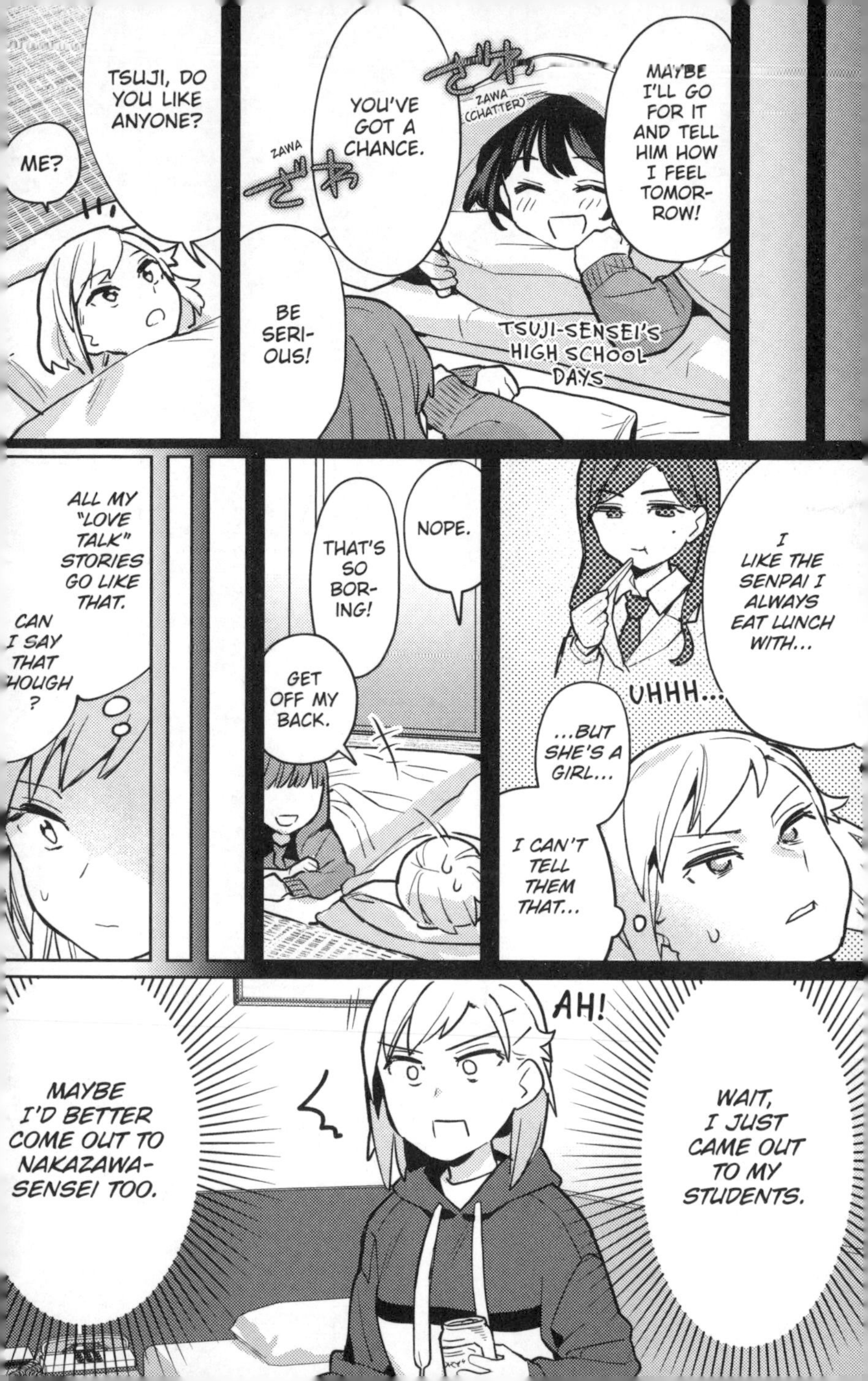
MAYBE I'LL GO FOR IT AND TELL HIM HOW I FEEL TOMORROW!
ZAWA (CHATTER)
YOU'VE GOT A CHANCE.
ZAWA
BE SERIOUS!
TSUJI-SENSEI'S HIGH SCHOOL DAYS
TSUJI, DO YOU LIKE ANYONE?
ME?
I LIKE THE SENPAI I ALWAYS EAT LUNCH WITH...
UHHH...
...BUT SHE'S A GIRL...
I CAN'T TELL THEM THAT...
NOPE.
THAT'S SO BORING!
GET OFF MY BACK.
ALL MY "LOVE TALK" STORIES GO LIKE THAT.
CAN I SAY THAT HOUGH ?
AH!
WAIT, I JUST CAME OUT TO MY STUDENTS.
MAYBE I'D BETTER COME OUT TO NAKAZAWA-SENSEI TOO.

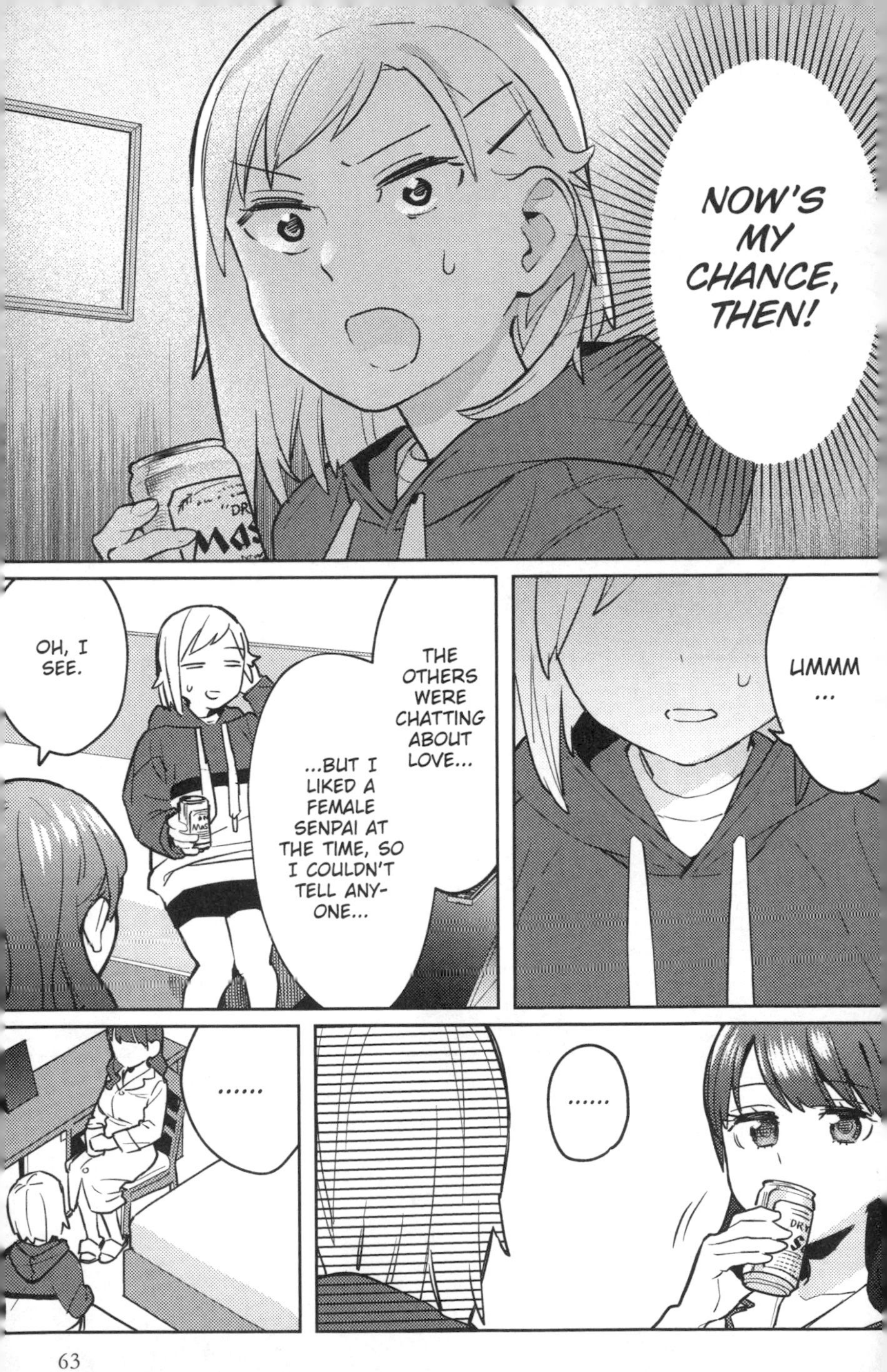
NOW'S MY CHANCE, THEN!
UMMM ...
THE OTHERS WERE CHATTING ABOUT LOVE...
...BUT I LIKED A FEMALE SENPAI AT THE TIME, SO I COULDN'T TELL ANY-ONE...
OH, I SEE.
......
......

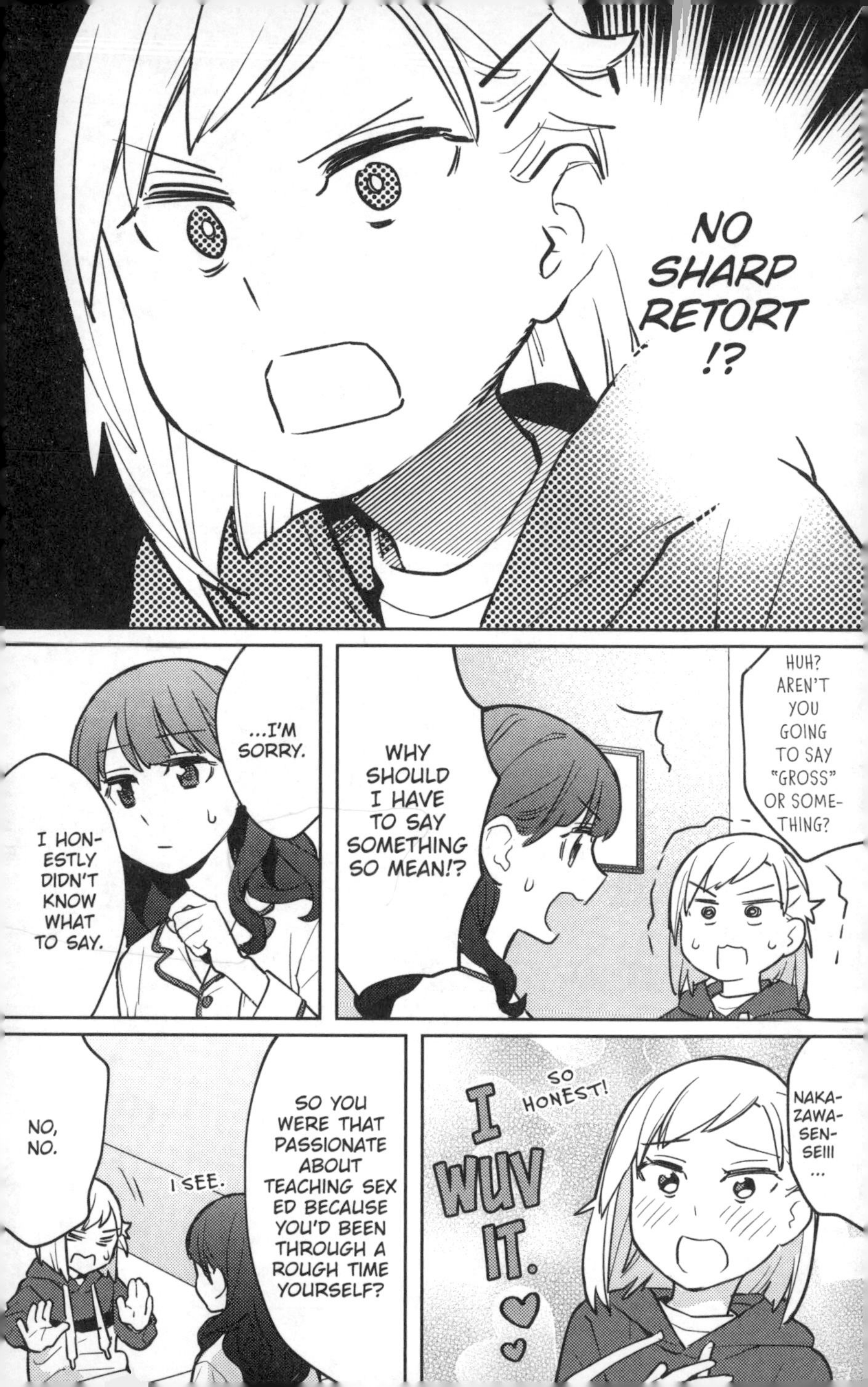
NO SHARP RETORT !?
HUH? AREN'T YOU GOING TO SAY "GROSS" OR SOME-THING?
WHY SHOULD I HAVE TO SAY SOMETHING SO MEAN!?
...I'M SORRY.
I HON-ESTLY DIDN'T KNOW WHAT TO SAY.
NAKA-ZAWA-SEN-SEIII ...
SO HONEST!
I WUV IT.
SO YOU WERE THAT PASSIONATE ABOUT TEACHING SEX ED BECAUSE YOU'D BEEN THROUGH A ROUGH TIME YOURSELF?
I SEE.
NO, NO.

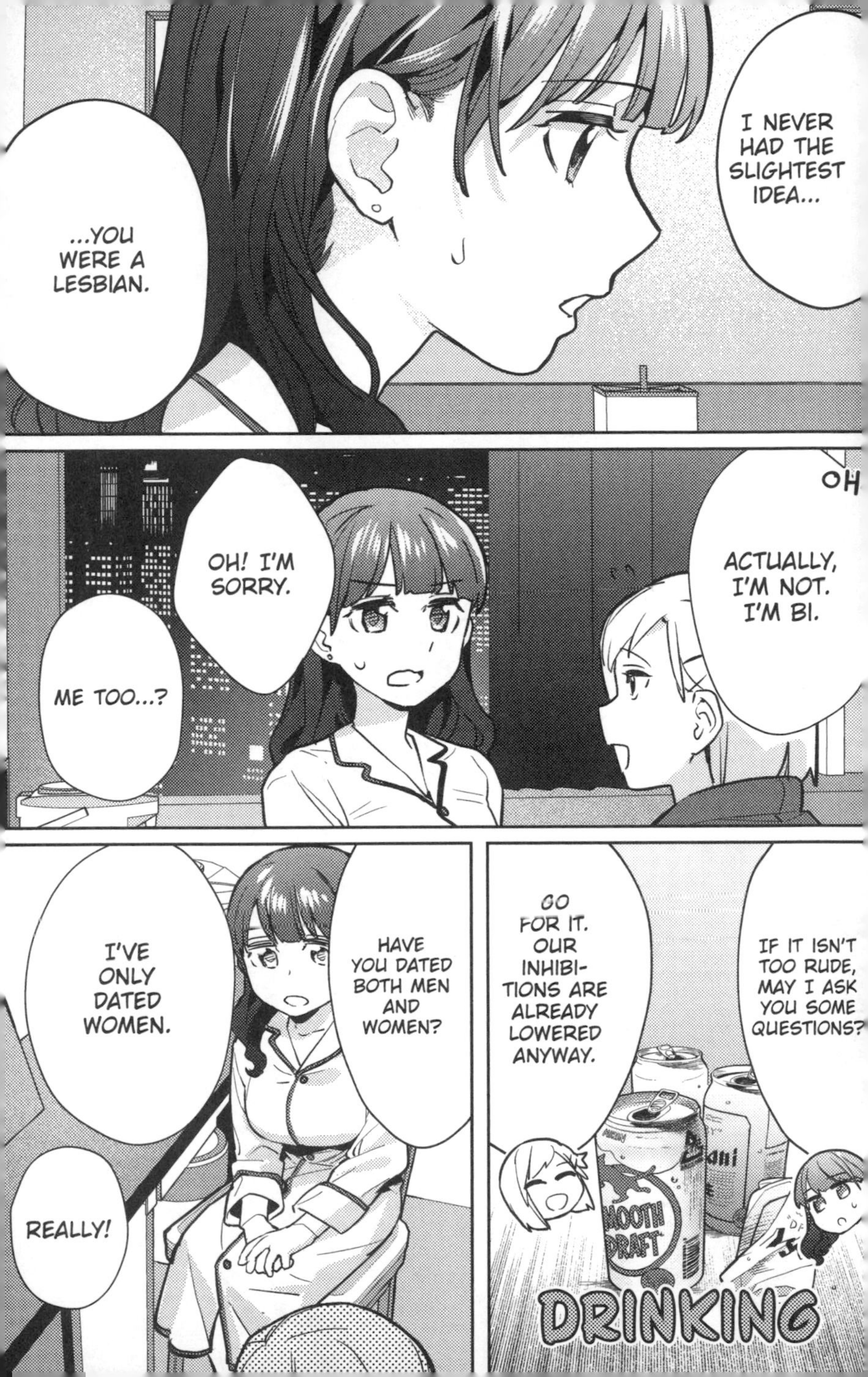
I NEVER HAD THE SLIGHTEST IDEA...
...YOU WERE A LESBIAN.
OH
ACTUALLY, I'M NOT. I'M BI.
OH! I'M SORRY.
ME TOO...?
IF IT ISN'T TOO RUDE, MAY I ASK YOU SOME QUESTIONS?
GO FOR IT. OUR INHIBI-TIONS ARE ALREADY LOWERED ANYWAY.
DRINKING
HAVE YOU DATED BOTH MEN AND WOMEN?
I'VE ONLY DATED WOMEN.
REALLY!

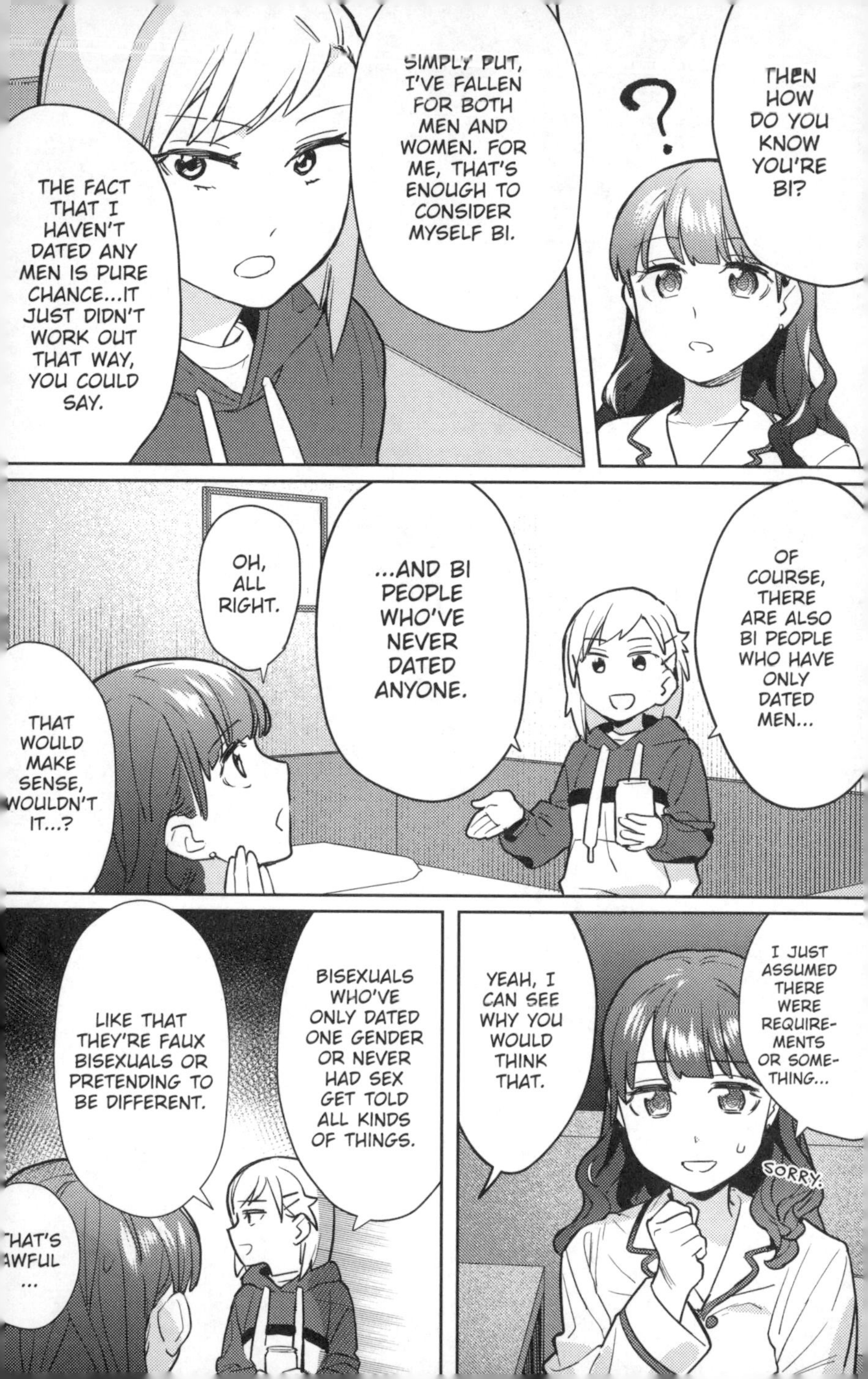
?
THEN HOW DO YOU KNOW YOU'RE BI?
SIMPLY PUT, I'VE FALLEN FOR BOTH MEN AND WOMEN. FOR ME, THAT'S ENOUGH TO CONSIDER MYSELF BI.
THE FACT THAT I HAVEN'T DATED ANY MEN IS PURE CHANCE...IT JUST DIDN'T WORK OUT THAT WAY, YOU COULD SAY.
OF COURSE, THERE ARE ALSO BI PEOPLE WHO HAVE ONLY DATED MEN...
...AND BI PEOPLE WHO'VE NEVER DATED ANYONE.
OH, ALL RIGHT.
THAT WOULD MAKE SENSE, WOULDN'T IT...?
I JUST ASSUMED THERE WERE REQUIREMENTS OR SOMETHING...
SORRY.
YEAH, I CAN SEE WHY YOU WOULD THINK THAT.
BISEXUALS WHO'VE ONLY DATED ONE GENDER OR NEVER HAD SEX GET TOLD ALL KINDS OF THINGS.
LIKE THAT THEY'RE FAUX BISEXUALS OR PRETENDING TO BE DIFFERENT.
THAT'S AWFUL ...

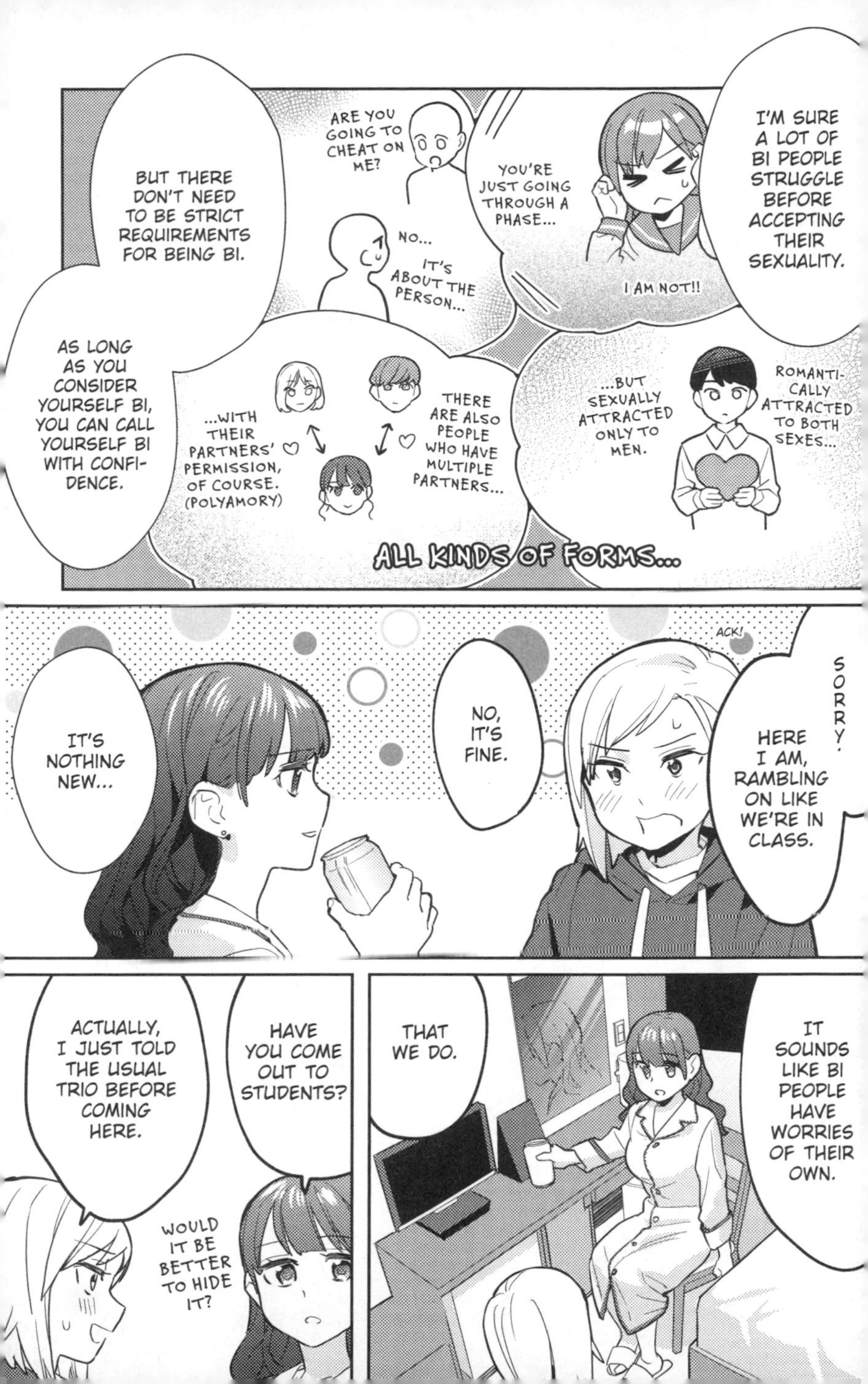
I'M SURE A LOT OF BI PEOPLE STRUGGLE BEFORE ACCEPTING THEIR SEXUALITY.
YOU'RE JUST GOING THROUGH A PHASE...
I AM NOT!!
ARE YOU GOING TO CHEAT ON ME?
NO...
IT'S ABOUT THE PERSON...
BUT THERE DON'T NEED TO BE STRICT REQUIREMENTS FOR BEING BI.
ROMANTICALLY ATTRACTED TO BOTH SEXES...
...BUT SEXUALLY ATTRACTED ONLY TO MEN.
THERE ARE ALSO PEOPLE WHO HAVE MULTIPLE PARTNERS...
...WITH THEIR PARTNERS' PERMISSION, OF COURSE. (POLYAMORY)
AS LONG AS YOU CONSIDER YOURSELF BI, YOU CAN CALL YOURSELF BI WITH CONFIDENCE.
ALL KINDS OF FORMS...
ACK!
SORRY.
HERE I AM, RAMBLING ON LIKE WE'RE IN CLASS.
NO, IT'S FINE.
IT'S NOTHING NEW...
IT SOUNDS LIKE BI PEOPLE HAVE WORRIES OF THEIR OWN.
THAT WE DO.
HAVE YOU COME OUT TO STUDENTS?
WOULD IT BE BETTER TO HIDE IT?
ACTUALLY, I JUST TOLD THE USUAL TRIO BEFORE COMING HERE.

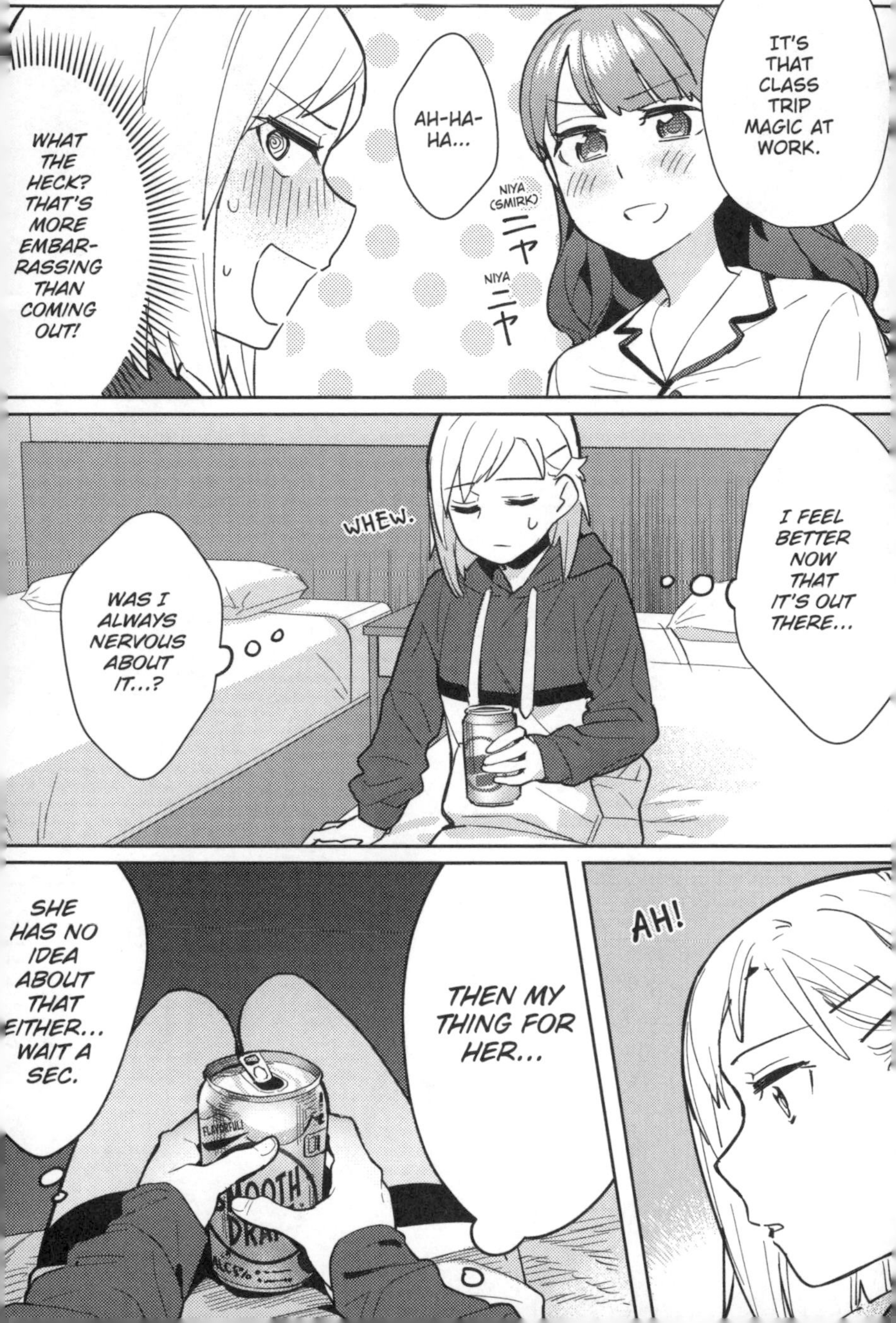
IT'S THAT CLASS TRIP MAGIC AT WORK.
NIYA (SMIRK)
ニヤ
NIYA
ニヤ
AH-HA-HA...
WHAT THE HECK? THAT'S MORE EMBARRASSING THAN COMING OUT!
I FEEL BETTER NOW THAT IT'S OUT THERE...
WHEW.
WAS I ALWAYS NERVOUS ABOUT IT...?
AH!
THEN MY THING FOR HER...
SHE HAS NO IDEA ABOUT THAT EITHER... WAIT A SEC.

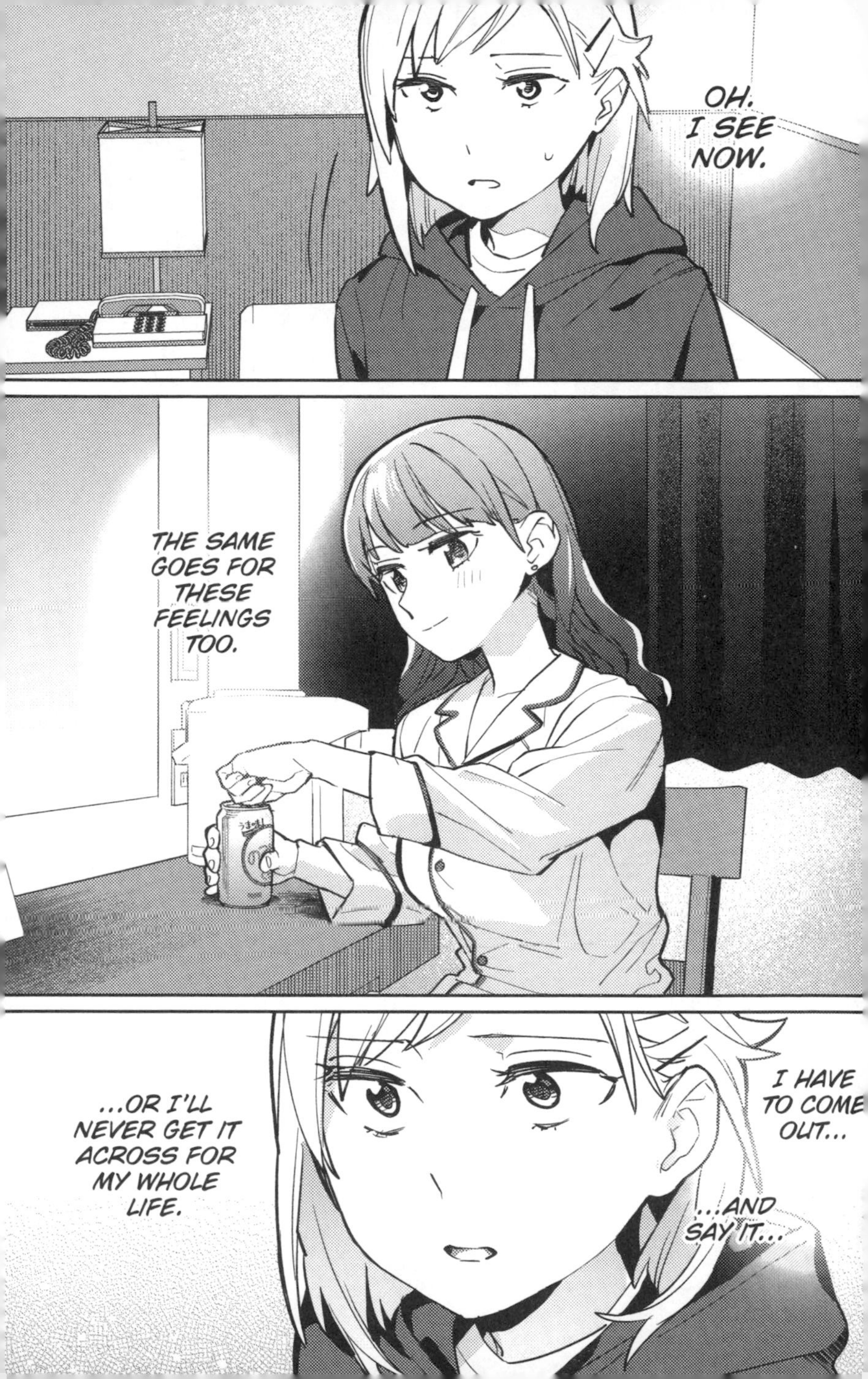
OH. I SEE NOW.
THE SAME GOES FOR THESE FEELINGS TOO.
I HAVE TO COME OUT...
...AND SAY IT...
...OR I'LL NEVER GET IT ACROSS FOR MY WHOLE LIFE.

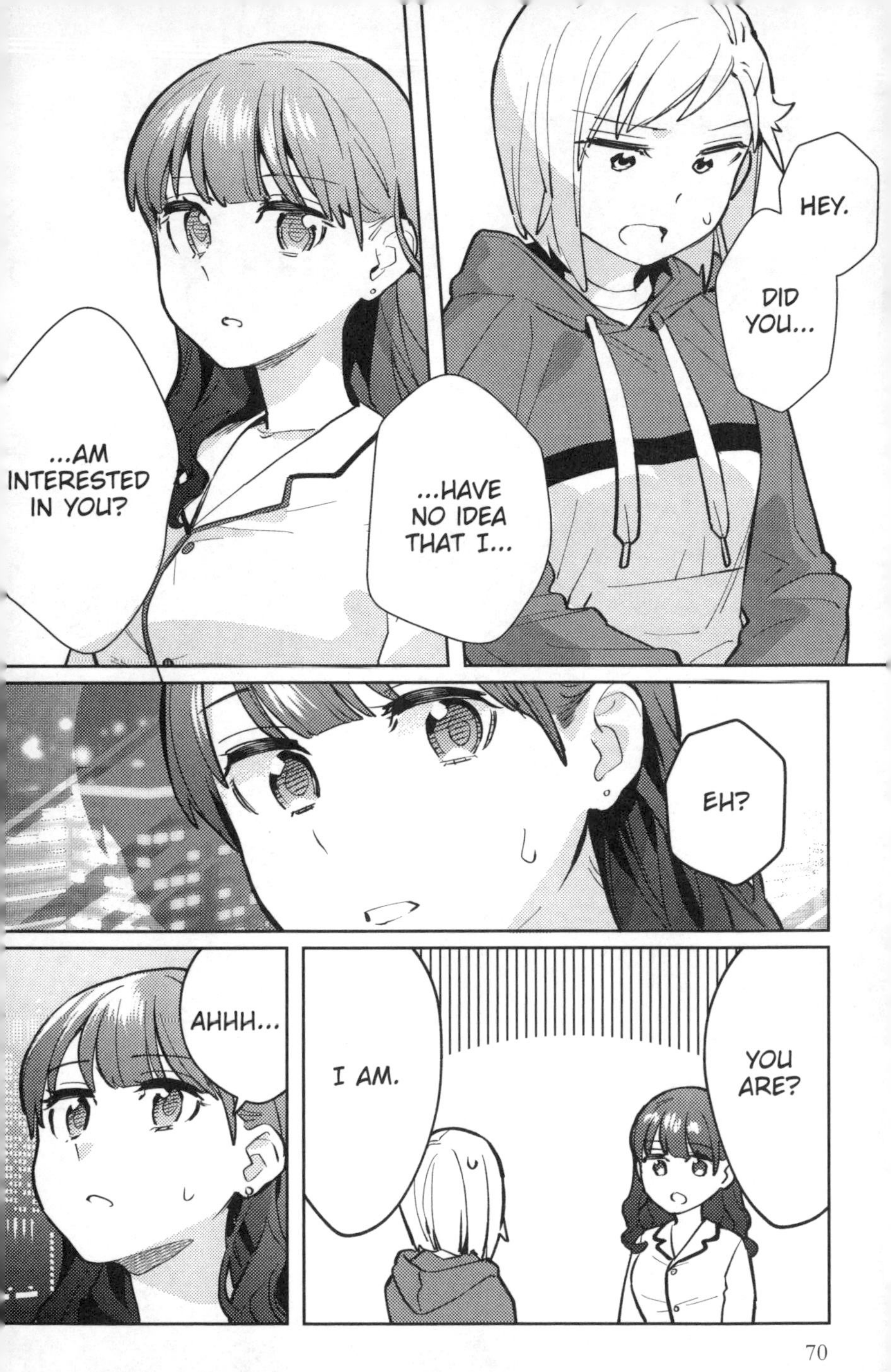
HEY.
DID YOU...
...HAVE NO IDEA THAT I...
...AM INTERESTED IN YOU?
EH?
YOU ARE?
I AM.
AHHH...

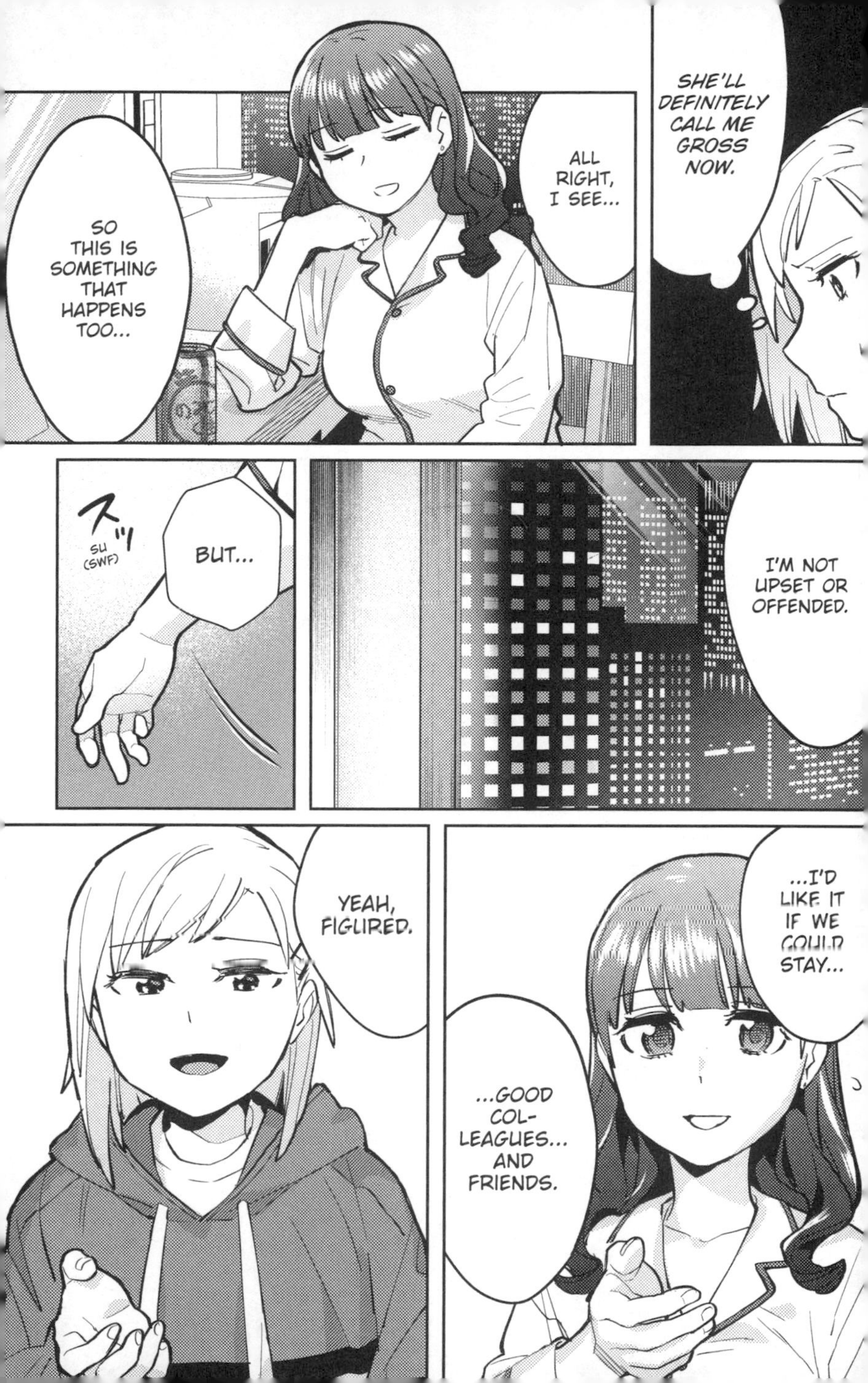
SHE'LL DEFINITELY CALL ME GROSS NOW.
ALL RIGHT, I SEE...
SO THIS IS SOMETHING THAT HAPPENS TOO...
I'M NOT UPSET OR OFFENDED.
BUT...
スッ
SU (SWF)
...I'D LIKE IT IF WE COULD STAY...
...GOOD COL-LEAGUES... AND FRIENDS.
YEAH, FIGURED.

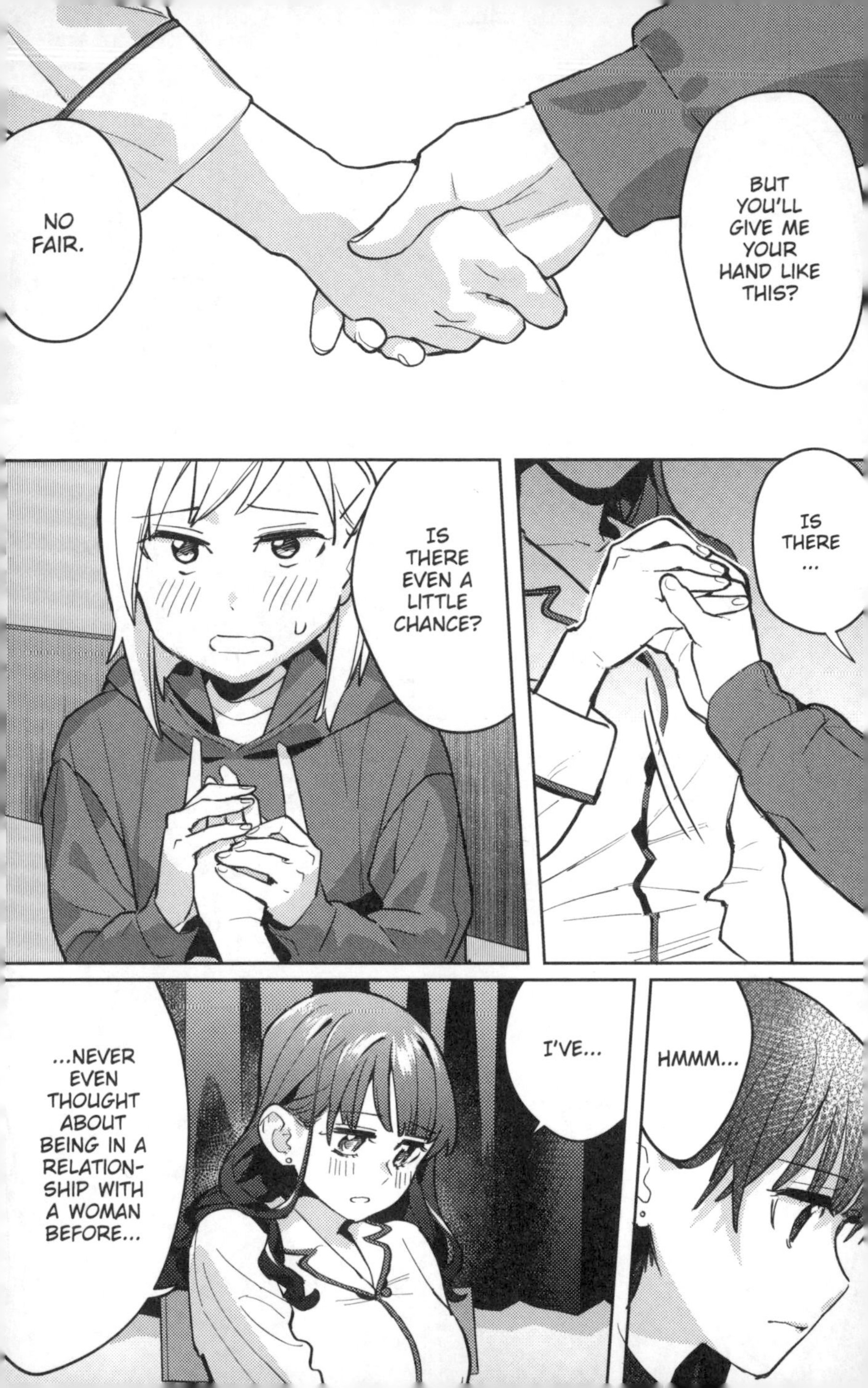
BUT YOU'LL GIVE ME YOUR HAND LIKE THIS?
NO FAIR.
IS THERE ...
IS THERE EVEN A LITTLE CHANCE?
HMMM...
I'VE...
...NEVER EVEN THOUGHT ABOUT BEING IN A RELATION-SHIP WITH A WOMAN BEFORE...

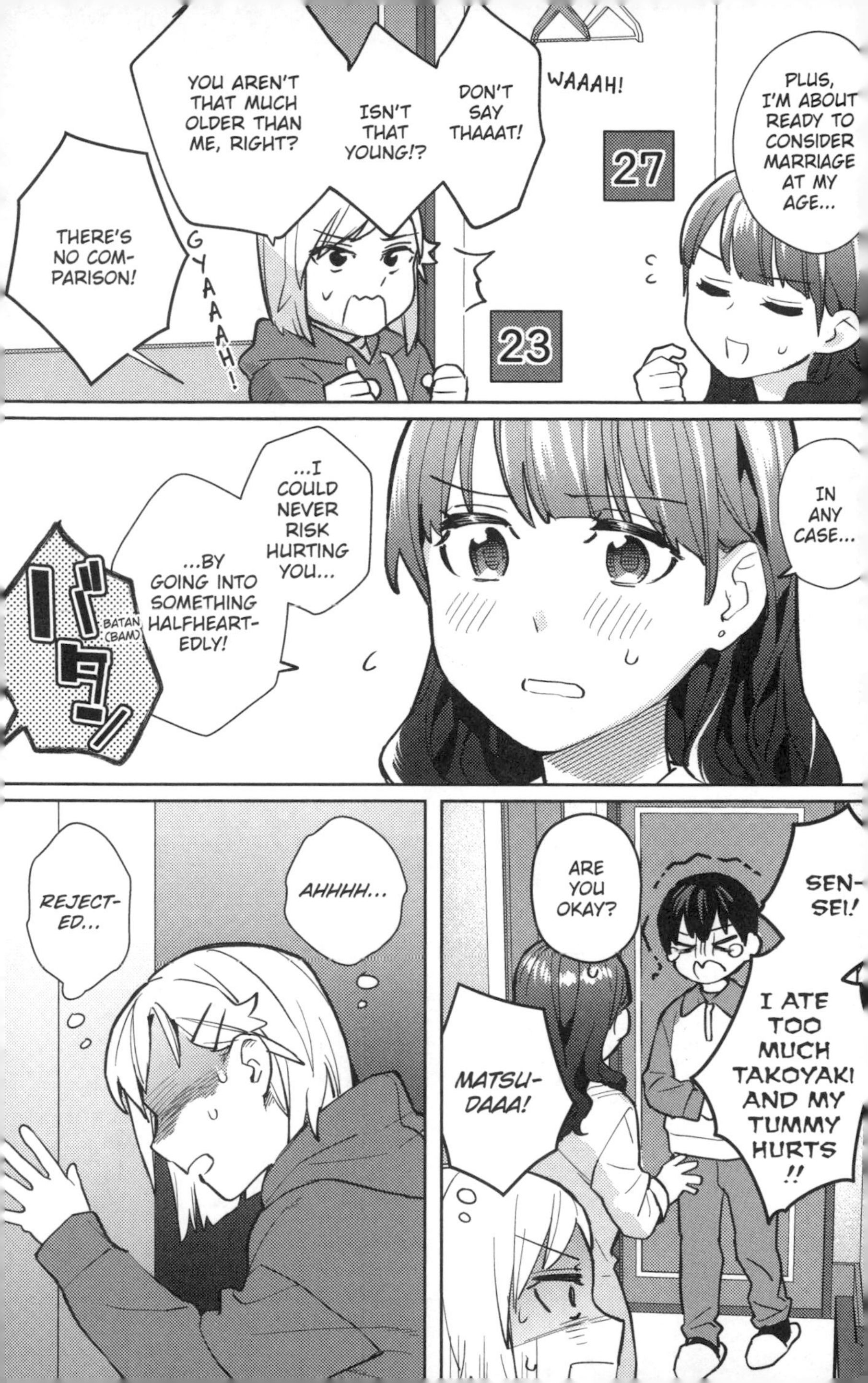
PLUS, I'M ABOUT READY TO CONSIDER MARRIAGE AT MY AGE...
27
WAAAH!
DON'T SAY THAAAT!
ISN'T THAT YOUNG!?
YOU AREN'T THAT MUCH OLDER THAN ME, RIGHT?
23
GYAAAAH!
THERE'S NO COM-PARISON!
IN ANY CASE...
...I COULD NEVER RISK HURTING YOU...
...BY GOING INTO SOMETHING HALFHEART-EDLY!
BATAN (BAM)
SEN-SEI!
I ATE TOO MUCH TAKOYAKI AND MY TUMMY HURTS !!
ARE YOU OKAY?
MATSU-DAAA!
AHHHH...
REJECT-ED...

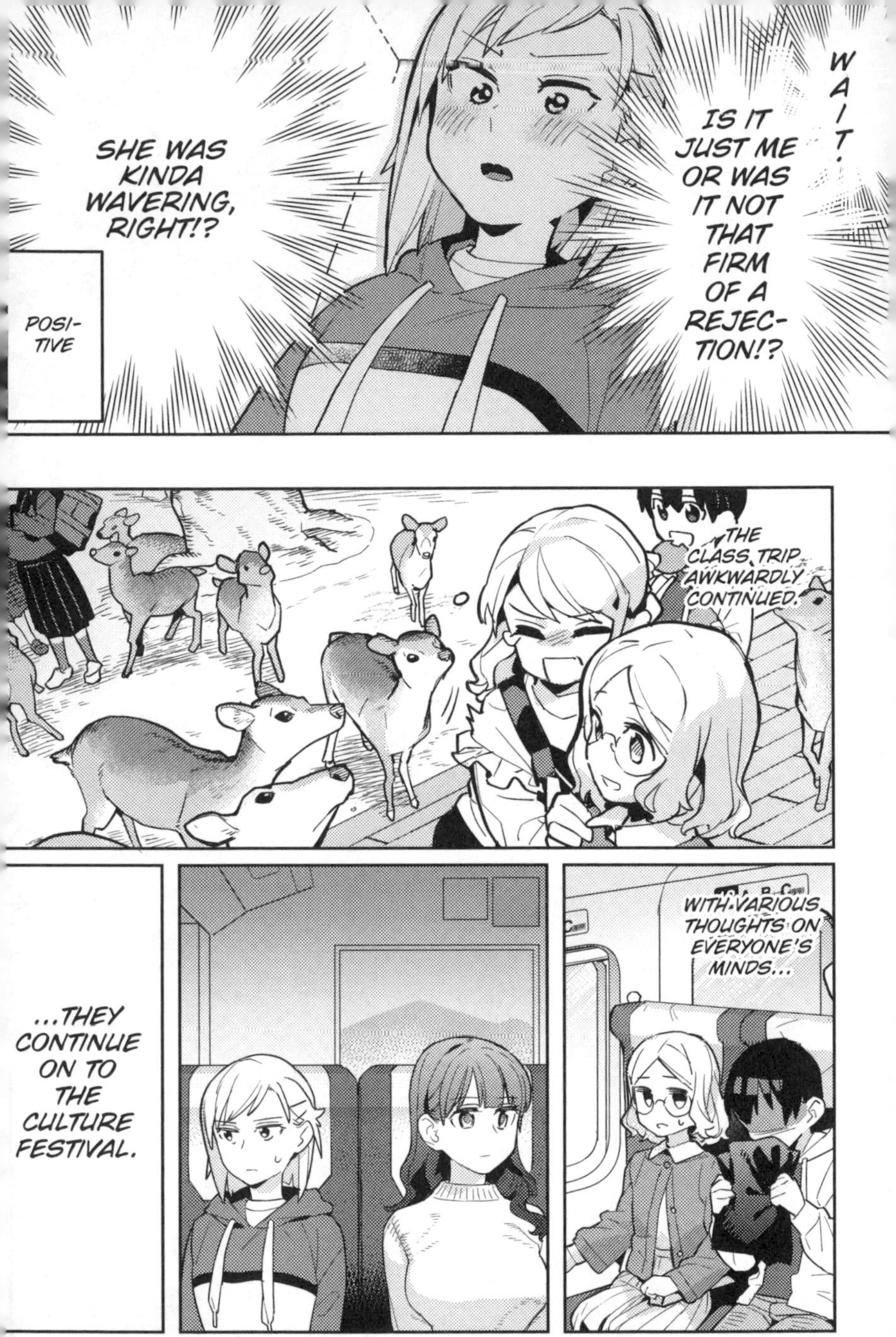
WAIT!
IS IT JUST ME OR WAS IT NOT THAT FIRM OF A REJECTION!?
SHE WAS KINDA WAVERING, RIGHT!?
POSITIVE
THE CLASS TRIP AWKWARDLY CONTINUED.
WITH VARIOUS THOUGHTS ON EVERYONE'S MINDS...
...THEY CONTINUE ON TO THE CULTURE FESTIVAL.

Class 16 **Candid Shot**

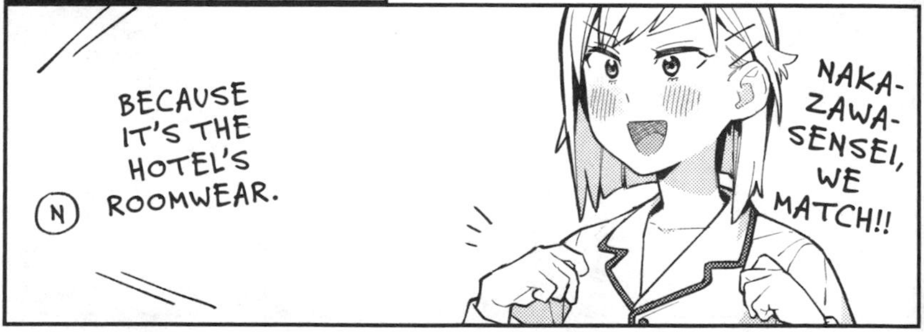
NAKA-ZAWA-SENSEI, WE MATCH!!
(N) BECAUSE IT'S THE HOTEL'S ROOMWEAR.

Knocking Out 12 Sex Concerns! 4

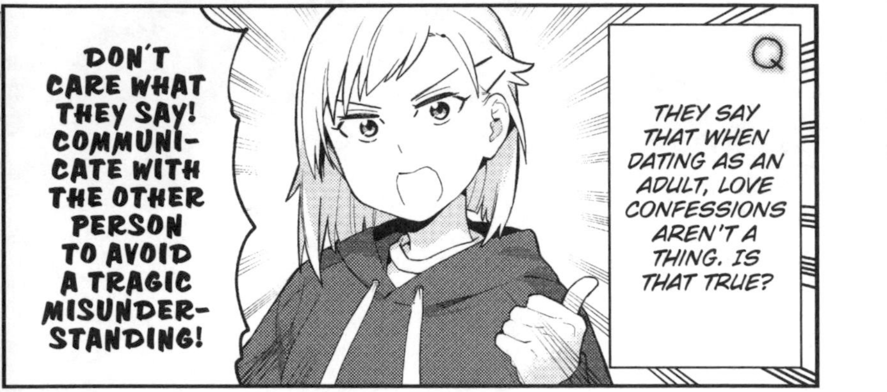
Q
THEY SAY THAT WHEN DATING AS AN ADULT, LOVE CONFESSIONS AREN'T A THING. IS THAT TRUE?
DON'T CARE WHAT THEY SAY! COMMUNI-CATE WITH THE OTHER PERSON TO AVOID A TRAGIC MISUNDER-STANDING!

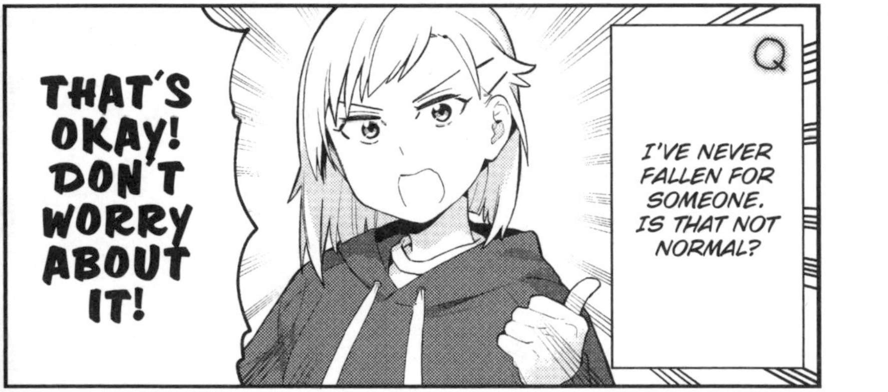
Q
I'VE NEVER FALLEN FOR SOMEONE. IS THAT NOT NORMAL?
THAT'S OKAY! DON'T WORRY ABOUT IT!

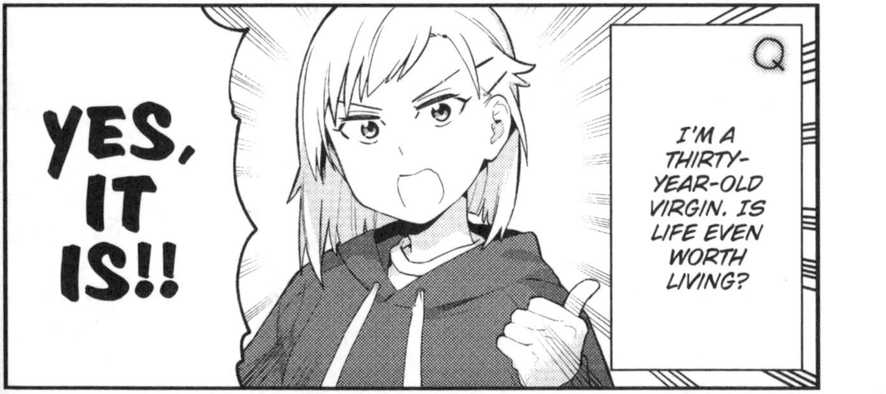
Q
I'M A THIRTY-YEAR-OLD VIRGIN. IS LIFE EVEN WORTH LIVING?
YES, IT IS!!

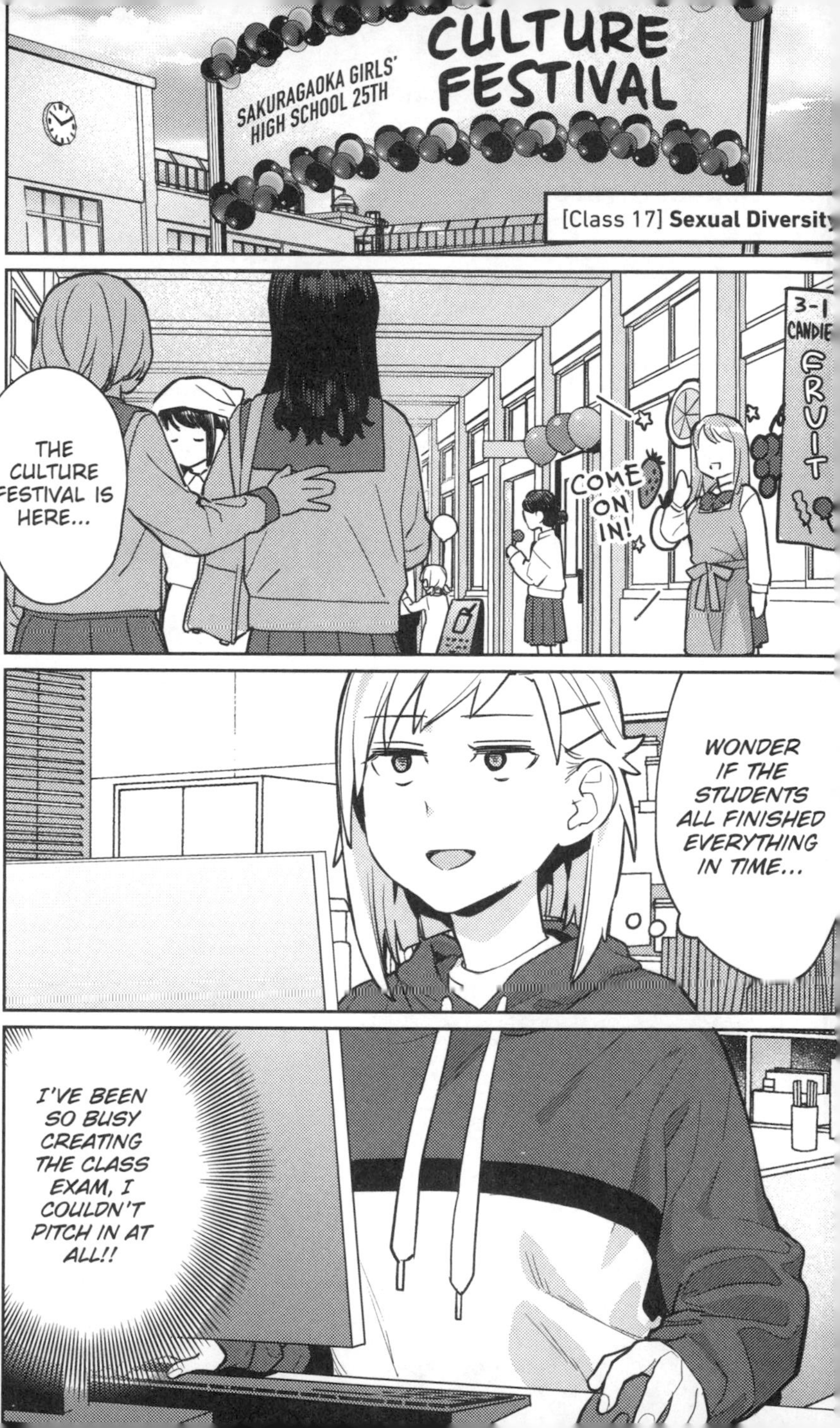
CULTURE FESTIVAL
SAKURAGAOKA GIRLS' HIGH SCHOOL 25TH
[Class 17] Sexual Diversit
3-1 CANDIE
FRUIT
COME ON IN!
THE CULTURE FESTIVAL IS HERE...
WONDER IF THE STUDENTS ALL FINISHED EVERYTHING IN TIME...
I'VE BEEN SO BUSY CREATING THE CLASS EXAM, I COULDN'T PITCH IN AT ALL!!

Class 17
Sexual Diversity

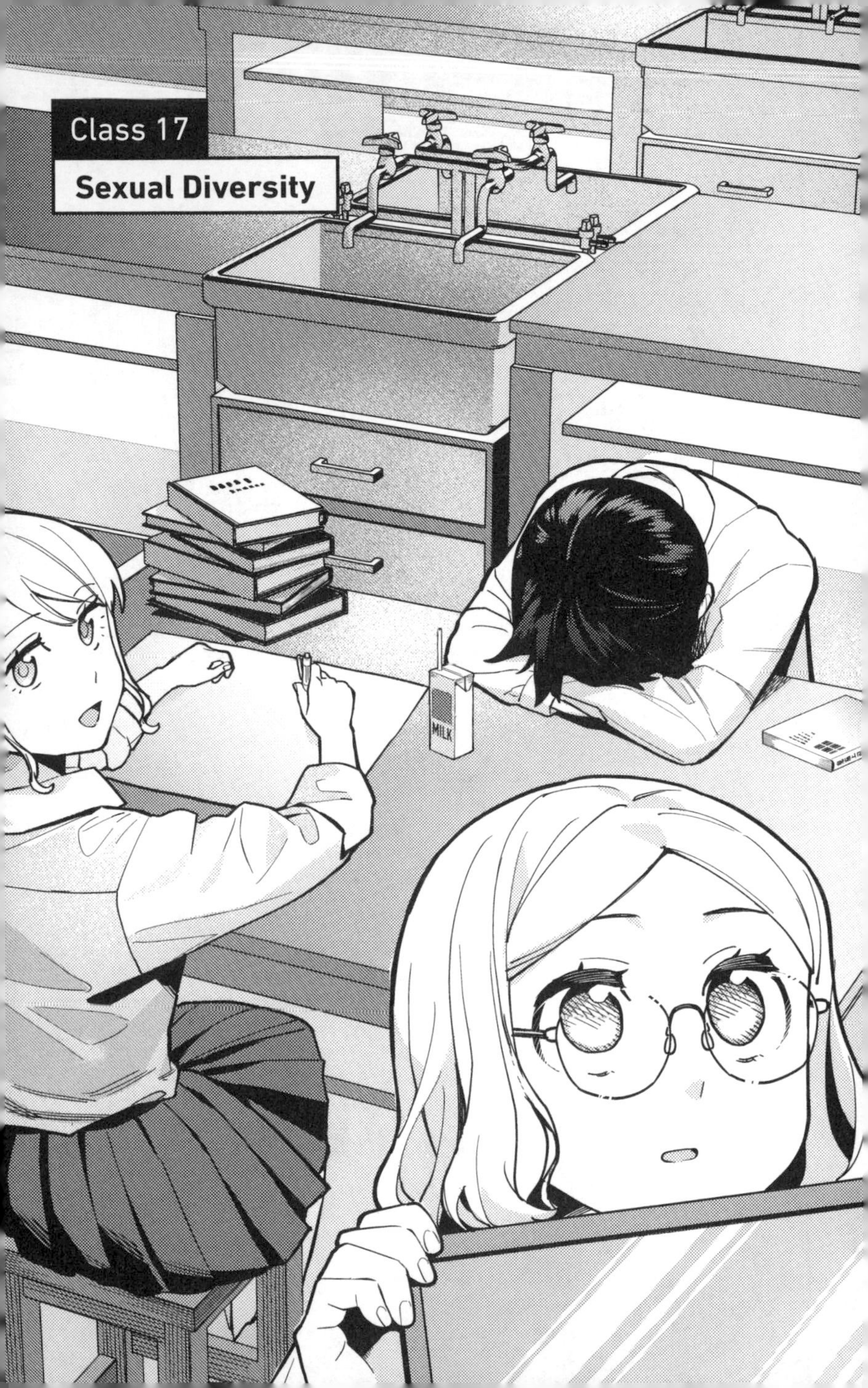
MILK

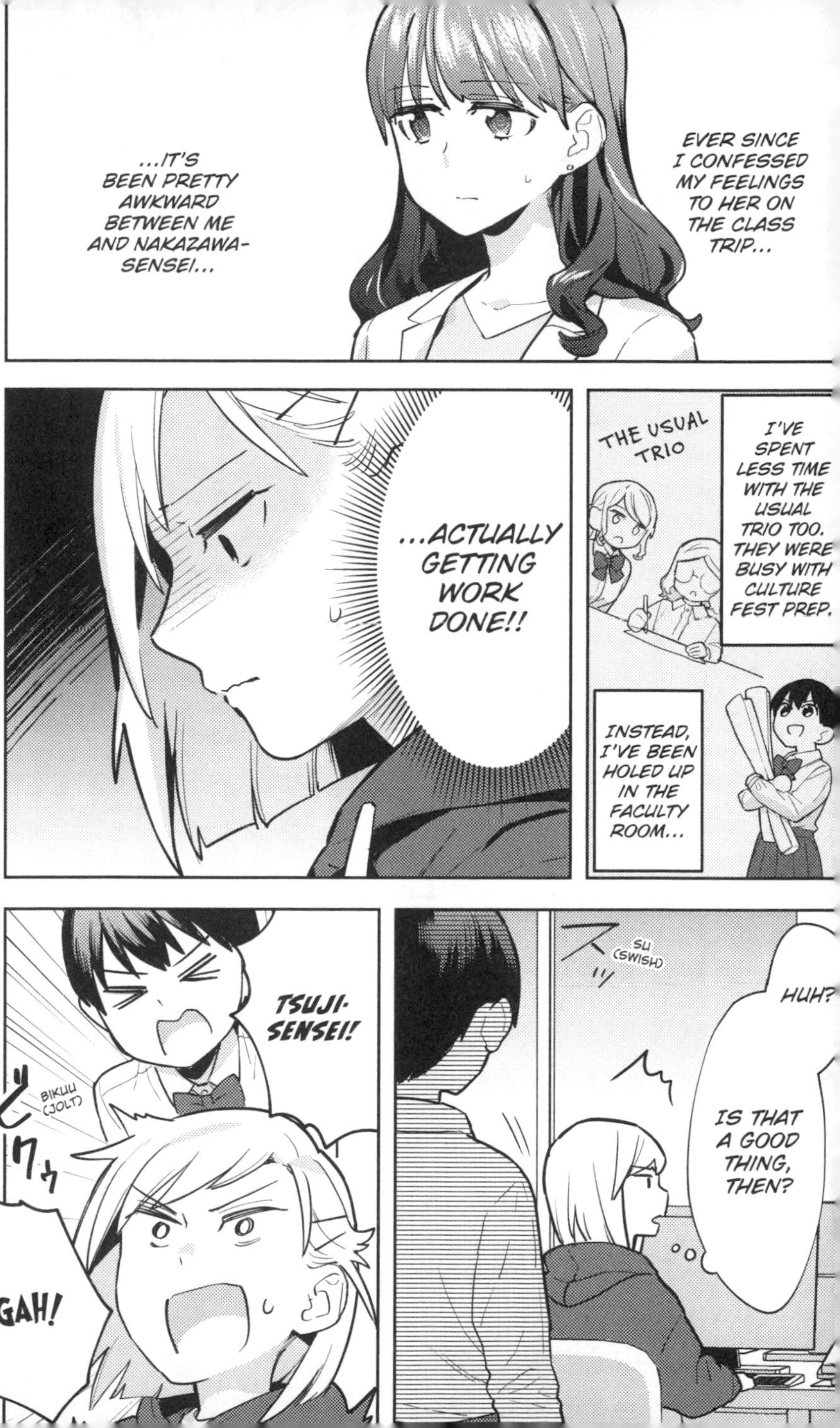
EVER SINCE I CONFESSED MY FEELINGS TO HER ON THE CLASS TRIP...
...IT'S BEEN PRETTY AWKWARD BETWEEN ME AND NAKAZAWA-SENSEI...
I'VE SPENT LESS TIME WITH THE USUAL TRIO TOO. THEY WERE BUSY WITH CULTURE FEST PREP.
THE USUAL TRIO
INSTEAD, I'VE BEEN HOLED UP IN THE FACULTY ROOM...
...ACTUALLY GETTING WORK DONE!!
SU (SWISH)
HUH?
IS THAT A GOOD THING, THEN?
TSUJI-SENSEI!
BIKUU (JOLT)
GAH!

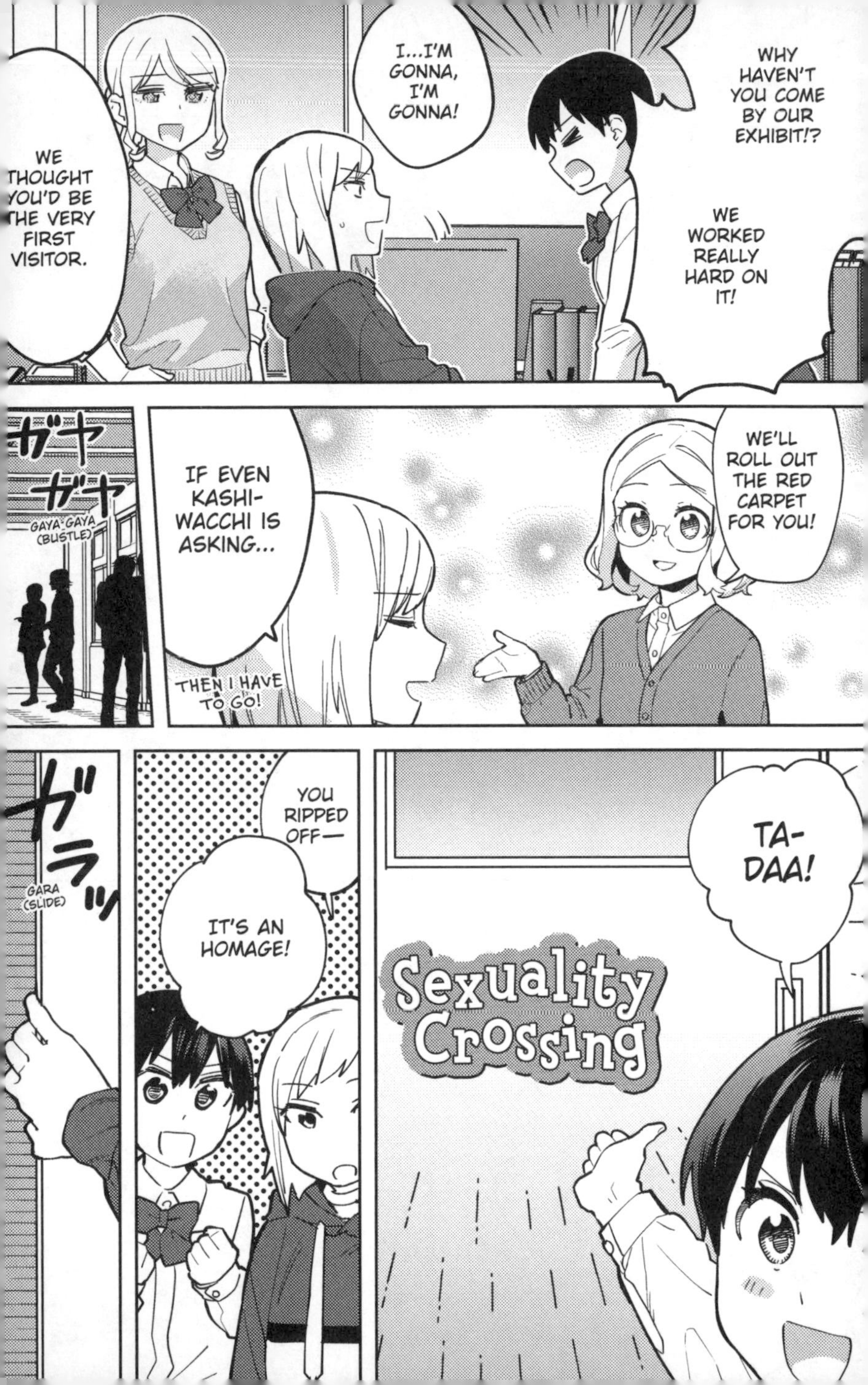
WHY HAVEN'T YOU COME BY OUR EXHIBIT!?
WE WORKED REALLY HARD ON IT!
I...I'M GONNA, I'M GONNA!
WE THOUGHT YOU'D BE THE VERY FIRST VISITOR.
WE'LL ROLL OUT THE RED CARPET FOR YOU!
IF EVEN KASHI-WACCHI IS ASKING...
THEN I HAVE TO GO!
ガヤガヤ
GAYA GAYA (BUSTLE)
TA-DAA!
Sexuality Crossing
YOU RIPPED OFF—
IT'S AN HOMAGE!
ガラッ
GARA (SLIDE)

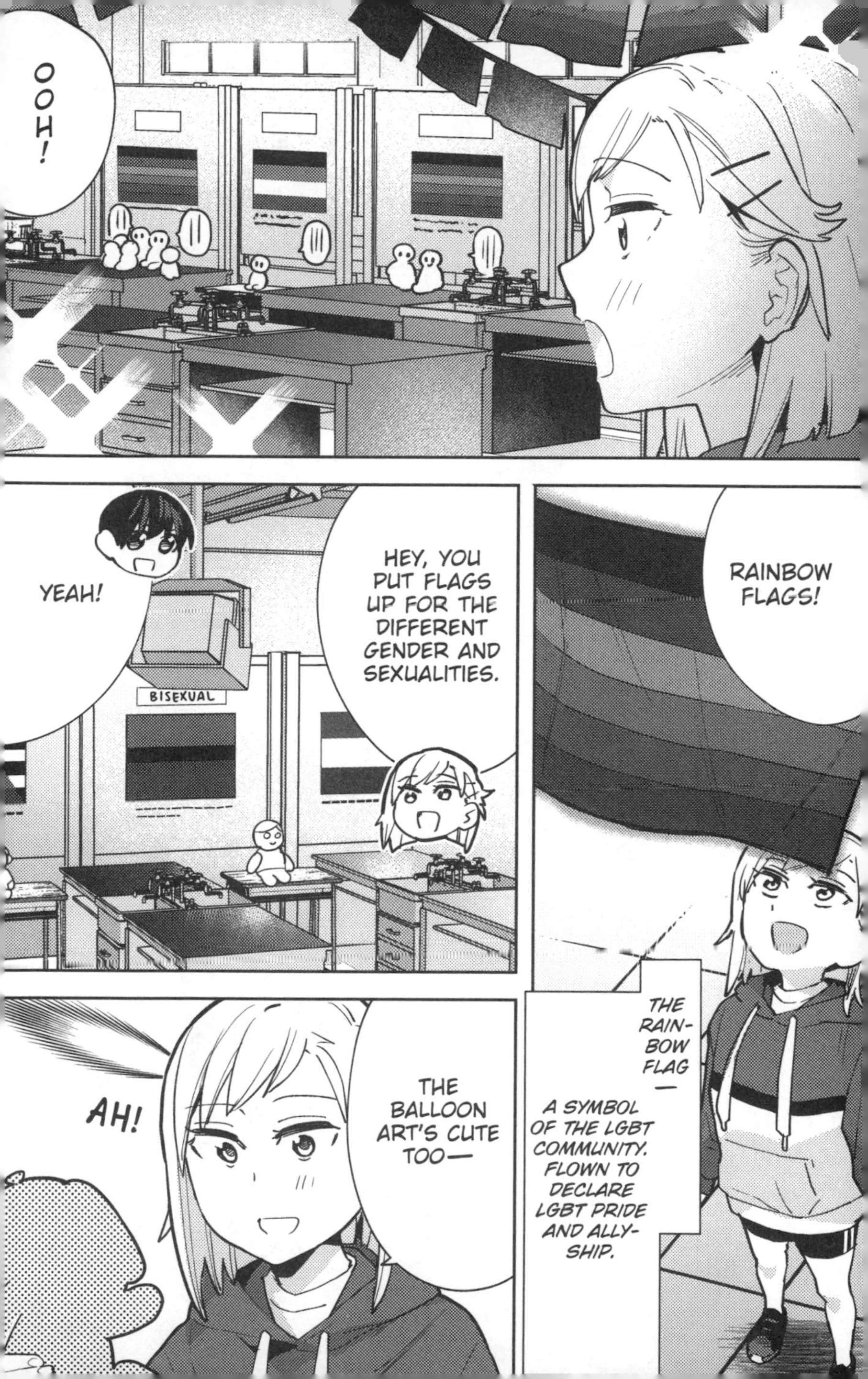
OOH!
RAINBOW FLAGS!
THE RAINBOW FLAG—
A SYMBOL OF THE LGBT COMMUNITY. FLOWN TO DECLARE LGBT PRIDE AND ALLYSHIP.
HEY, YOU PUT FLAGS UP FOR THE DIFFERENT GENDER AND SEXUALITIES.
YEAH!
BISEXUAL
THE BALLOON ART'S CUTE TOO—
AH!

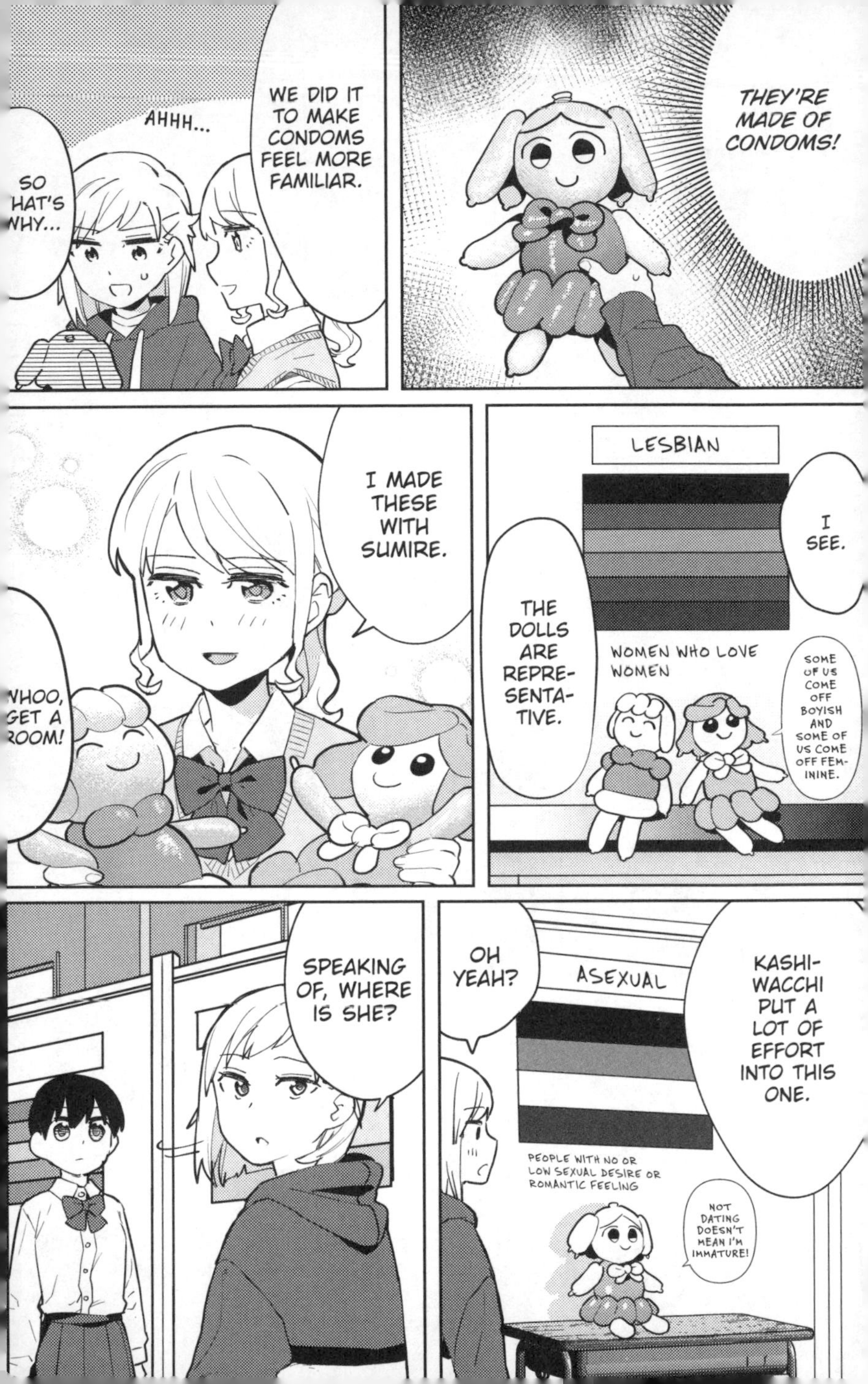
THEY'RE MADE OF CONDOMS!
WE DID IT TO MAKE CONDOMS FEEL MORE FAMILIAR.
AHHH...
SO HAT'S WHY...
LESBIAN
I SEE.
THE DOLLS ARE REPRE-SENTA-TIVE.
WOMEN WHO LOVE WOMEN
SOME OF US COME OFF BOYISH AND SOME OF US COME OFF FEM-ININE.
I MADE THESE WITH SUMIRE.
WHOO, GET A ROOM!
KASHI-WACCHI PUT A LOT OF EFFORT INTO THIS ONE.
ASEXUAL
OH YEAH?
PEOPLE WITH NO OR LOW SEXUAL DESIRE OR ROMANTIC FEELING
NOT DATING DOESN'T MEAN I'M IMMATURE!
SPEAKING OF, WHERE IS SHE?

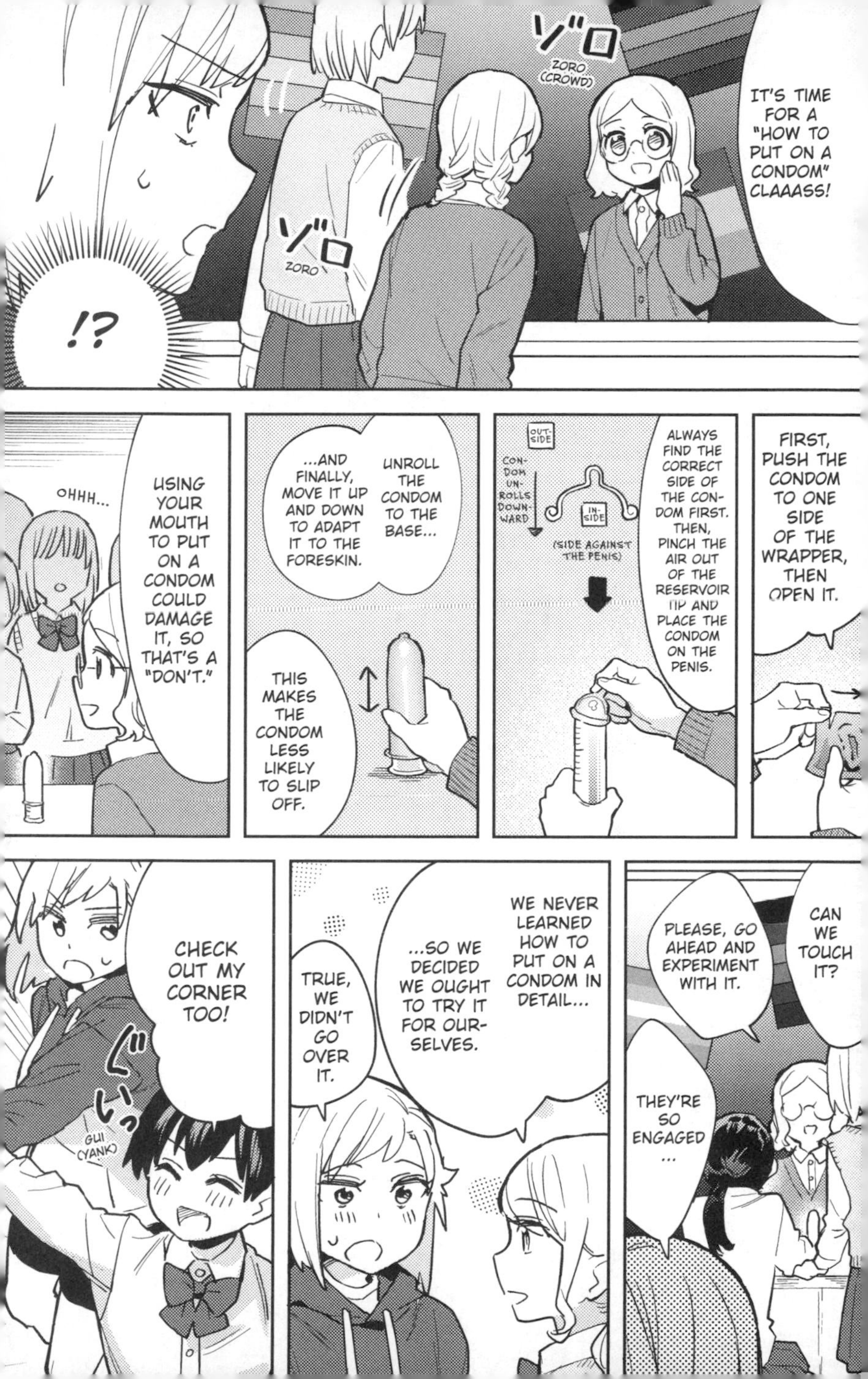
ゾロ
ZORO (CROWD)
IT'S TIME FOR A "HOW TO PUT ON A CONDOM" CLAAASS!
ゾロ
ZORO
!?
FIRST, PUSH THE CONDOM TO ONE SIDE OF THE WRAPPER, THEN OPEN IT.
ALWAYS FIND THE CORRECT SIDE OF THE CONDOM FIRST. THEN, PINCH THE AIR OUT OF THE RESERVOIR TIP AND PLACE THE CONDOM ON THE PENIS.
OUTSIDE
CONDOM UNROLLS DOWNWARD
INSIDE
(SIDE AGAINST THE PENIS)
UNROLL THE CONDOM TO THE BASE...
...AND FINALLY, MOVE IT UP AND DOWN TO ADAPT IT TO THE FORESKIN.
THIS MAKES THE CONDOM LESS LIKELY TO SLIP OFF.
USING YOUR MOUTH TO PUT ON A CONDOM COULD DAMAGE IT, SO THAT'S A "DON'T."
OHHH...
CAN WE TOUCH IT?
PLEASE, GO AHEAD AND EXPERIMENT WITH IT.
THEY'RE SO ENGAGED...
WE NEVER LEARNED HOW TO PUT ON A CONDOM IN DETAIL...
...SO WE DECIDED WE OUGHT TO TRY IT FOR OURSELVES.
TRUE, WE DIDN'T GO OVER IT.
CHECK OUT MY CORNER TOO!
ぐいっ
GUI (YANK)

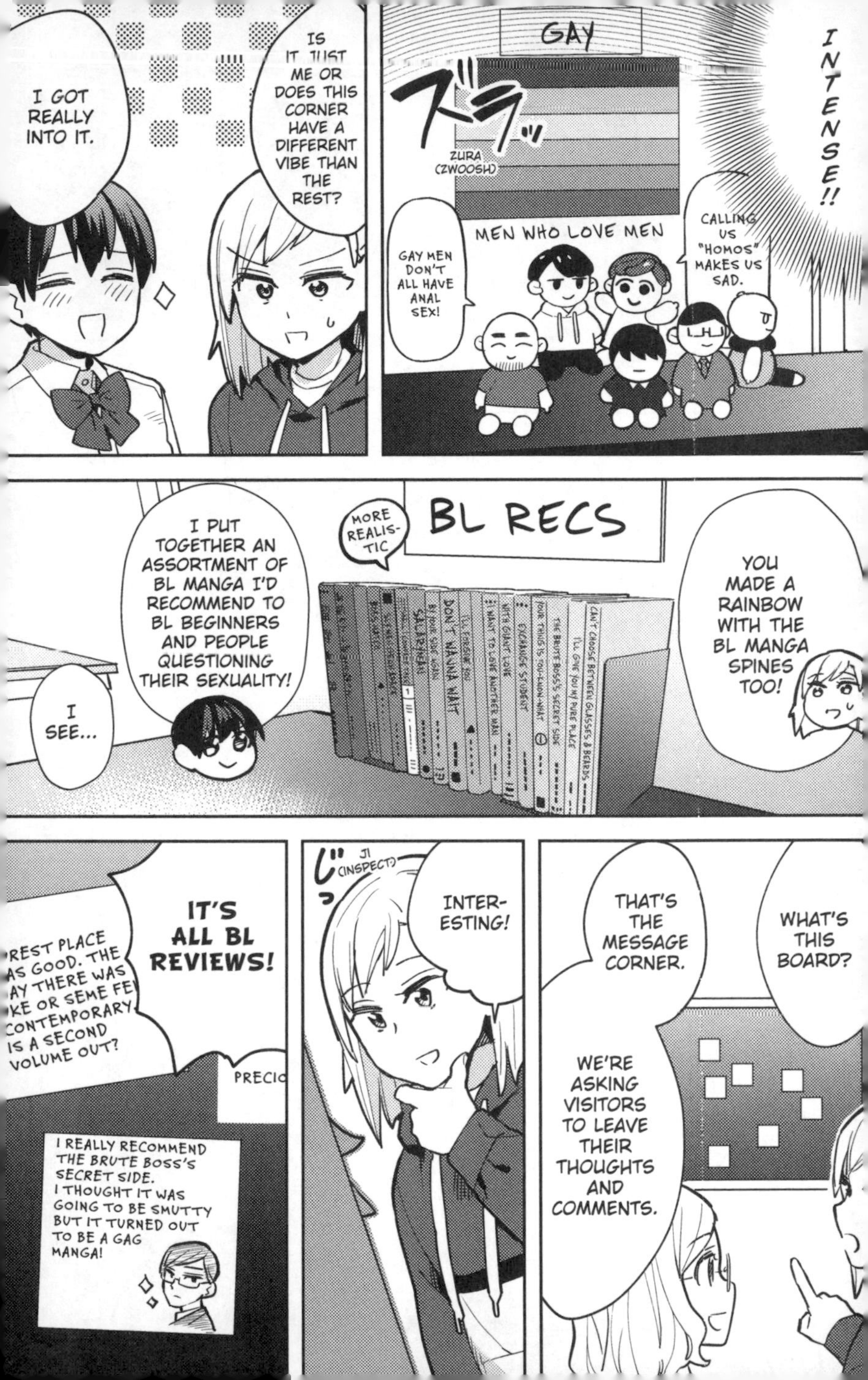
INTENSE!!
GAY
ZURA (ZWOOSH)
CALLING US "HOMOS" MAKES US SAD.
MEN WHO LOVE MEN
GAY MEN DON'T ALL HAVE ANAL SEX!
IS IT JUST ME OR DOES THIS CORNER HAVE A DIFFERENT VIBE THAN THE REST?
I GOT REALLY INTO IT.
YOU MADE A RAINBOW WITH THE BL MANGA SPINES TOO!
BL RECS
MORE REALISTIC
I PUT TOGETHER AN ASSORTMENT OF BL MANGA I'D RECOMMEND TO BL BEGINNERS AND PEOPLE QUESTIONING THEIR SEXUALITY!
I SEE...
CAN'T CHOOSE BETWEEN GLASSES & BEARDS
I'LL GIVE YOU MY PURE PLACE
THE BRUTE BOSS'S SECRET SIDE
YOUR THING IS YOU-KNOW-WHAT
EXCHANGE STUDENT
WITH GIANT LOVE
I WANT TO LOVE ANOTHER MAN
DON'T WANNA WAIT
BY YOUR SIDE AGAIN
SALARYMAN
WHAT'S THIS BOARD?
THAT'S THE MESSAGE CORNER.
WE'RE ASKING VISITORS TO LEAVE THEIR THOUGHTS AND COMMENTS.
JI (INSPECT)
INTER-ESTING!
IT'S ALL BL REVIEWS!
REST PLACE AS GOOD. THE AY THERE WAS KE OR SEME FE CONTEMPORARY IS A SECOND VOLUME OUT?
PRECIO
I REALLY RECOMMEND THE BRUTE BOSS'S SECRET SIDE. I THOUGHT IT WAS GOING TO BE SMUTTY BUT IT TURNED OUT TO BE A GAG MANGA!

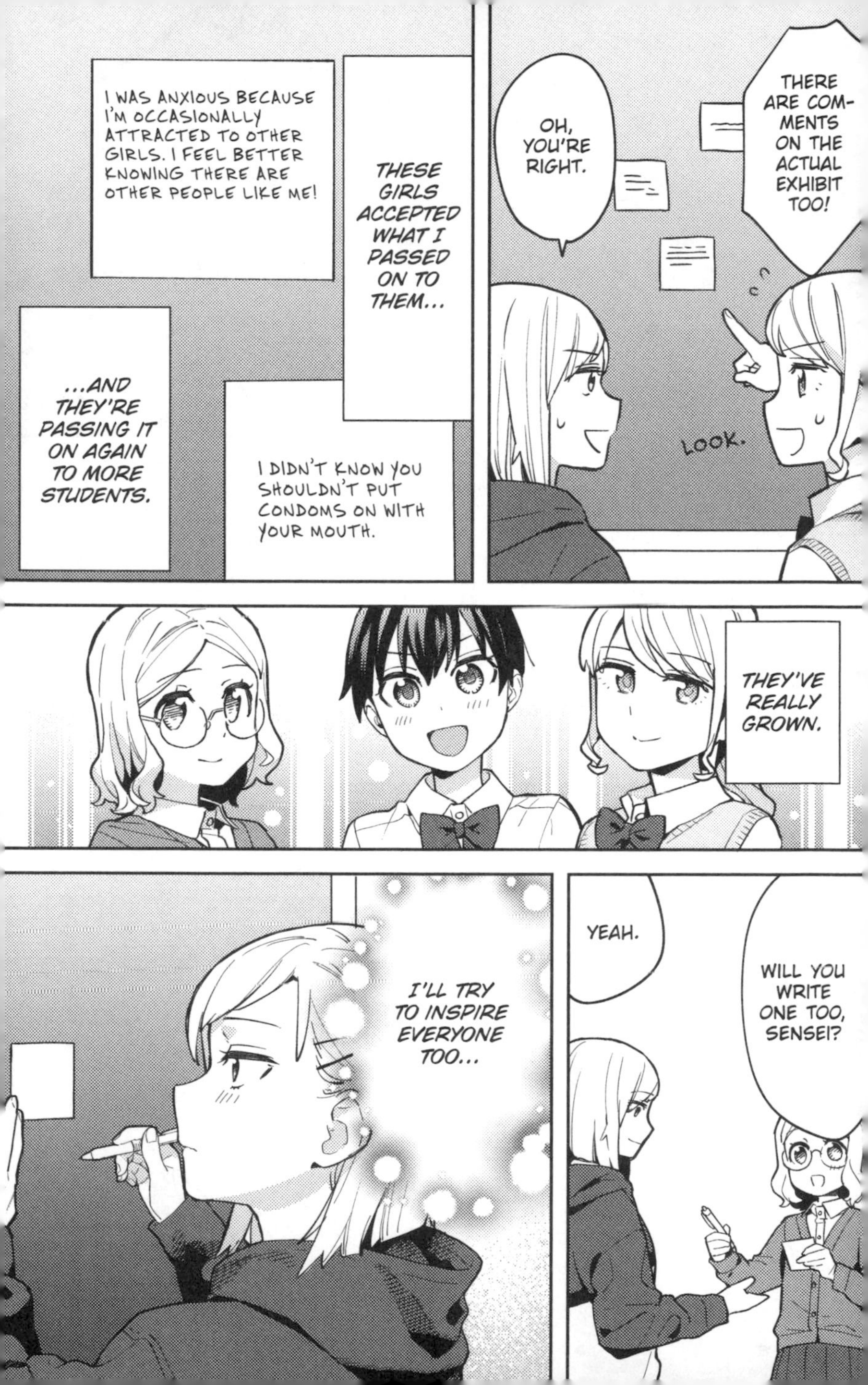
THERE ARE COM-MENTS ON THE ACTUAL EXHIBIT TOO!
OH, YOU'RE RIGHT.
LOOK.
THESE GIRLS ACCEPTED WHAT I PASSED ON TO THEM...
I WAS ANXIOUS BECAUSE I'M OCCASIONALLY ATTRACTED TO OTHER GIRLS. I FEEL BETTER KNOWING THERE ARE OTHER PEOPLE LIKE ME!
I DIDN'T KNOW YOU SHOULDN'T PUT CONDOMS ON WITH YOUR MOUTH.
...AND THEY'RE PASSING IT ON AGAIN TO MORE STUDENTS.
THEY'VE REALLY GROWN.
WILL YOU WRITE ONE TOO, SENSEI?
YEAH.
I'LL TRY TO INSPIRE EVERYONE TOO...

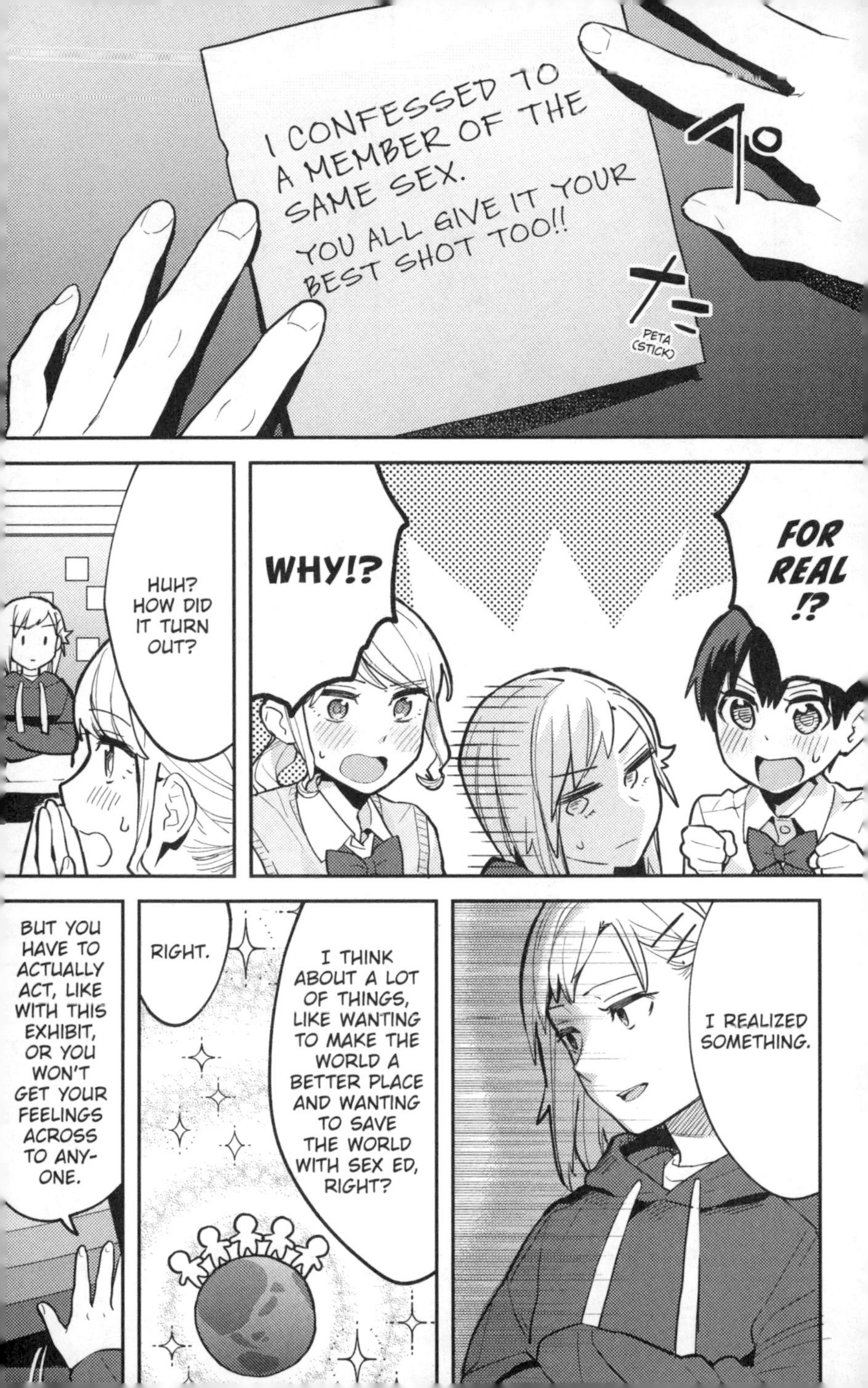
I CONFESSED TO A MEMBER OF THE SAME SEX.
YOU ALL GIVE IT YOUR BEST SHOT TOO!!
PETA (STICK)
FOR REAL!?
WHY!?
HUH? HOW DID IT TURN OUT?
I REALIZED SOMETHING.
I THINK ABOUT A LOT OF THINGS, LIKE WANTING TO MAKE THE WORLD A BETTER PLACE AND WANTING TO SAVE THE WORLD WITH SEX ED, RIGHT?
RIGHT.
BUT YOU HAVE TO ACTUALLY ACT, LIKE WITH THIS EXHIBIT, OR YOU WON'T GET YOUR FEELINGS ACROSS TO ANY-ONE.

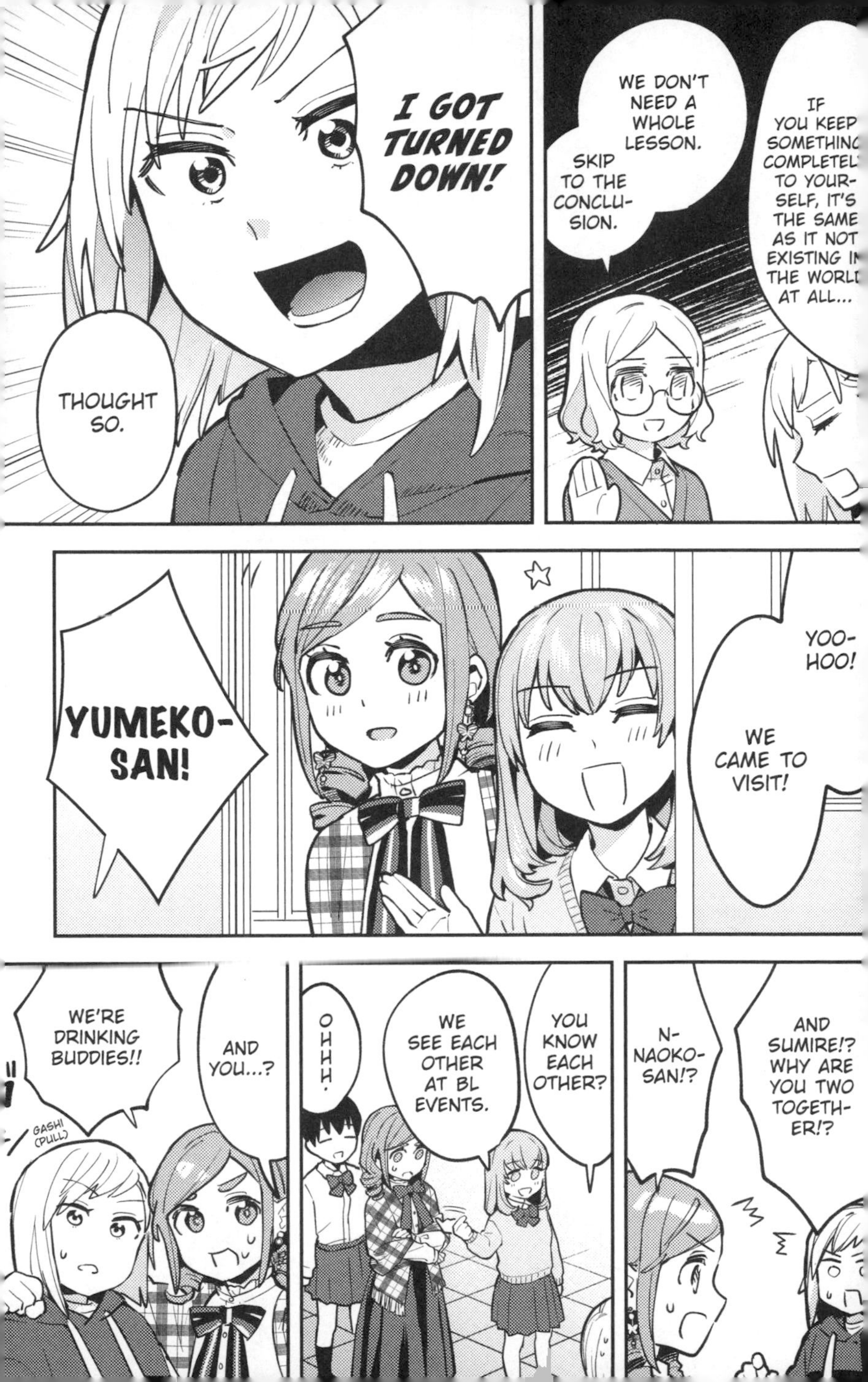
IF YOU KEEP SOMETHING COMPLETELY TO YOURSELF, IT'S THE SAME AS IT NOT EXISTING IN THE WORLD AT ALL...
WE DON'T NEED A WHOLE LESSON.
SKIP TO THE CONCLUSION.
I GOT TURNED DOWN!
THOUGHT SO.
YOO-HOO!
WE CAME TO VISIT!
YUMEKO-SAN!
AND SUMIRE!? WHY ARE YOU TWO TOGETHER!?
N-NAOKO-SAN!?
YOU KNOW EACH OTHER?
WE SEE EACH OTHER AT BL EVENTS.
OHHH.
AND YOU...?
WE'RE DRINKING BUDDIES!!
GASHI (PULL)

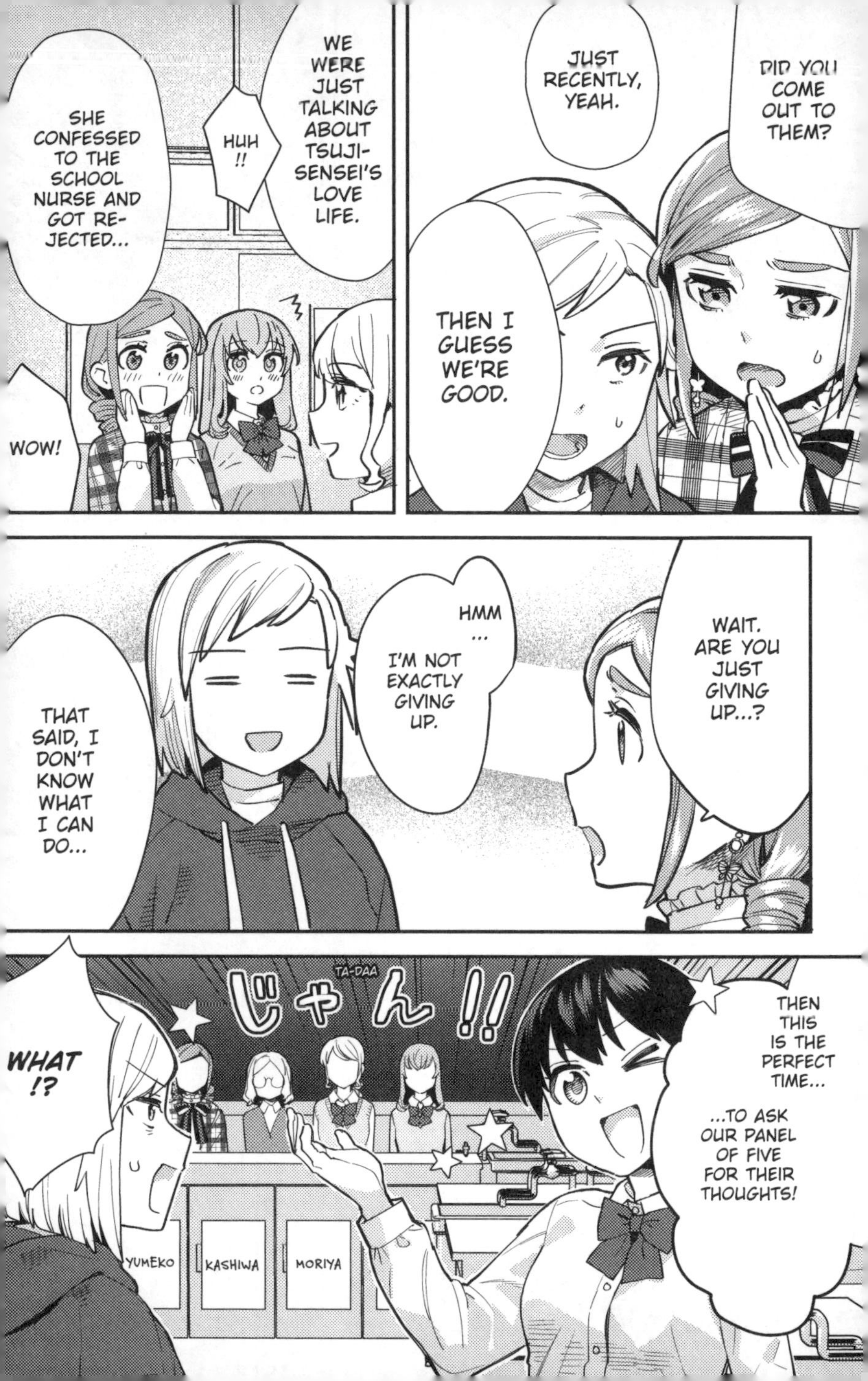
DID YOU COME OUT TO THEM?
JUST RECENTLY, YEAH.
THEN I GUESS WE'RE GOOD.
WE WERE JUST TALKING ABOUT TSUJI-SENSEI'S LOVE LIFE.
HUH !!
SHE CONFESSED TO THE SCHOOL NURSE AND GOT RE-JECTED...
WOW!
WAIT. ARE YOU JUST GIVING UP...?
HMM ...
I'M NOT EXACTLY GIVING UP.
THAT SAID, I DON'T KNOW WHAT I CAN DO...
THEN THIS IS THE PERFECT TIME...
...TO ASK OUR PANEL OF FIVE FOR THEIR THOUGHTS!
じゃん!!
TA-DAA
WHAT !?
YUMEKO
KASHIWA
MORIYA

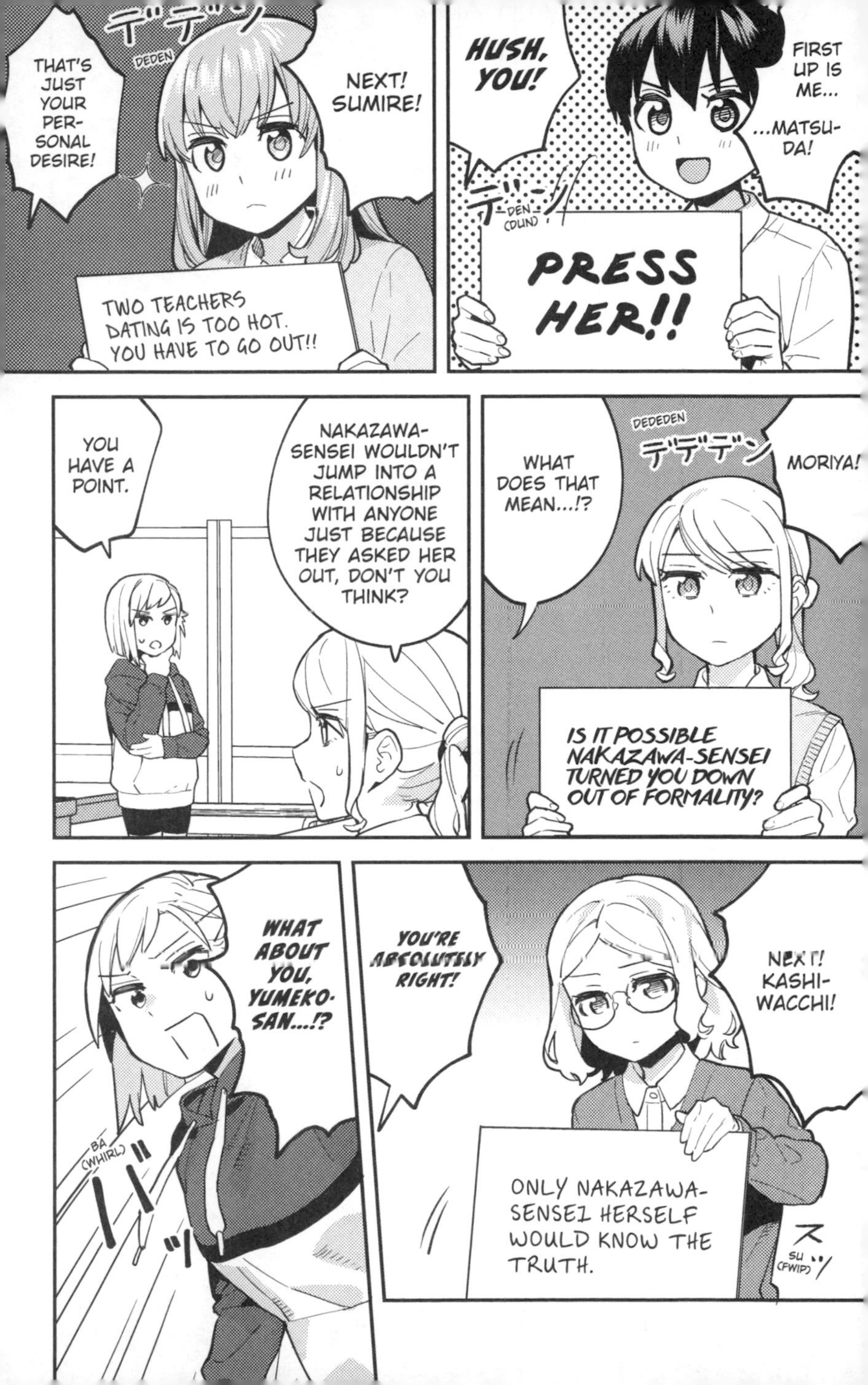
FIRST UP IS ME...
...MATSUDA!
デーン
DEN (DUN)
PRESS HER!!
HUSH, YOU!
NEXT! SUMIRE!
DEDEN
TWO TEACHERS DATING IS TOO HOT. YOU HAVE TO GO OUT!!
THAT'S JUST YOUR PERSONAL DESIRE!
MORIYA!
デデデン
DEDEDEN
IS IT POSSIBLE NAKAZAWA-SENSEI TURNED YOU DOWN OUT OF FORMALITY?
WHAT DOES THAT MEAN...!?
NAKAZAWA-SENSEI WOULDN'T JUMP INTO A RELATIONSHIP WITH ANYONE JUST BECAUSE THEY ASKED HER OUT, DON'T YOU THINK?
YOU HAVE A POINT.
NEXT! KASHIWACCHI!
ス
SU (FWIP)
ONLY NAKAZAWA-SENSEI HERSELF WOULD KNOW THE TRUTH.
YOU'RE ABSOLUTELY RIGHT!
バッ
BA (WHIRL)
WHAT ABOUT YOU, YUMEKO-SAN...!?

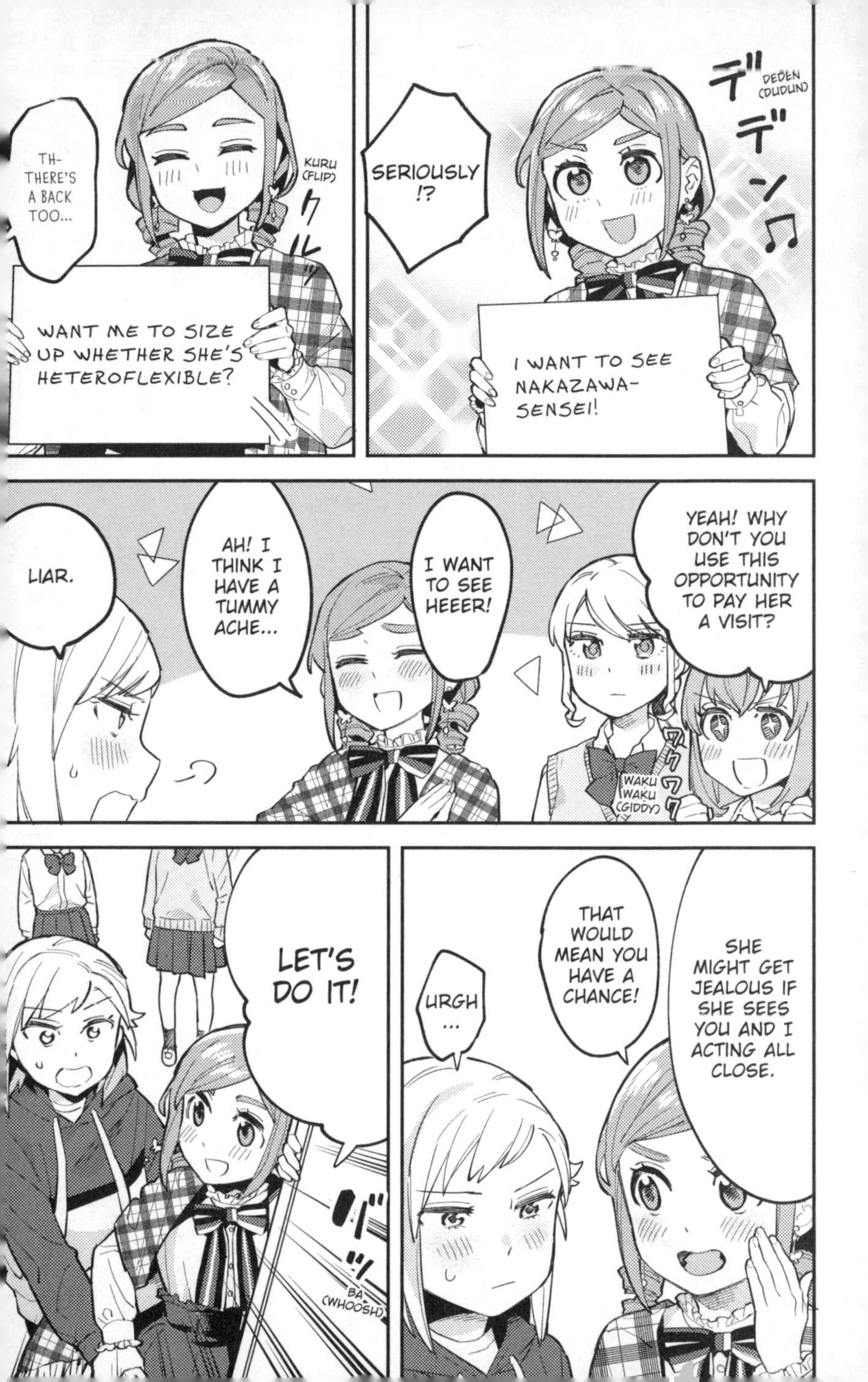
DEDEN (DUDUN)
SERIOUSLY !?
I WANT TO SEE NAKAZAWA-SENSEI!
KURU (FLIP)
TH- THERE'S A BACK TOO...
WANT ME TO SIZE UP WHETHER SHE'S HETEROFLEXIBLE?
YEAH! WHY DON'T YOU USE THIS OPPORTUNITY TO PAY HER A VISIT?
WAKU WAKU (GIDDY)
I WANT TO SEE HEEER!
AH! I THINK I HAVE A TUMMY ACHE...
LIAR.
SHE MIGHT GET JEALOUS IF SHE SEES YOU AND I ACTING ALL CLOSE.
THAT WOULD MEAN YOU HAVE A CHANCE!
URGH ...
LET'S DO IT!
BA (WHOOSH)

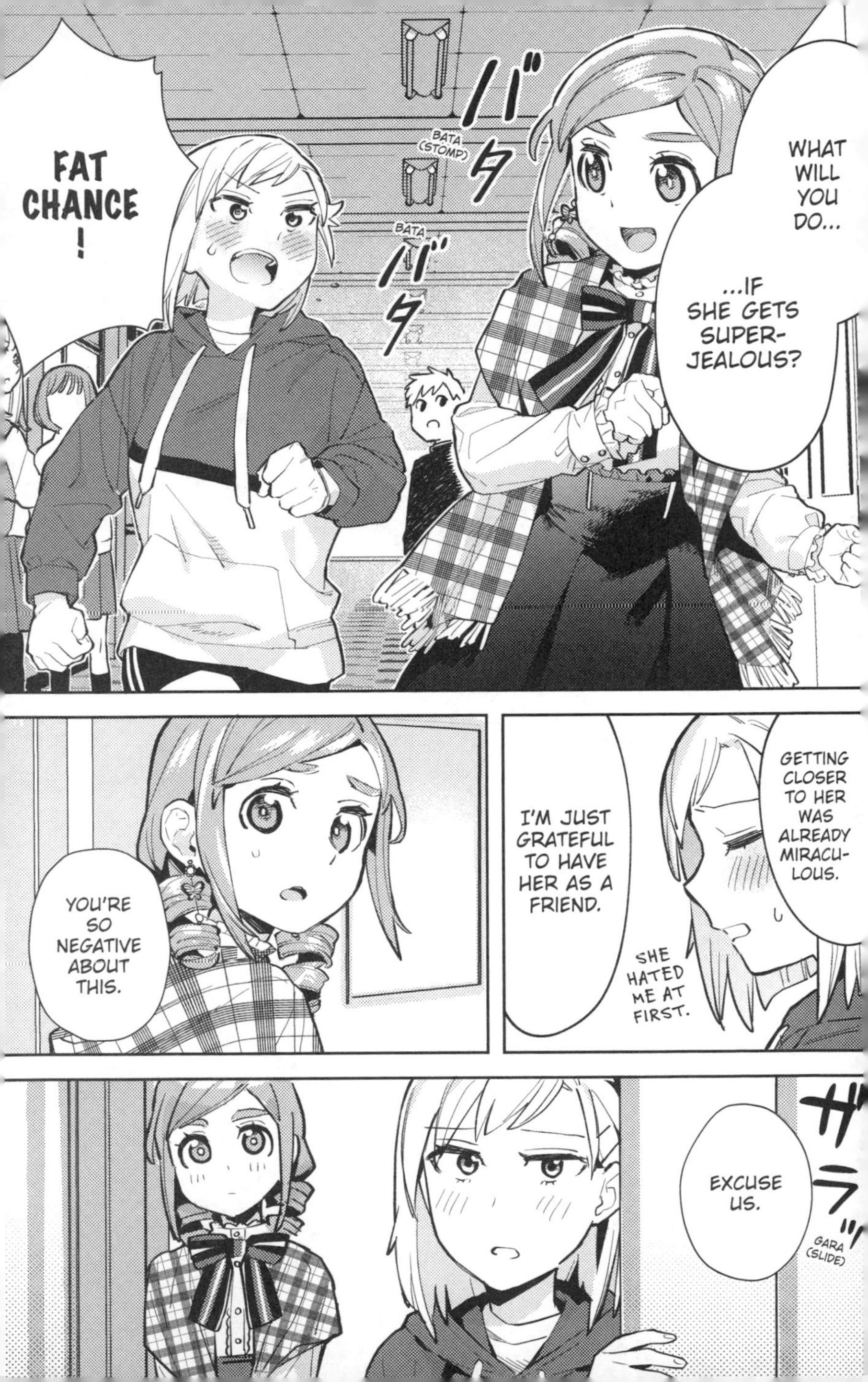
WHAT WILL YOU DO...
...IF SHE GETS SUPER-JEALOUS?
BATA (STOMP)
BATA
FAT CHANCE!
GETTING CLOSER TO HER WAS ALREADY MIRACULOUS.
I'M JUST GRATEFUL TO HAVE HER AS A FRIEND.
SHE HATED ME AT FIRST.
YOU'RE SO NEGATIVE ABOUT THIS.
GARA (SLIDE)
EXCUSE US.

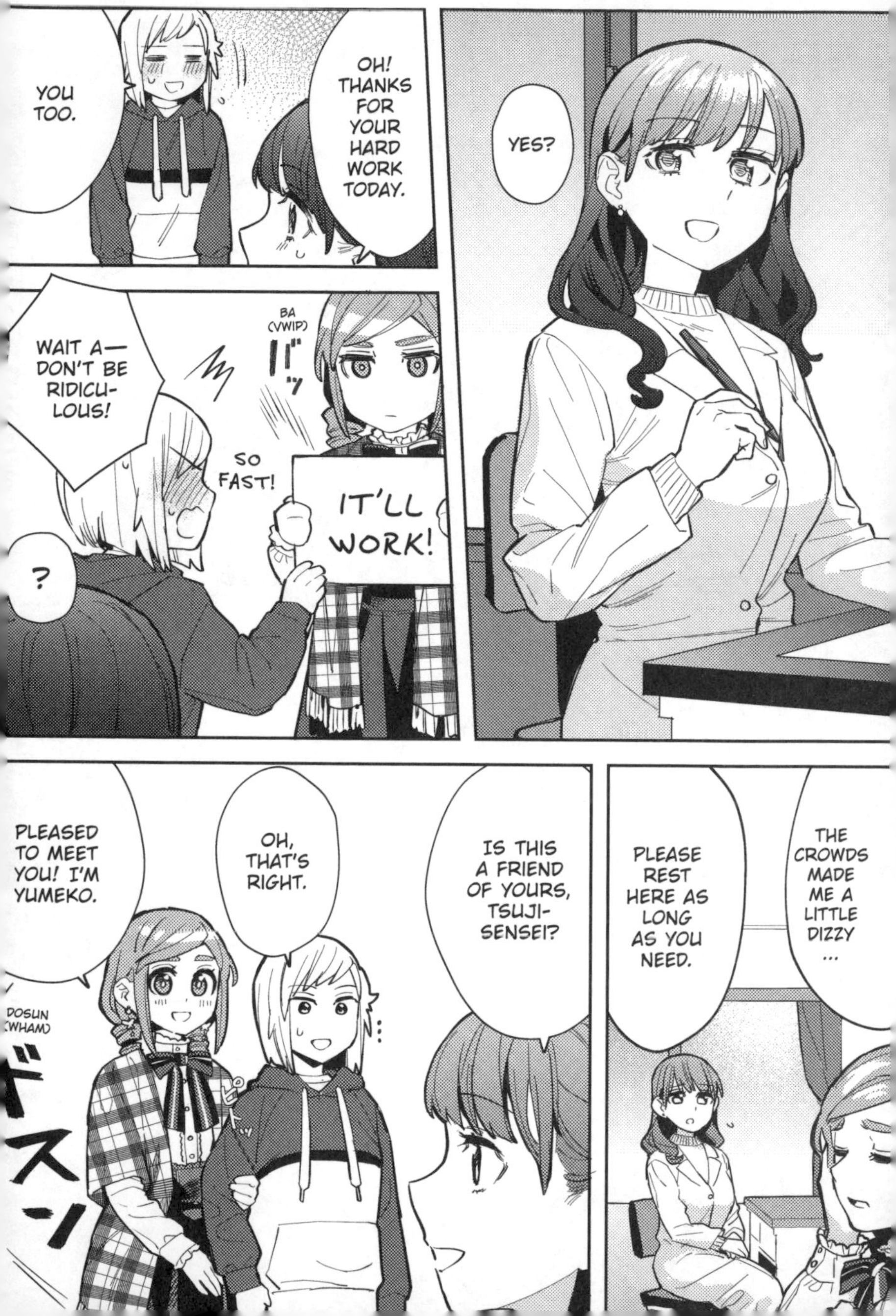
YES?
OH! THANKS FOR YOUR HARD WORK TODAY.
YOU TOO.
BA (VWIP)
WAIT A— DON'T BE RIDICULOUS!
SO FAST!
IT'LL WORK!
?
THE CROWDS MADE ME A LITTLE DIZZY...
PLEASE REST HERE AS LONG AS YOU NEED.
IS THIS A FRIEND OF YOURS, TSUJI-SENSEI?
OH, THAT'S RIGHT.
PLEASED TO MEET YOU! I'M YUMEKO.
DOSUN (WHAM)

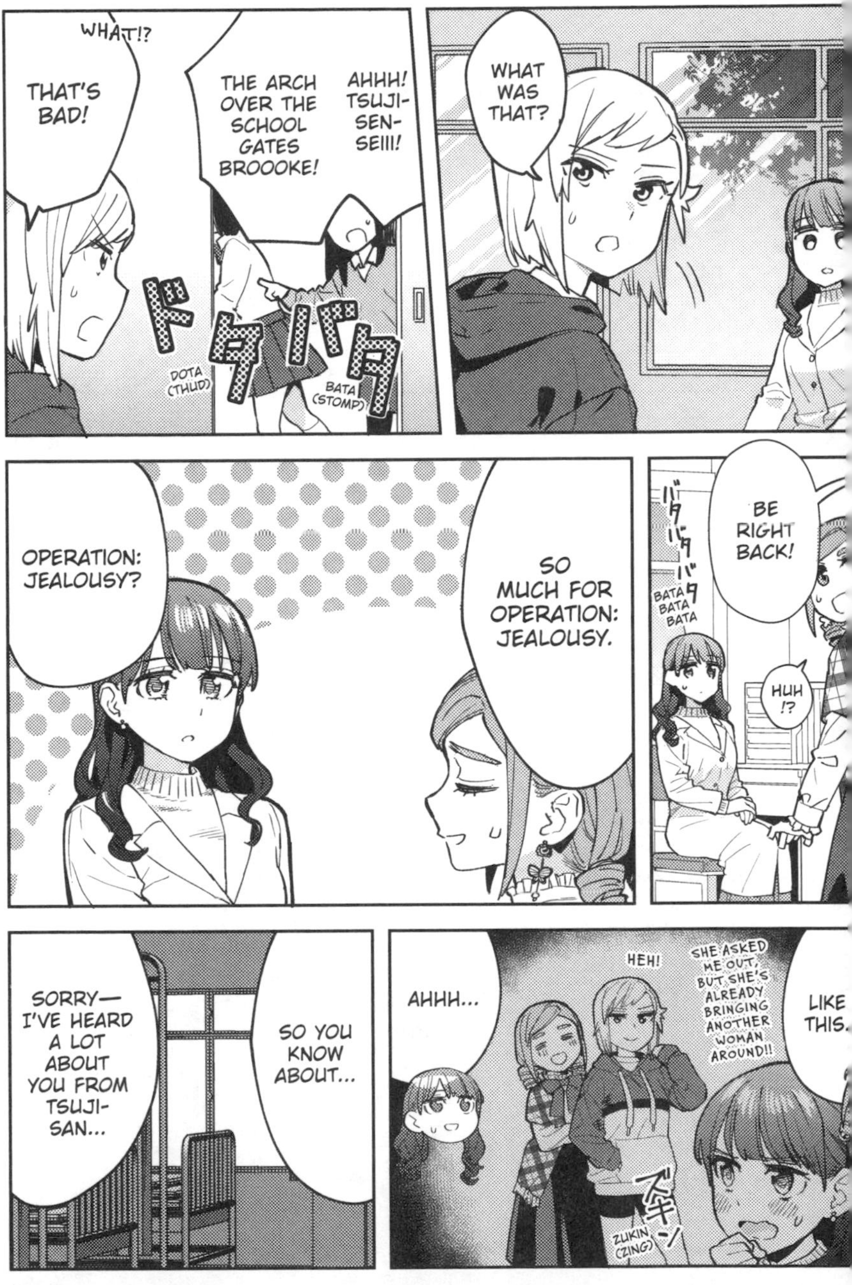
WHAT WAS THAT?
AHHH! TSUJI-SENSEIII!
THE ARCH OVER THE SCHOOL GATES BROOOKE!
WHAT!?
THAT'S BAD!
ドタバタ
DOTA (THUD)
BATA (STOMP)
BE RIGHT BACK!
バタバタバタ
BATA BATA BATA
HUH!?
SO MUCH FOR OPERATION: JEALOUSY.
OPERATION: JEALOUSY?
LIKE THIS.
SHE ASKED ME OUT, BUT SHE'S ALREADY BRINGING ANOTHER WOMAN AROUND!!
HEH!
AHHH...
ズキン
ZUKIN (ZING)
SO YOU KNOW ABOUT...
SORRY— I'VE HEARD A LOT ABOUT YOU FROM TSUJI-SAN...

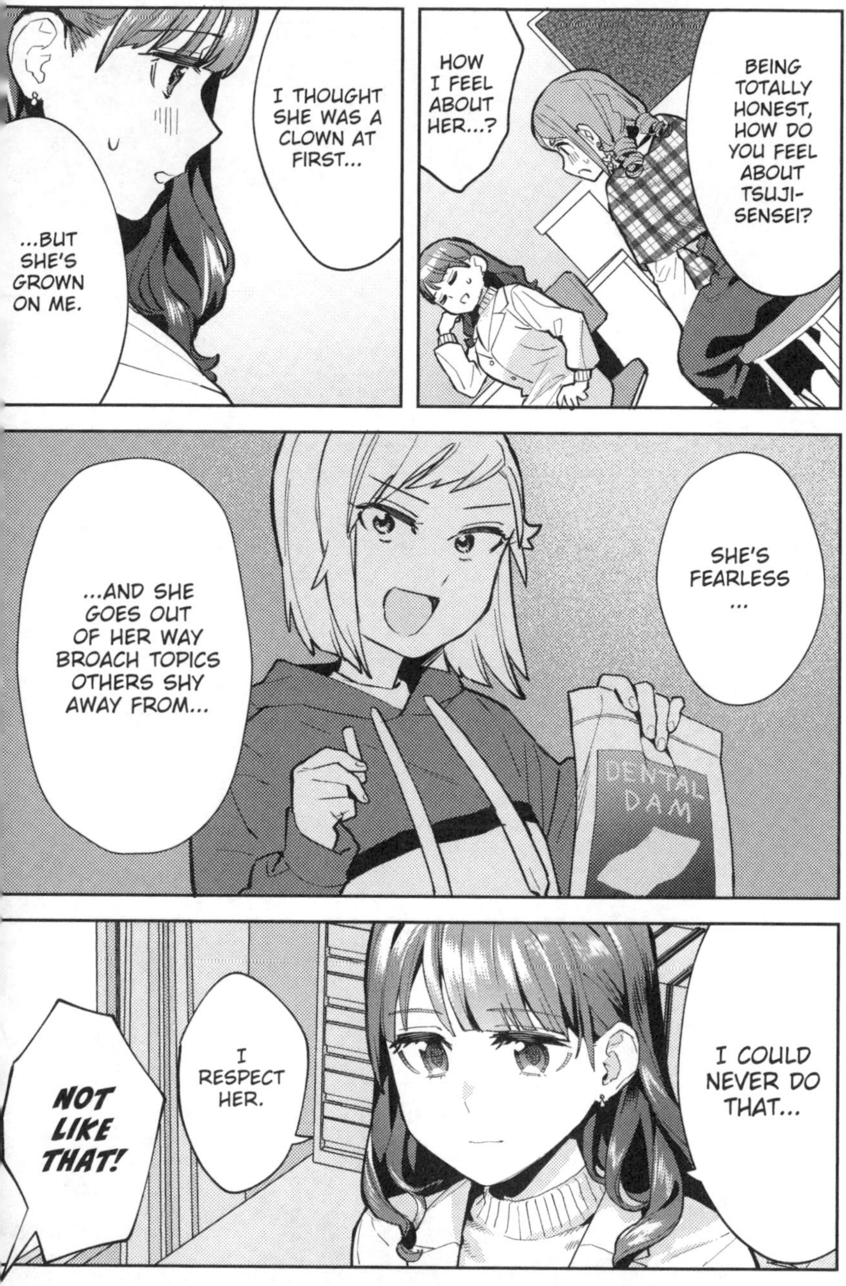
BEING TOTALLY HONEST, HOW DO YOU FEEL ABOUT TSUJI-SENSEI?
HOW I FEEL ABOUT HER...?
I THOUGHT SHE WAS A CLOWN AT FIRST...
...BUT SHE'S GROWN ON ME.
SHE'S FEARLESS ...
...AND SHE GOES OUT OF HER WAY BROACH TOPICS OTHERS SHY AWAY FROM...
DENTAL DAM
I COULD NEVER DO THAT...
I RESPECT HER.
NOT LIKE THAT!

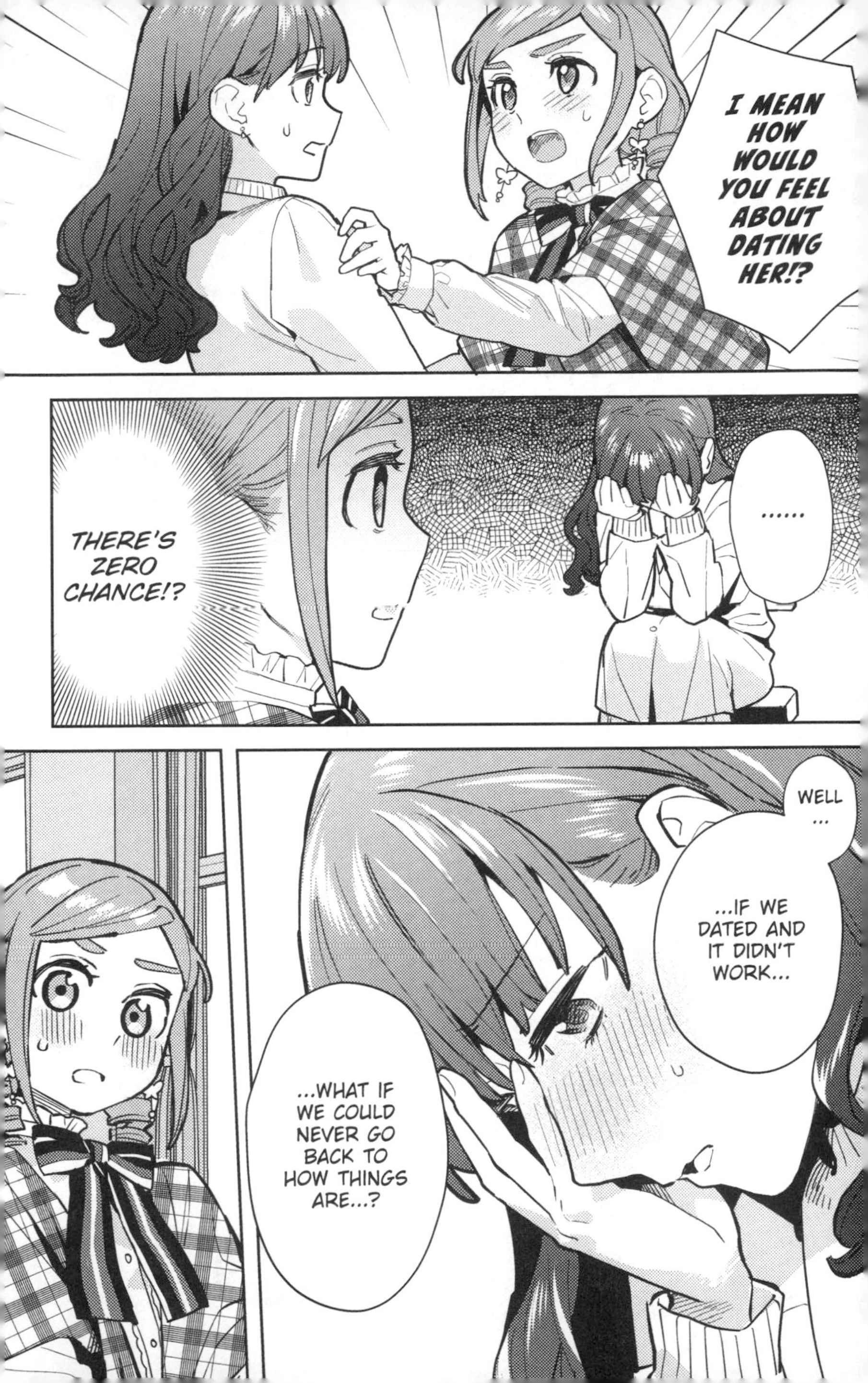
I MEAN HOW WOULD YOU FEEL ABOUT DATING HER!?
......
THERE'S ZERO CHANCE!?
WELL ...
...IF WE DATED AND IT DIDN'T WORK...
...WHAT IF WE COULD NEVER GO BACK TO HOW THINGS ARE...?

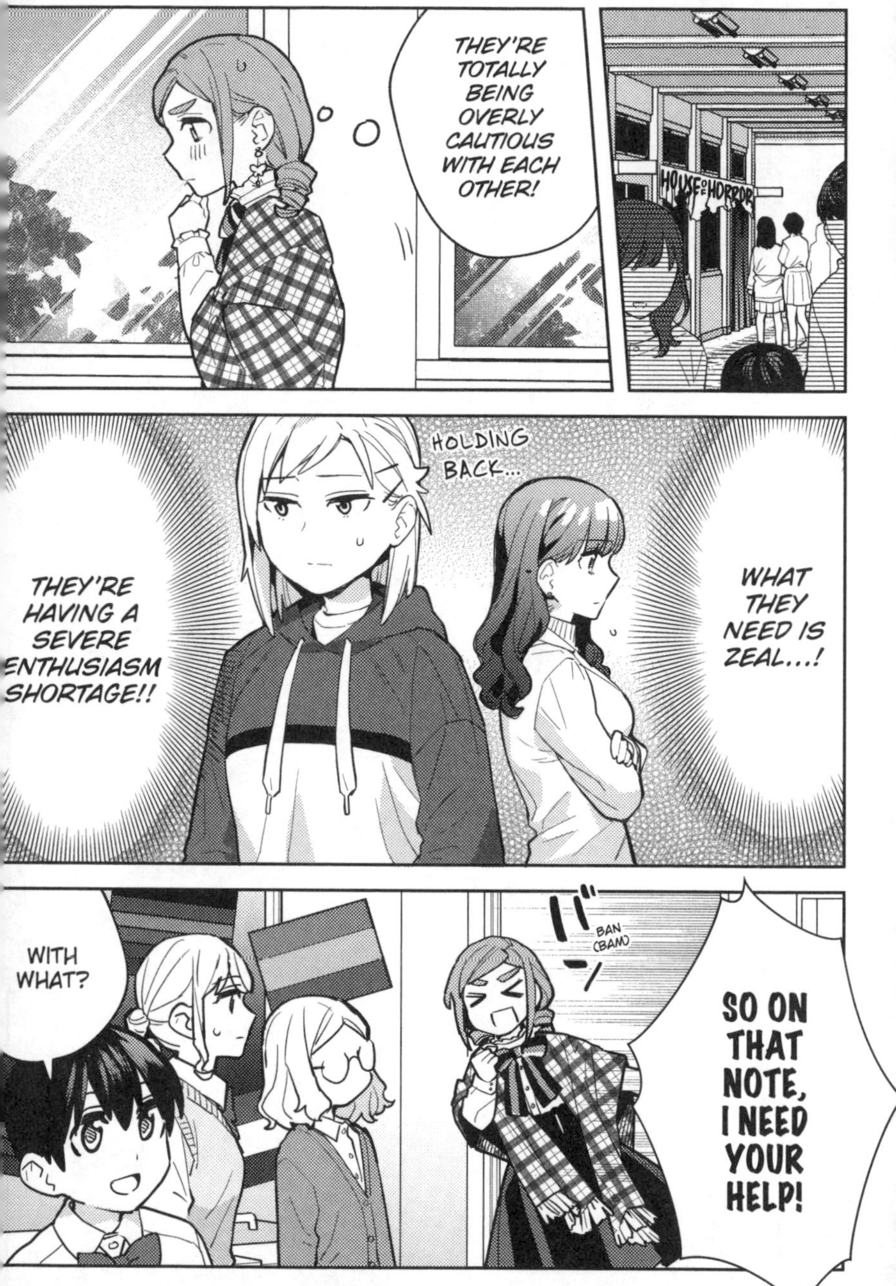
HOUSE OF HORROR
THEY'RE TOTALLY BEING OVERLY CAUTIOUS WITH EACH OTHER!
WHAT THEY NEED IS ZEAL...!
HOLDING BACK...
THEY'RE HAVING A SEVERE ENTHUSIASM SHORTAGE!!
SO ON THAT NOTE, I NEED YOUR HELP!
BAN (BAM)
WITH WHAT?

TRANSLATION NOTES

Page 3
Comiket, short for Comic Market, is a biannual convention centered around the sale of amateur and fan works.

Page 8
100 yen = roughly 1 USD.

Page 24
When the character says, "I want to call myself a boy," in the original Japanese, he says he wants to use the personal pronoun *ore*, a masculine way to refer to oneself.

Page 25
Doujinshi is a term referring to self-published works, usually derivative content created by fans.

BL is an acronym for "boys' love," a genre focused on romantic relationships between male characters.

Page 26
The term used for **genderqueer** in Japanese is "x-gender," which refers to a person who identifies as neither a man nor woman.

Page 41
Doyama is a district in Osaka famous for its nightlife and gay scene. In Tokyo, a similar district is Shinjuku **Ni-chome.**

Page 47
Takosen, short for *takosenbei* or *takoyaki senbei*, is a snack popular in Osaka, made by sandwiching *takoyaki* (round octopus dumplings) between two rice crackers (*senbei*).

Page 62
A **senpai** is an upperclassman or more experienced coworker.

Page 76
There's a popular saying in Japan that if a man is still a **virgin at thirty years old**, he becomes a wizard.

Page 84
In BL, *seme* is the term for the "top" or dominant/leading partner. *Uke* is the term for the "bottom" or more submissive partner.

Page 89
In Japan, everyone is considered to have two voices: *honne*, referring to one's true feelings, and *tatemae*, one's public face. Moriya is suggesting that Nakazawa rejected Tsuji out of societal expectations and that she may actually feel differently.

Page 127
In Japanese, using another person's **given name** typically indicates a close relationship.

Class 17 | **Candid Shot**

WHAT'S THAT ABOUT...?

Extra Lesson 15

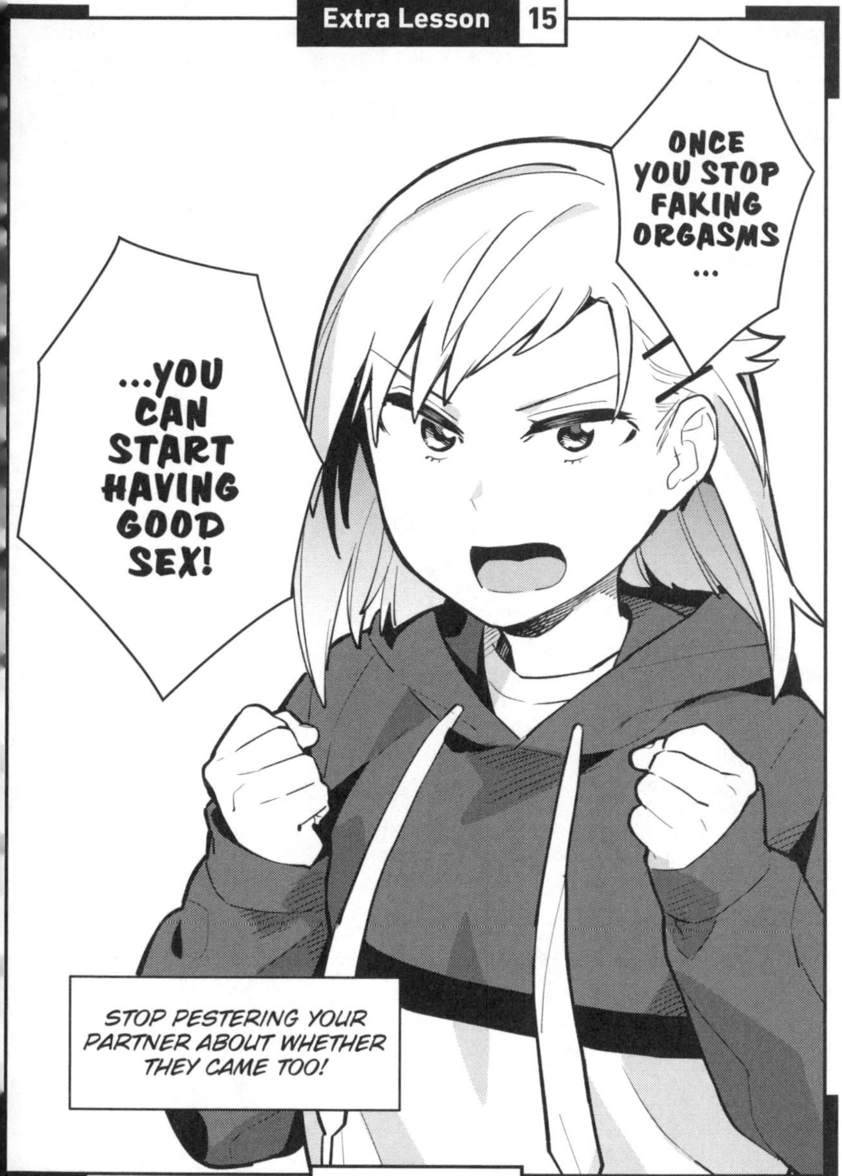
ONCE YOU STOP FAKING ORGASMS ...
...YOU CAN START HAVING GOOD SEX!
STOP PESTERING YOUR PARTNER ABOUT WHETHER THEY CAME TOO!

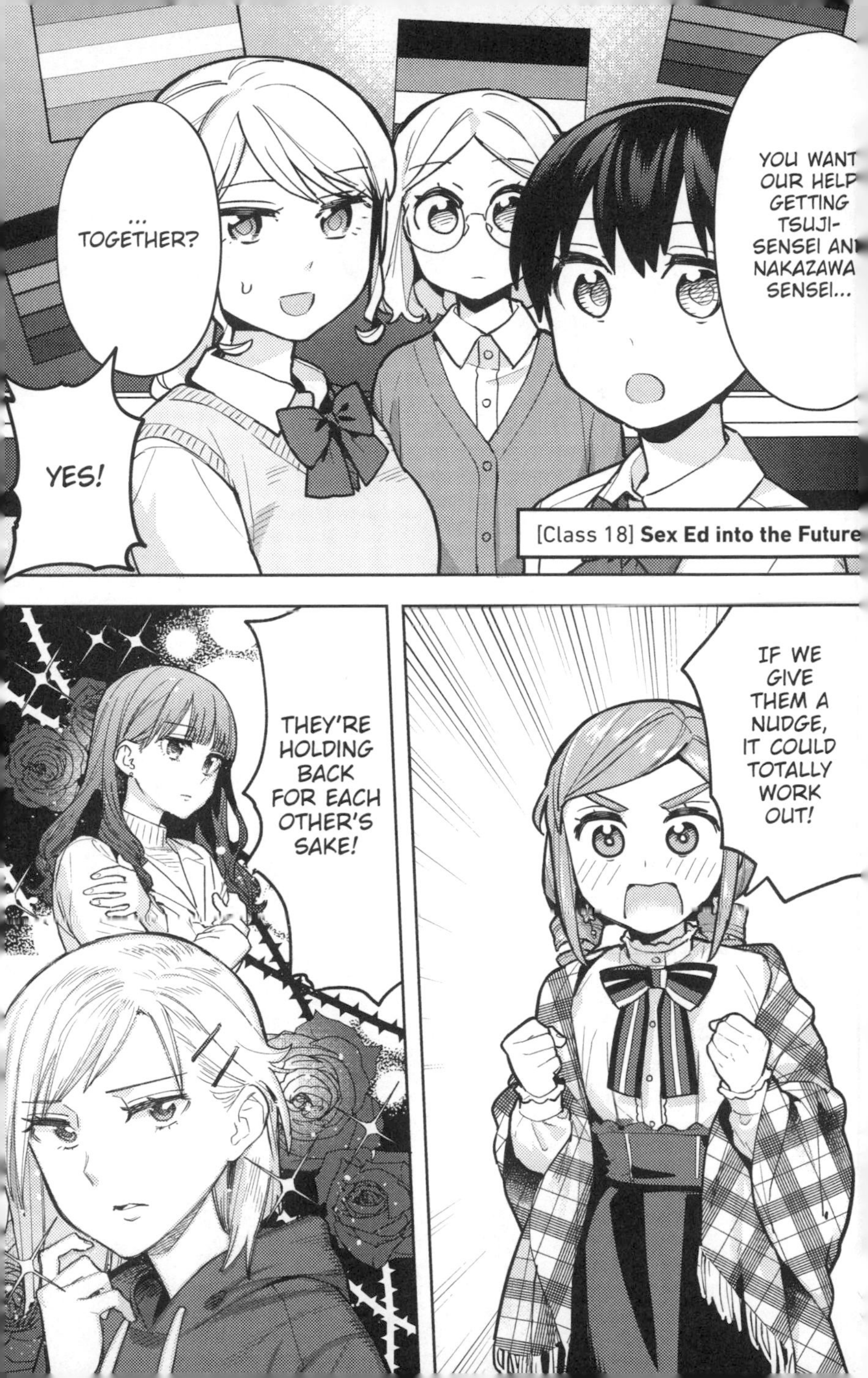
YOU WANT OUR HELP GETTING TSUJI-SENSEI AN NAKAZAWA SENSEI...
... TOGETHER?
YES!
[Class 18] Sex Ed into the Future
IF WE GIVE THEM A NUDGE, IT COULD TOTALLY WORK OUT!
THEY'RE HOLDING BACK FOR EACH OTHER'S SAKE!

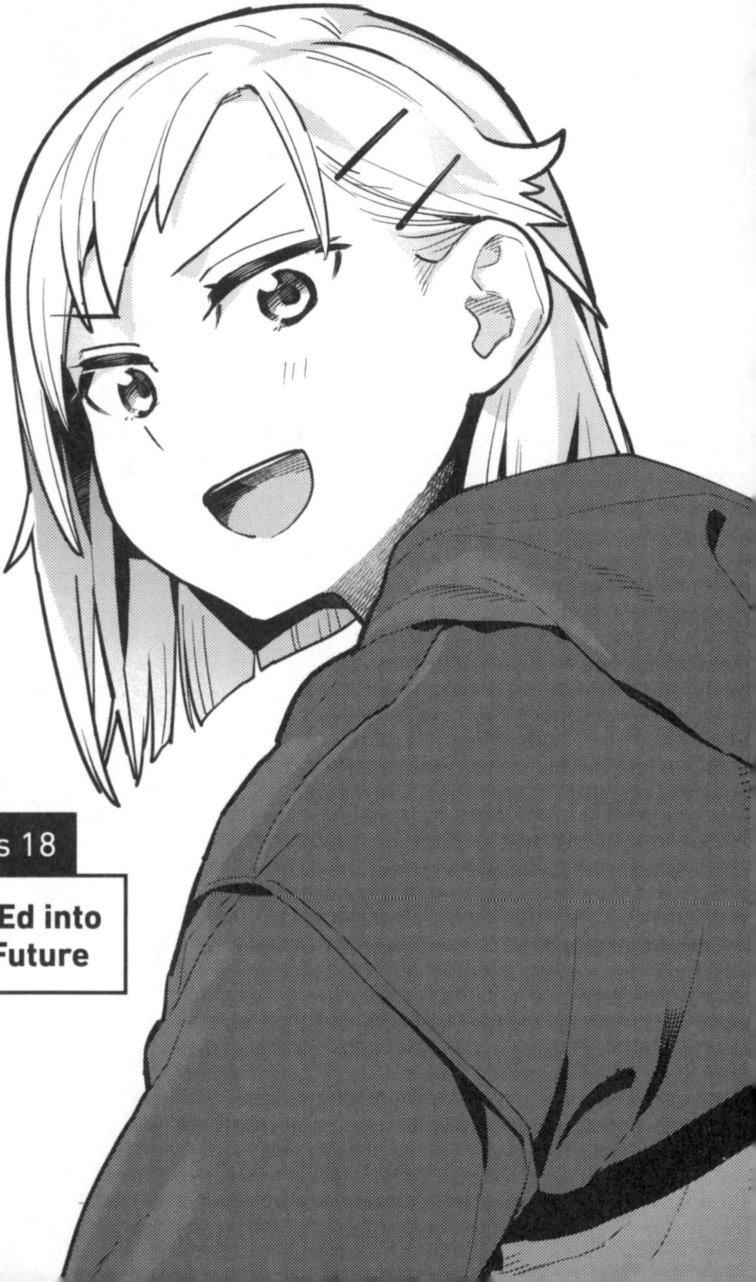

Class 18

Sex Ed into the Future

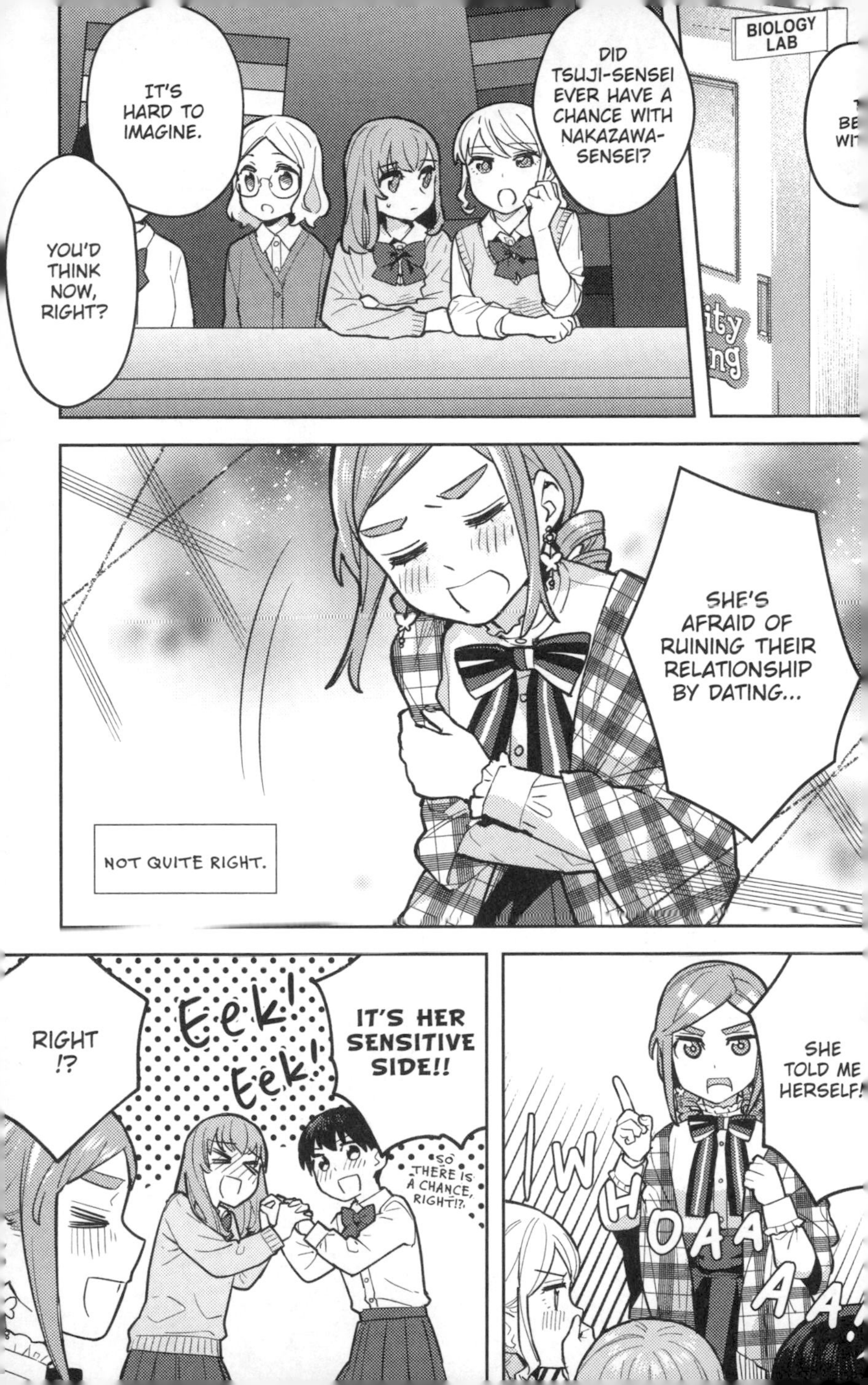
BIOLOGY LAB
DID TSUJI-SENSEI EVER HAVE A CHANCE WITH NAKAZAWA-SENSEI?
IT'S HARD TO IMAGINE.
YOU'D THINK NOW, RIGHT?
SHE'S AFRAID OF RUINING THEIR RELATIONSHIP BY DATING...
NOT QUITE RIGHT.
SHE TOLD ME HERSELF!
WHOAAAAAA!
IT'S HER SENSITIVE SIDE!!
Eek! Eek!
SO THERE IS A CHANCE, RIGHT!?
RIGHT!?

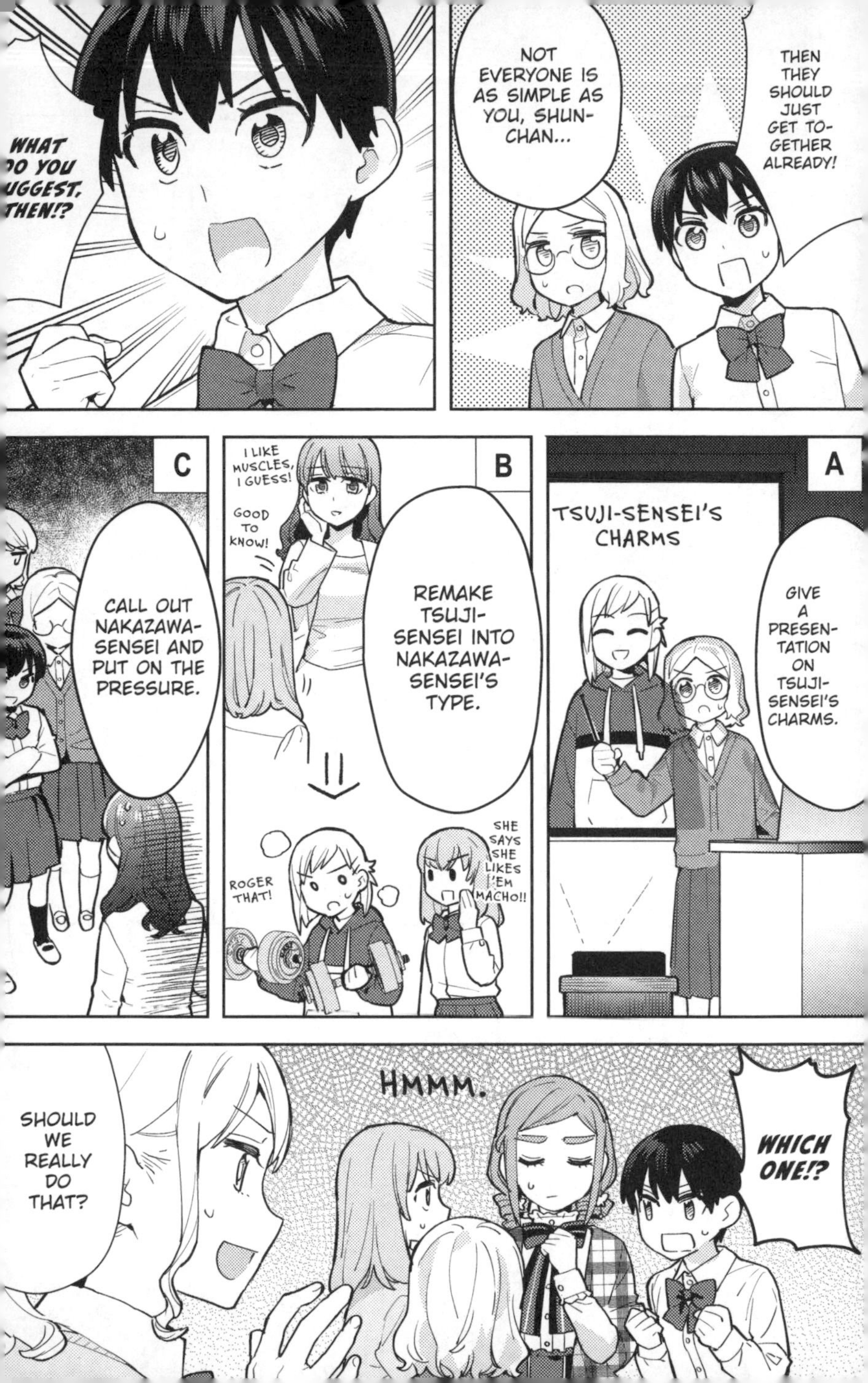
THEN THEY SHOULD JUST GET TO-GETHER ALREADY!
NOT EVERYONE IS AS SIMPLE AS YOU, SHUN-CHAN...
WHAT DO YOU SUGGEST, THEN!?
A
TSUJI-SENSEI'S CHARMS
GIVE A PRESEN-TATION ON TSUJI-SENSEI'S CHARMS.
B
I LIKE MUSCLES, I GUESS!
GOOD TO KNOW!
REMAKE TSUJI-SENSEI INTO NAKAZAWA-SENSEI'S TYPE.
SHE SAYS SHE LIKES 'EM MACHO!!
ROGER THAT!
C
CALL OUT NAKAZAWA-SENSEI AND PUT ON THE PRESSURE.
WHICH ONE!?
HMMM.
SHOULD WE REALLY DO THAT?

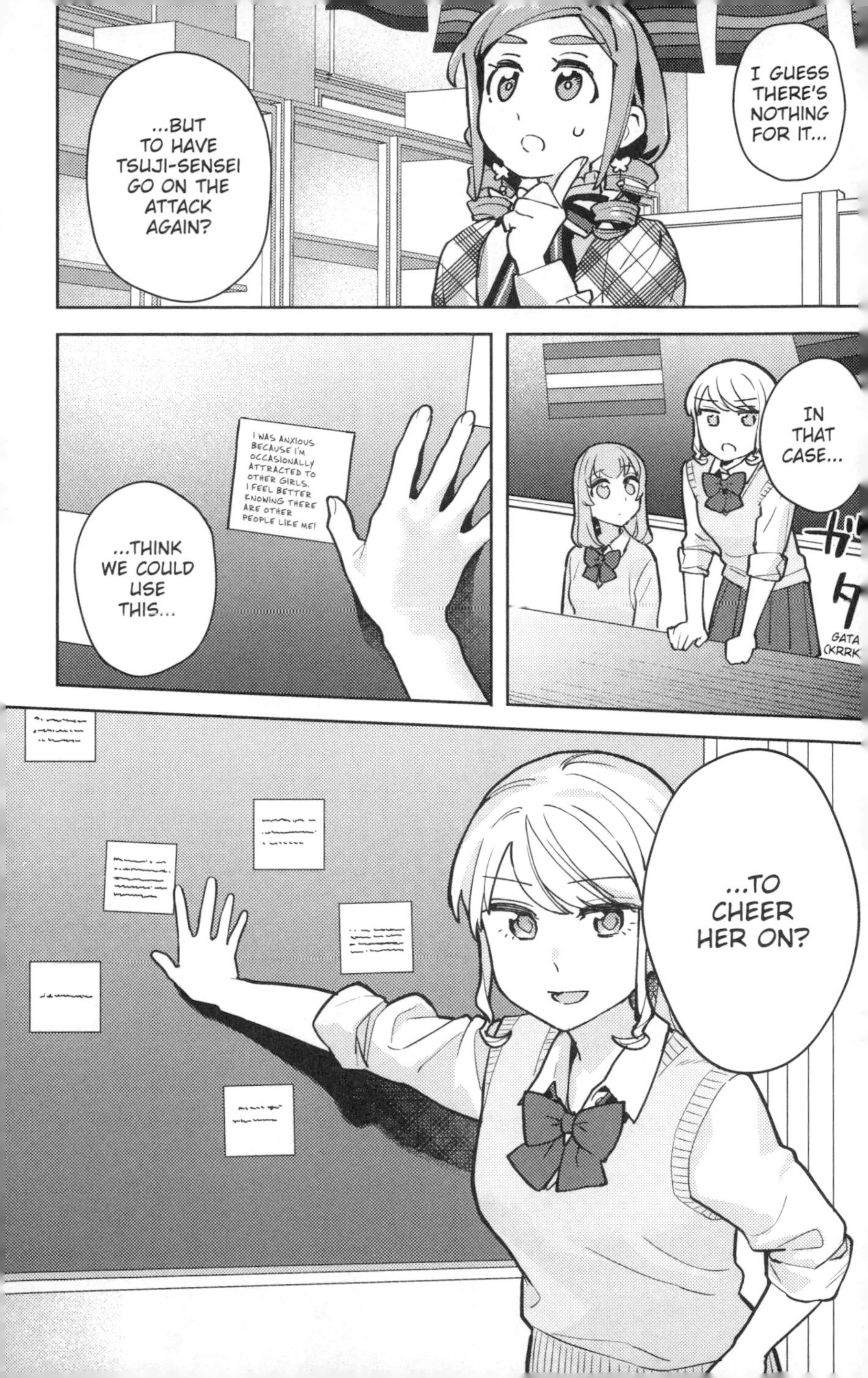
I GUESS THERE'S NOTHING FOR IT...
...BUT TO HAVE TSUJI-SENSEI GO ON THE ATTACK AGAIN?
IN THAT CASE...
GATA (KRRK
I WAS ANXIOUS BECAUSE I'M OCCASIONALLY ATTRACTED TO OTHER GIRLS. I FEEL BETTER KNOWING THERE ARE OTHER PEOPLE LIKE ME!
...THINK WE COULD USE THIS...
...TO CHEER HER ON?

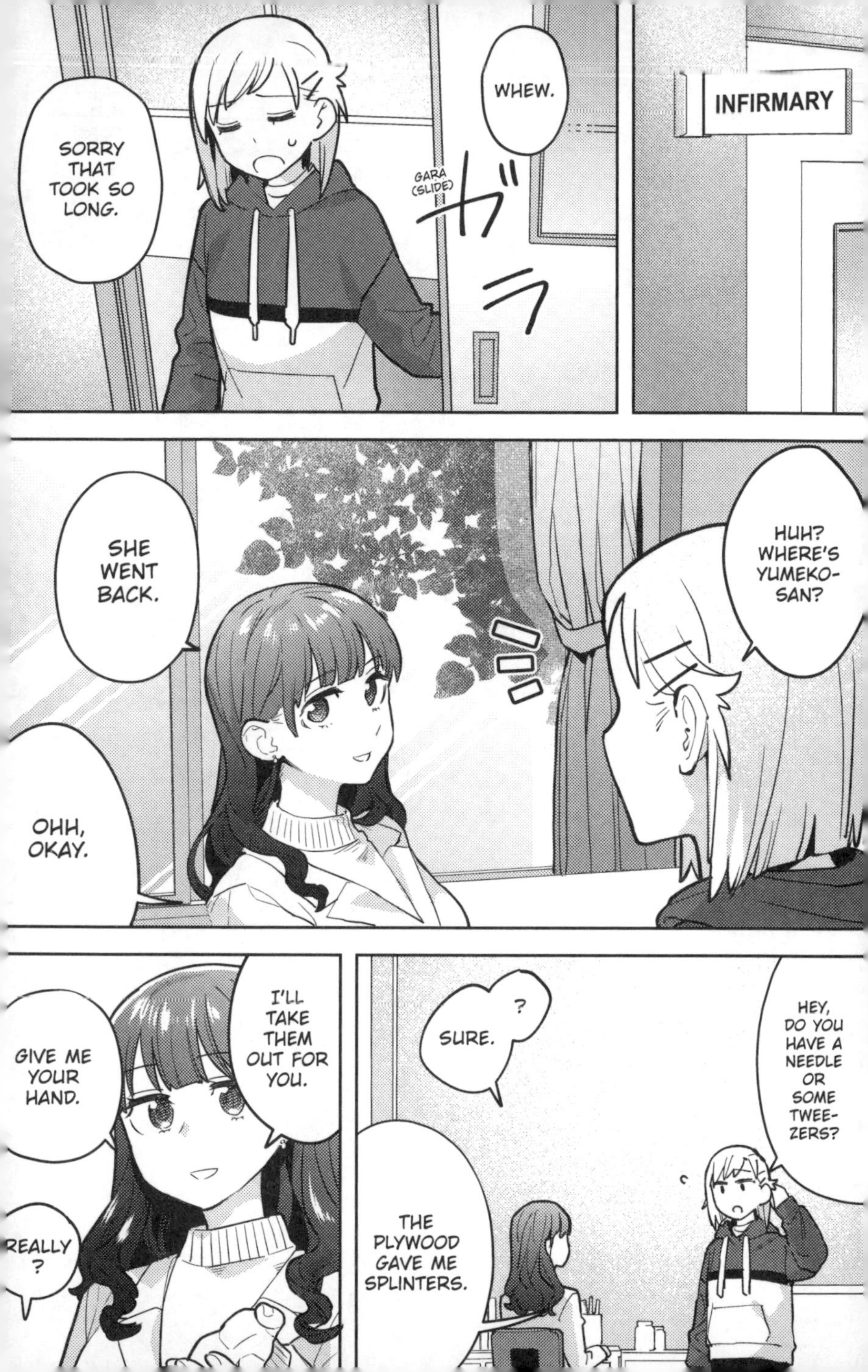
INFIRMARY
WHEW.
GARA (SLIDE)
ガラ
SORRY THAT TOOK SO LONG.
HUH? WHERE'S YUMEKO-SAN?
SHE WENT BACK.
OHH, OKAY.
HEY, DO YOU HAVE A NEEDLE OR SOME TWEE-ZERS?
? SURE.
THE PLYWOOD GAVE ME SPLINTERS.
I'LL TAKE THEM OUT FOR YOU.
GIVE ME YOUR HAND.
REALLY?

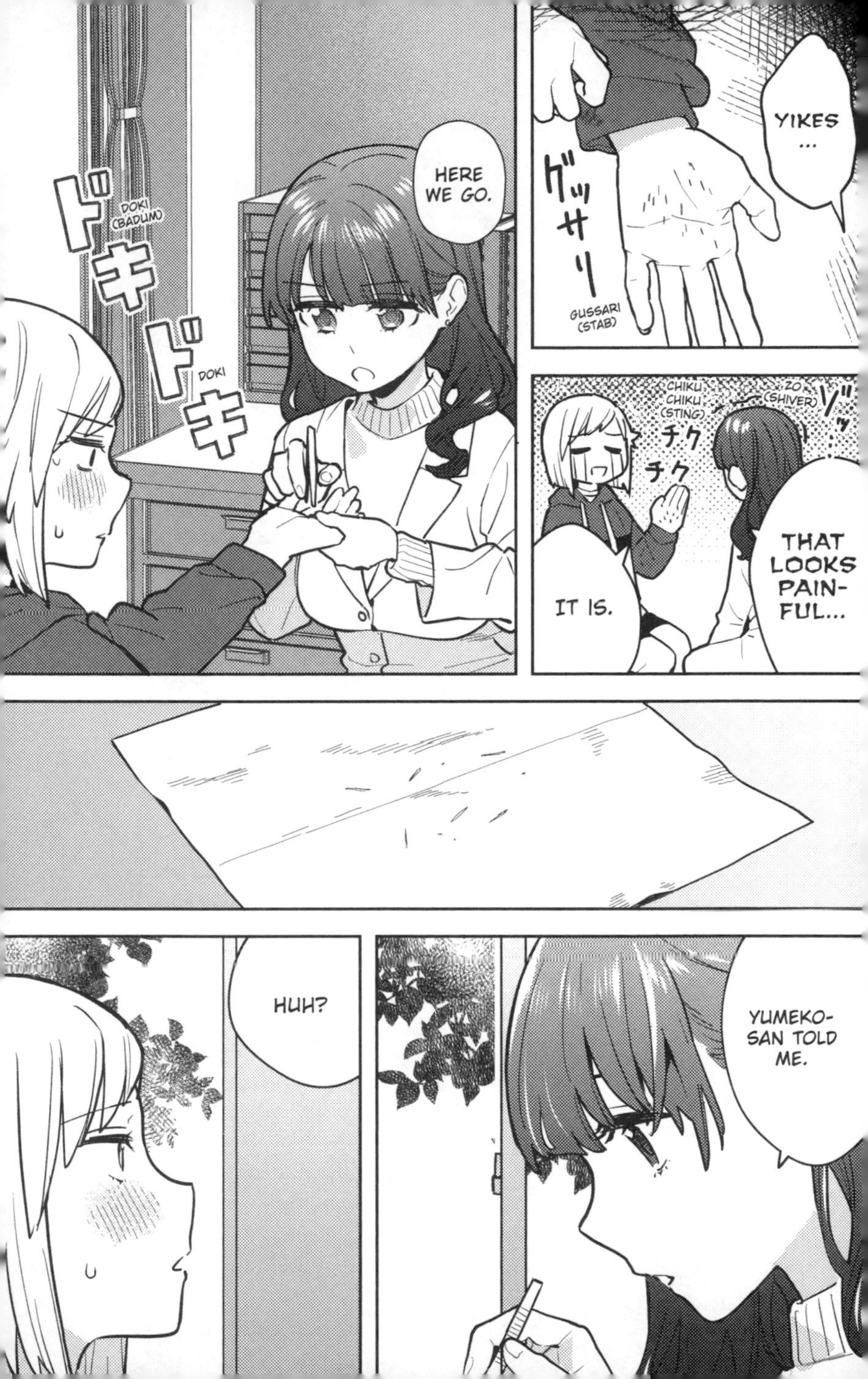

YIKES...
グッサリ
GUSSARI (STAB)
ゾッ
ZO (SHIVER)
チクチク
CHIKU CHIKU (STING)
THAT LOOKS PAIN-FUL...
IT IS.
HERE WE GO.
ドキドキ
DOKI (BADUM)
DOKI
YUMEKO-SAN TOLD ME.
HUH?

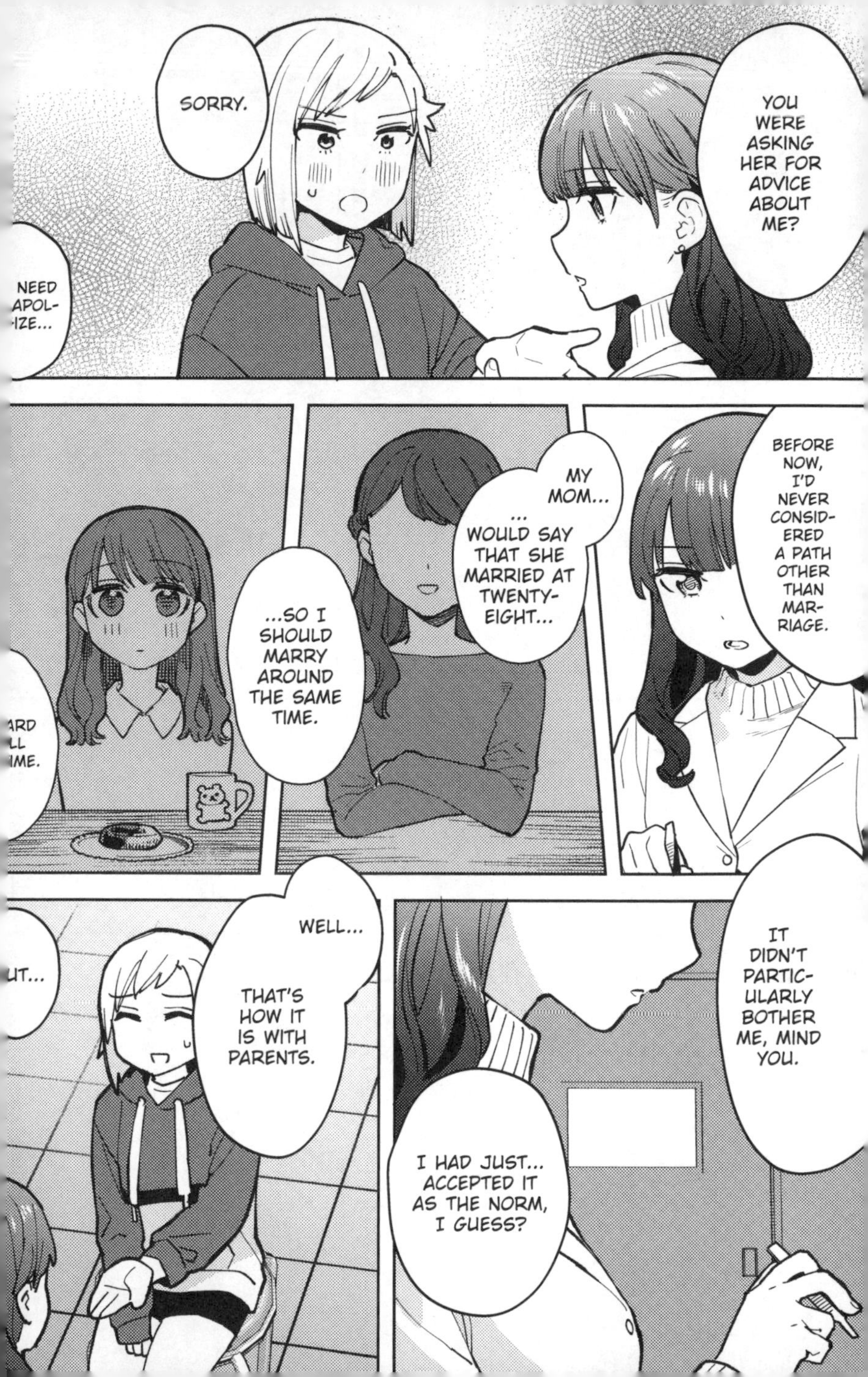
YOU WERE ASKING HER FOR ADVICE ABOUT ME?
SORRY.
NEED APOL-IZE...
BEFORE NOW, I'D NEVER CONSIDERED A PATH OTHER THAN MARRIAGE.
MY MOM...
...WOULD SAY THAT SHE MARRIED AT TWENTY-EIGHT...
...SO I SHOULD MARRY AROUND THE SAME TIME.
IT DIDN'T PARTICULARLY BOTHER ME, MIND YOU.
I HAD JUST... ACCEPTED IT AS THE NORM, I GUESS?
WELL...
THAT'S HOW IT IS WITH PARENTS.

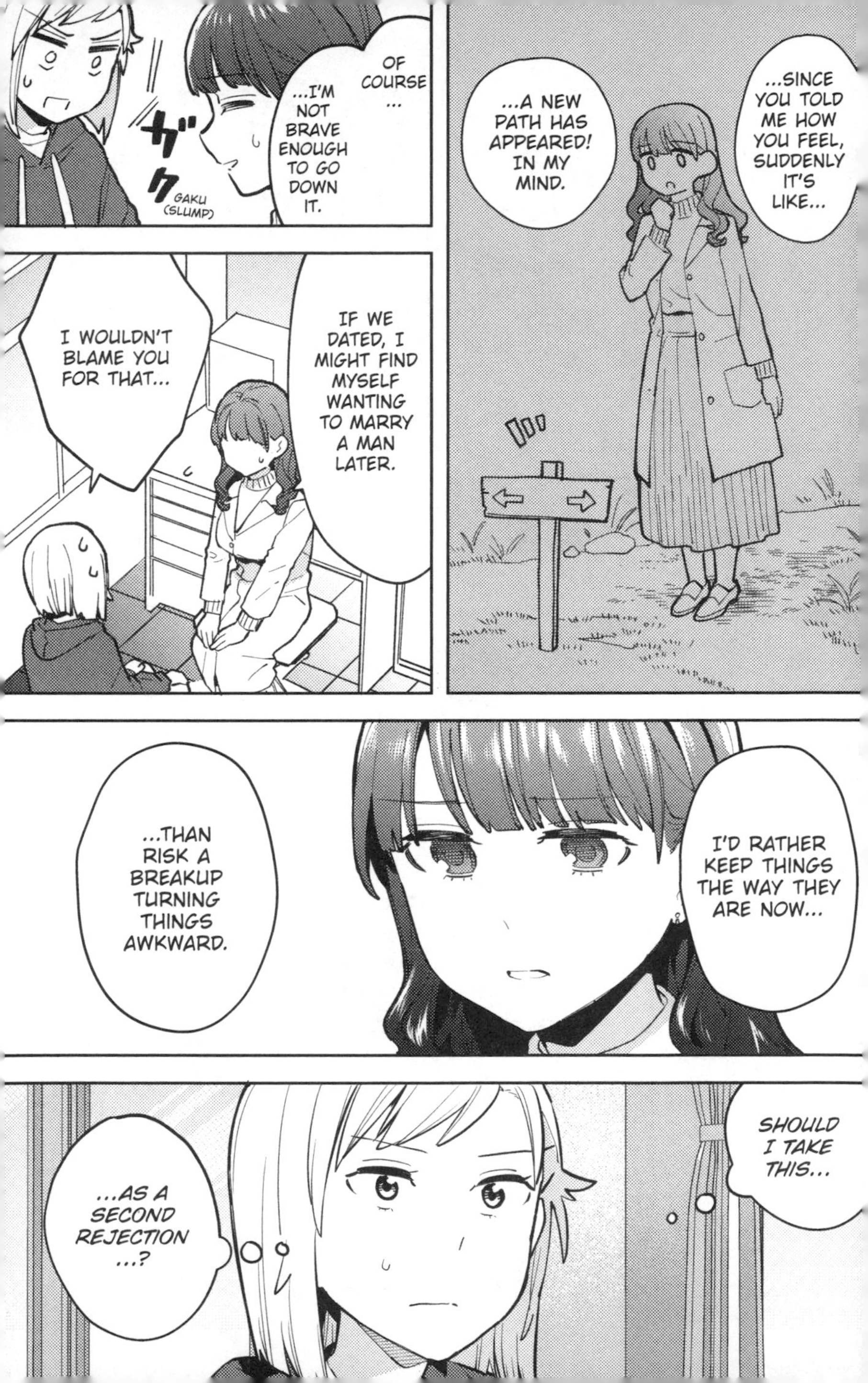
...SINCE YOU TOLD ME HOW YOU FEEL, SUDDENLY IT'S LIKE...
...A NEW PATH HAS APPEARED! IN MY MIND.
OF COURSE...
...I'M NOT BRAVE ENOUGH TO GO DOWN IT.
GAKU (SLUMP)
IF WE DATED, I MIGHT FIND MYSELF WANTING TO MARRY A MAN LATER.
I WOULDN'T BLAME YOU FOR THAT...
I'D RATHER KEEP THINGS THE WAY THEY ARE NOW...
...THAN RISK A BREAKUP TURNING THINGS AWKWARD.
SHOULD I TAKE THIS...
...AS A SECOND REJECTION...?

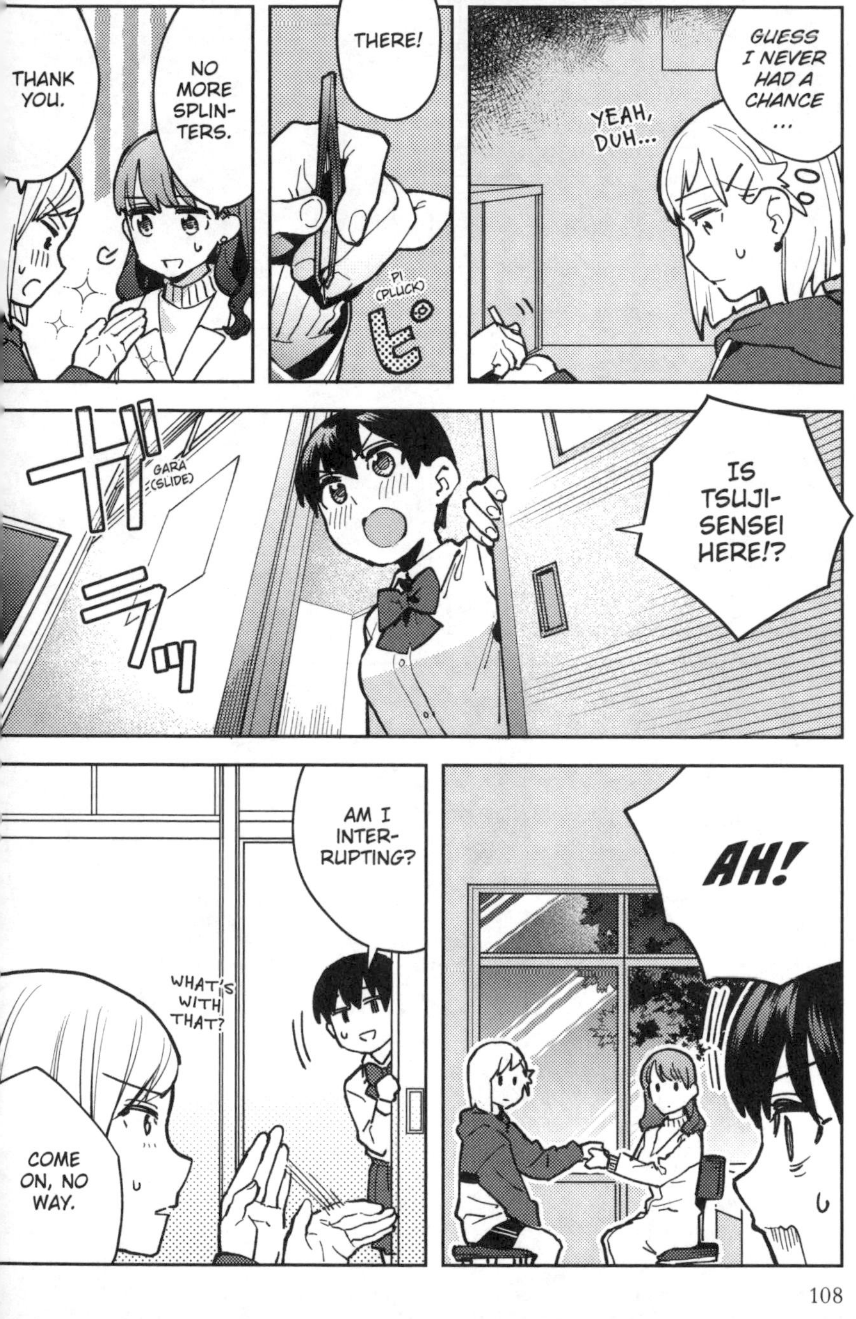
GUESS I NEVER HAD A CHANCE ...
YEAH, DUH...
THERE!
PI (PLUCK)
NO MORE SPLINTERS.
THANK YOU.
IS TSUJI-SENSEI HERE!?
GARA (SLIDE)
AH!
AM I INTERRUPTING?
WHAT'S WITH THAT?
COME ON, NO WAY.

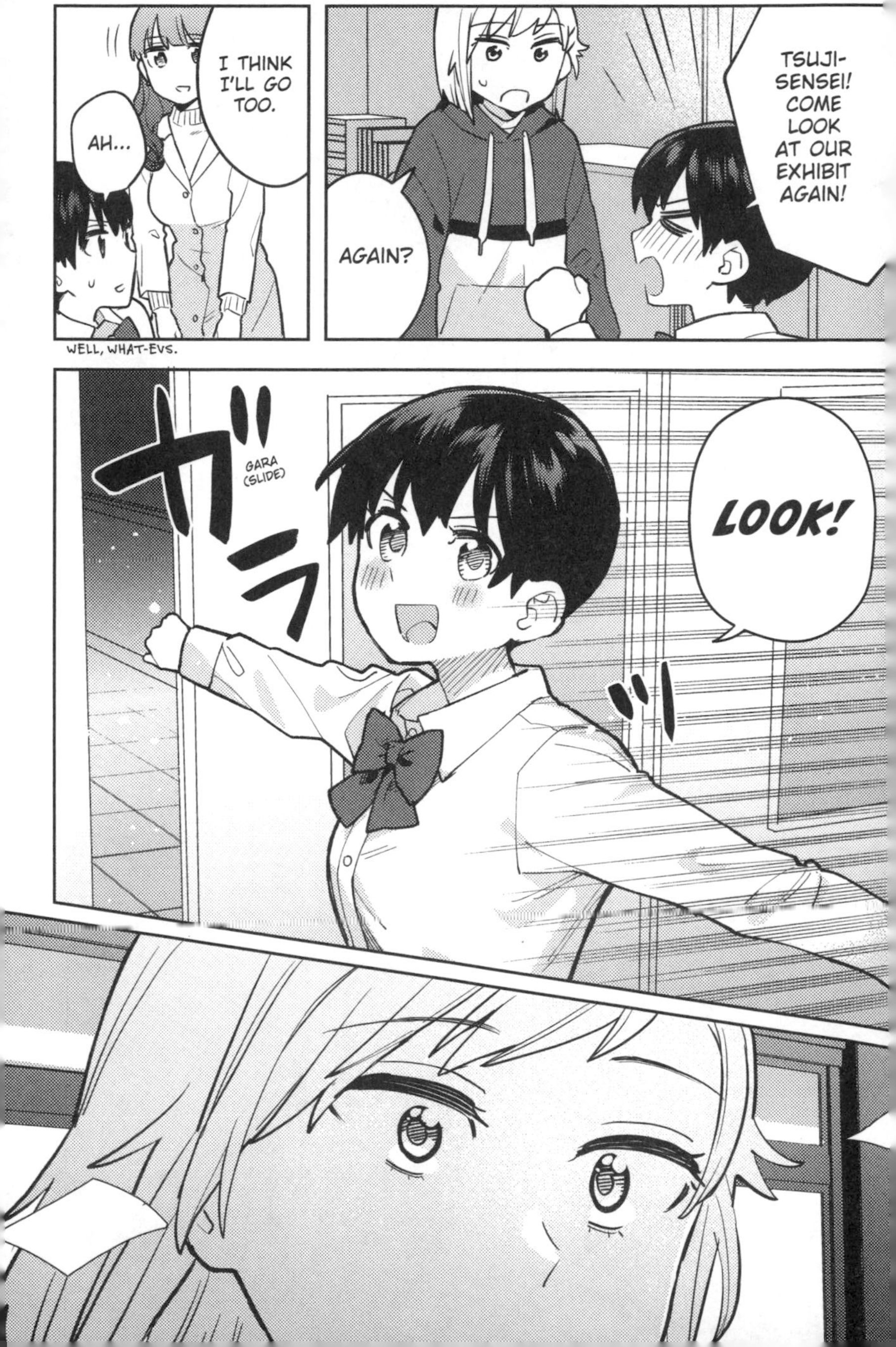
TSUJI-SENSEI! COME LOOK AT OUR EXHIBIT AGAIN!
AGAIN?
I THINK I'LL GO TOO.
AH...
WELL, WHAT-EVS.
LOOK!
GARA (SLIDE)

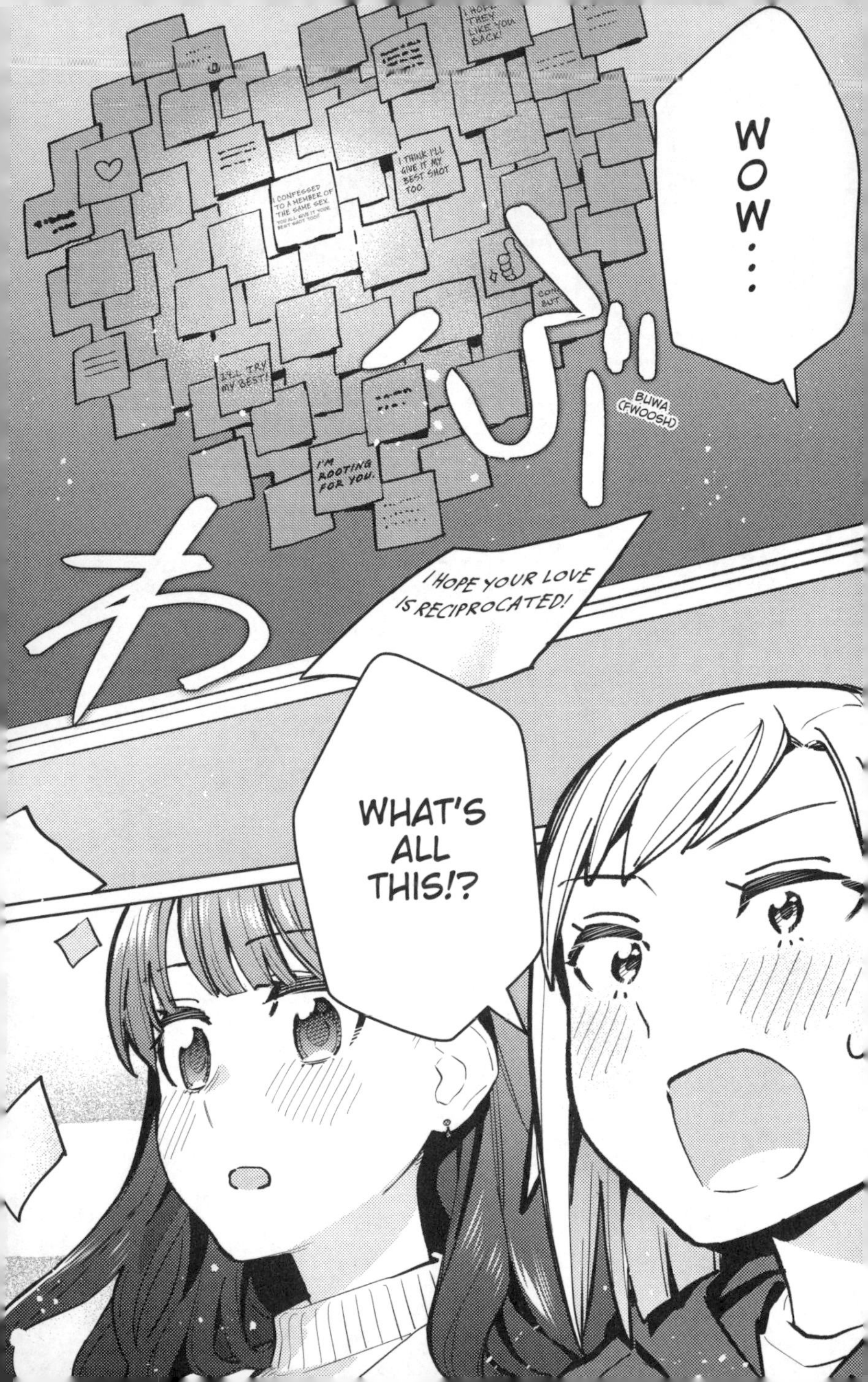
WOW...
I HOPE THEY LIKE YOU BACK!
I THINK I'LL GIVE IT MY BEST SHOT TOO.
I CONFESSED TO A MEMBER OF THE SAME SEX. YOU ALL GIVE IT YOUR BEST SHOT TOO!!
BUWA (FWOOSH)
I'LL TRY MY BEST!
I'M ROOTING FOR YOU.
I HOPE YOUR LOVE IS RECIPROCATED!
WHAT'S ALL THIS!?

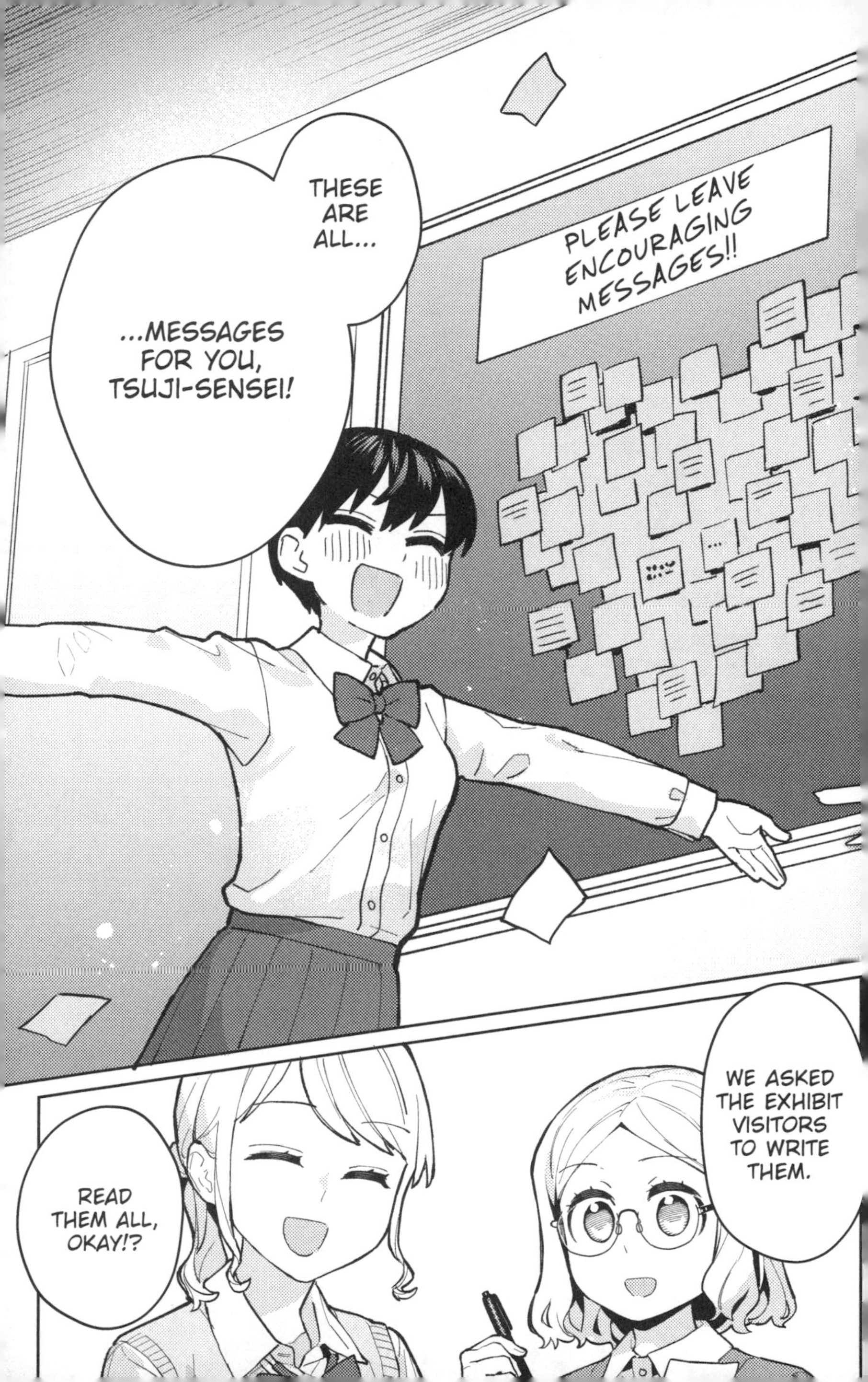
PLEASE LEAVE ENCOURAGING MESSAGES!!
THESE ARE ALL...
...MESSAGES FOR YOU, TSUJI-SENSEI!
WE ASKED THE EXHIBIT VISITORS TO WRITE THEM.
READ THEM ALL, OKAY!?

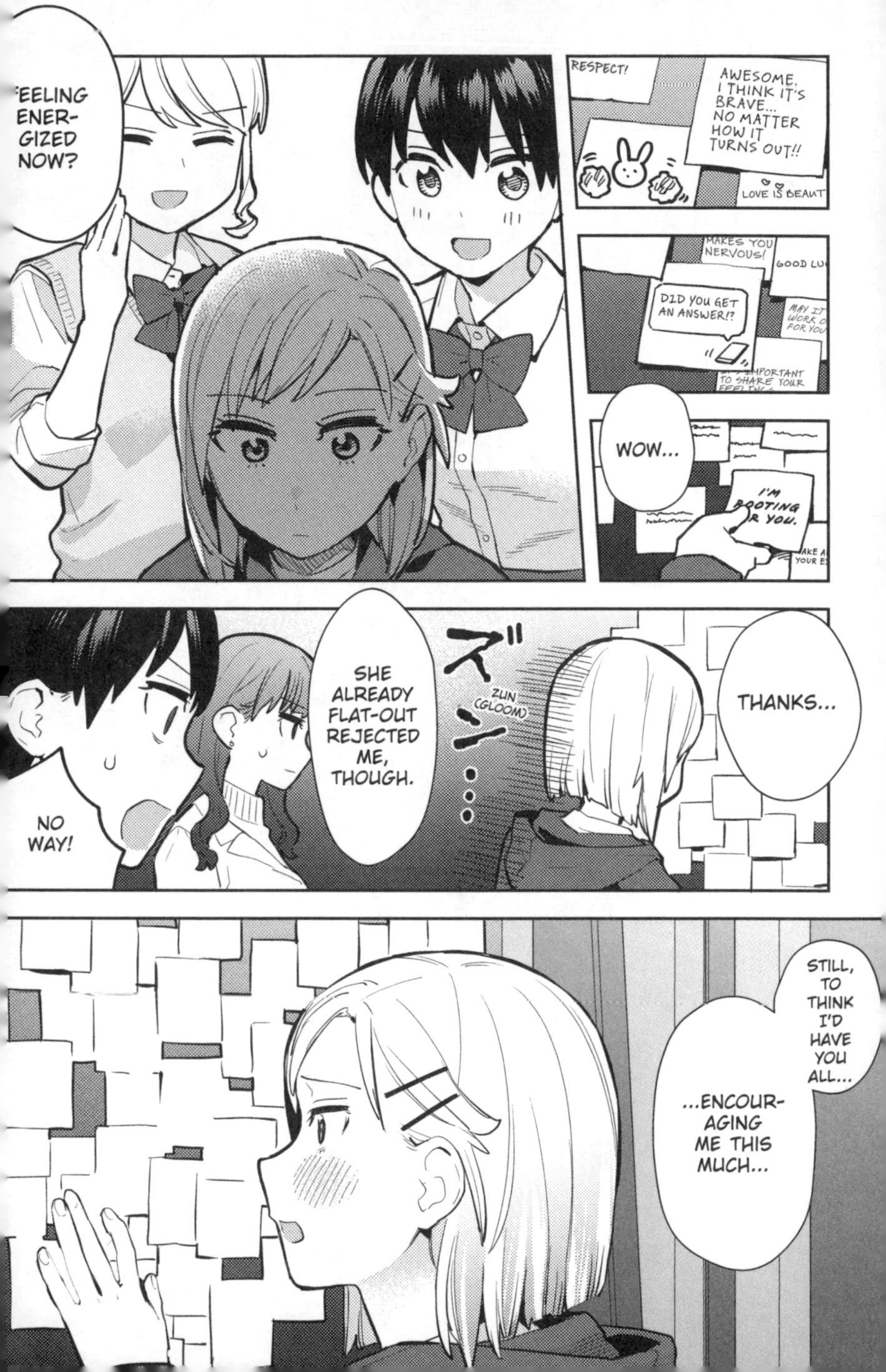
RESPECT!
AWESOME. I THINK IT'S BRAVE... NO MATTER HOW IT TURNS OUT!!
MAKES YOU NERVOUS!
DID YOU GET AN ANSWER!?
TO SHARE YOUR
WOW...
FEELING ENERGIZED NOW?
THANKS...
ZUN (GLOOM)
SHE ALREADY FLAT-OUT REJECTED ME, THOUGH.
NO WAY!
STILL, TO THINK I'D HAVE YOU ALL...
...ENCOURAGING ME THIS MUCH...

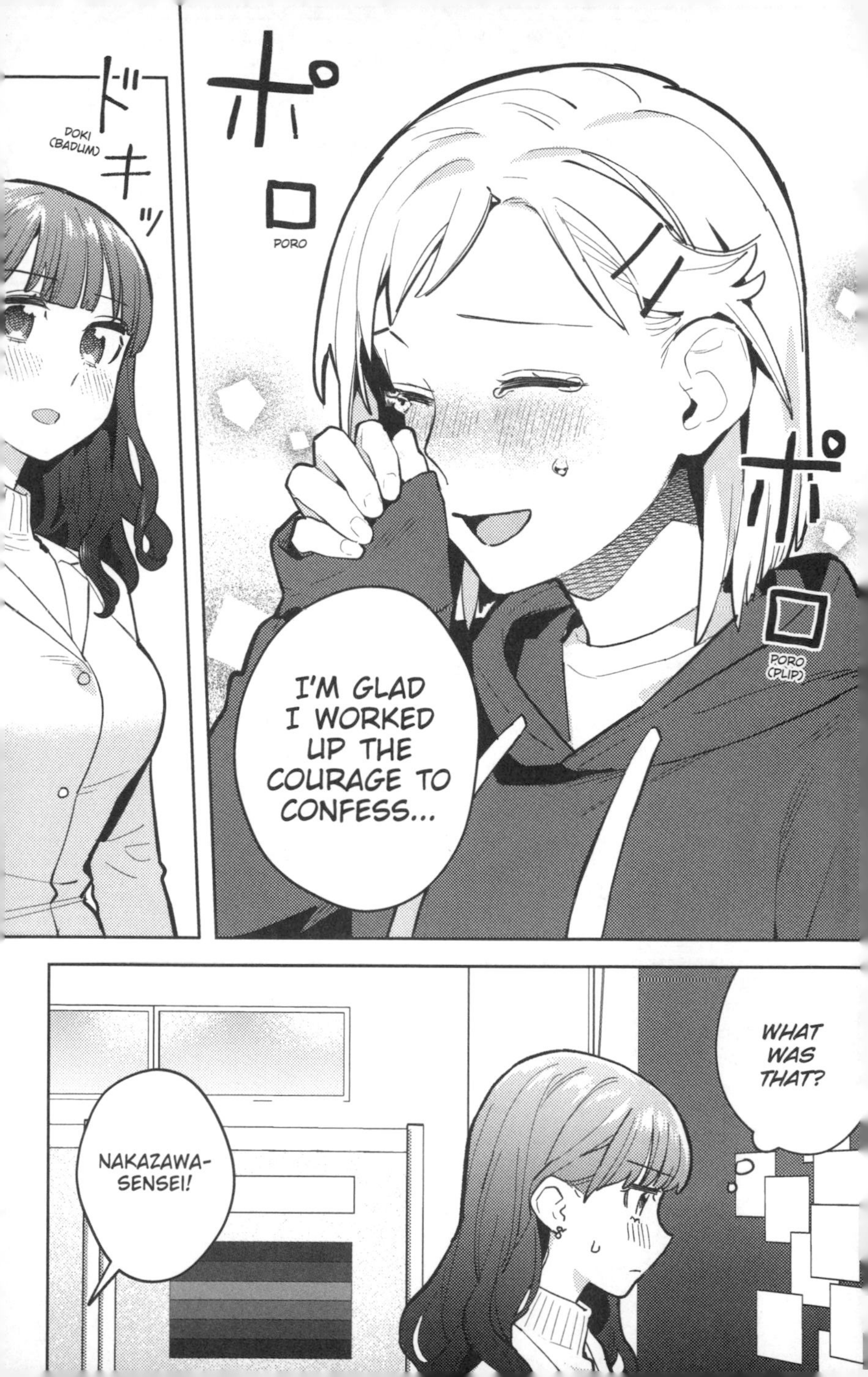
ポロ
PORO
I'M GLAD I WORKED UP THE COURAGE TO CONFESS...
ポロ
PORO (PLIP)
ドキッ
DOKI (BADUM)
WHAT WAS THAT?
NAKAZAWA-SENSEI!

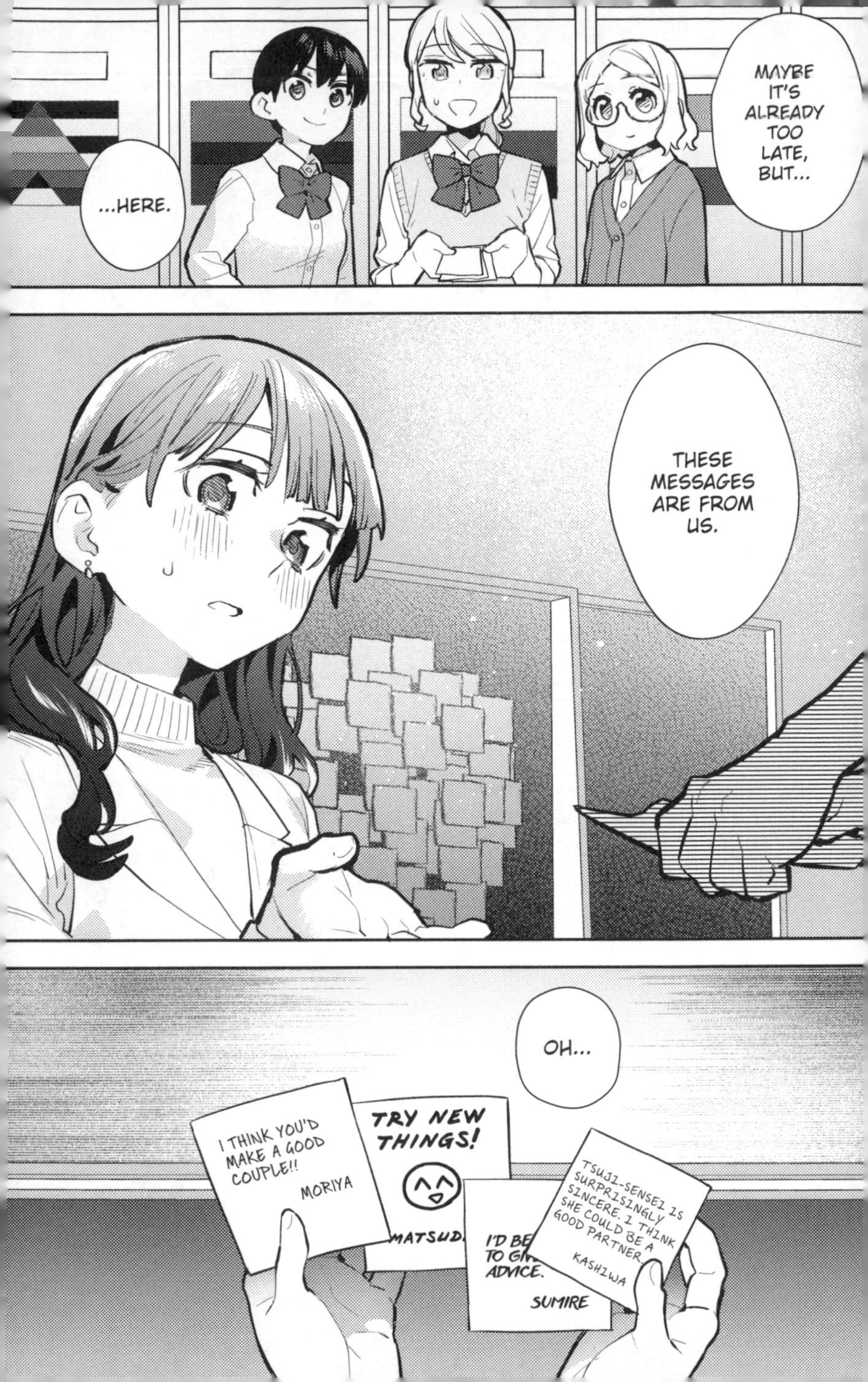
MAYBE IT'S ALREADY TOO LATE, BUT...
...HERE.
THESE MESSAGES ARE FROM US.
OH...
TSUJI-SENSEI IS SURPRISINGLY SINCERE. I THINK SHE COULD BE A GOOD PARTNER.
KASHIWA
I'D BE
TO GIV
ADVICE.
SUMIRE
TRY NEW THINGS!
MATSUD
I THINK YOU'D MAKE A GOOD COUPLE!!
MORIYA

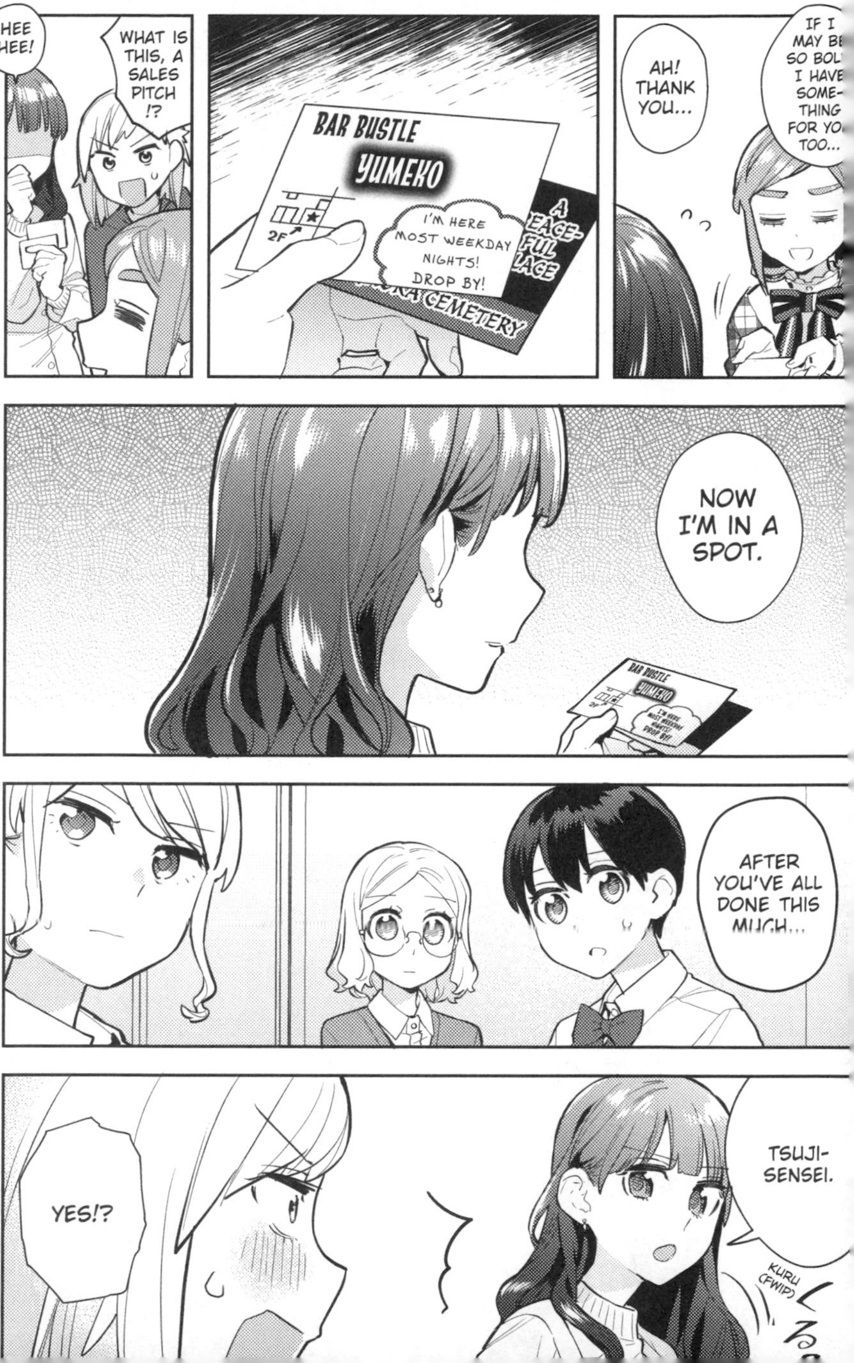
IF I MAY BE SO BOL I HAVE SOME-THING FOR YO TOO...
AH! THANK YOU...
BAR BUSTLE
YUMEKO
I'M HERE MOST WEEKDAY NIGHTS! DROP BY!
WHAT IS THIS, A SALES PITCH!?
HEE HEE!
NOW I'M IN A SPOT.
AFTER YOU'VE ALL DONE THIS MUCH...
TSUJI-SENSEI.
KURU (FWIP)
YES!?

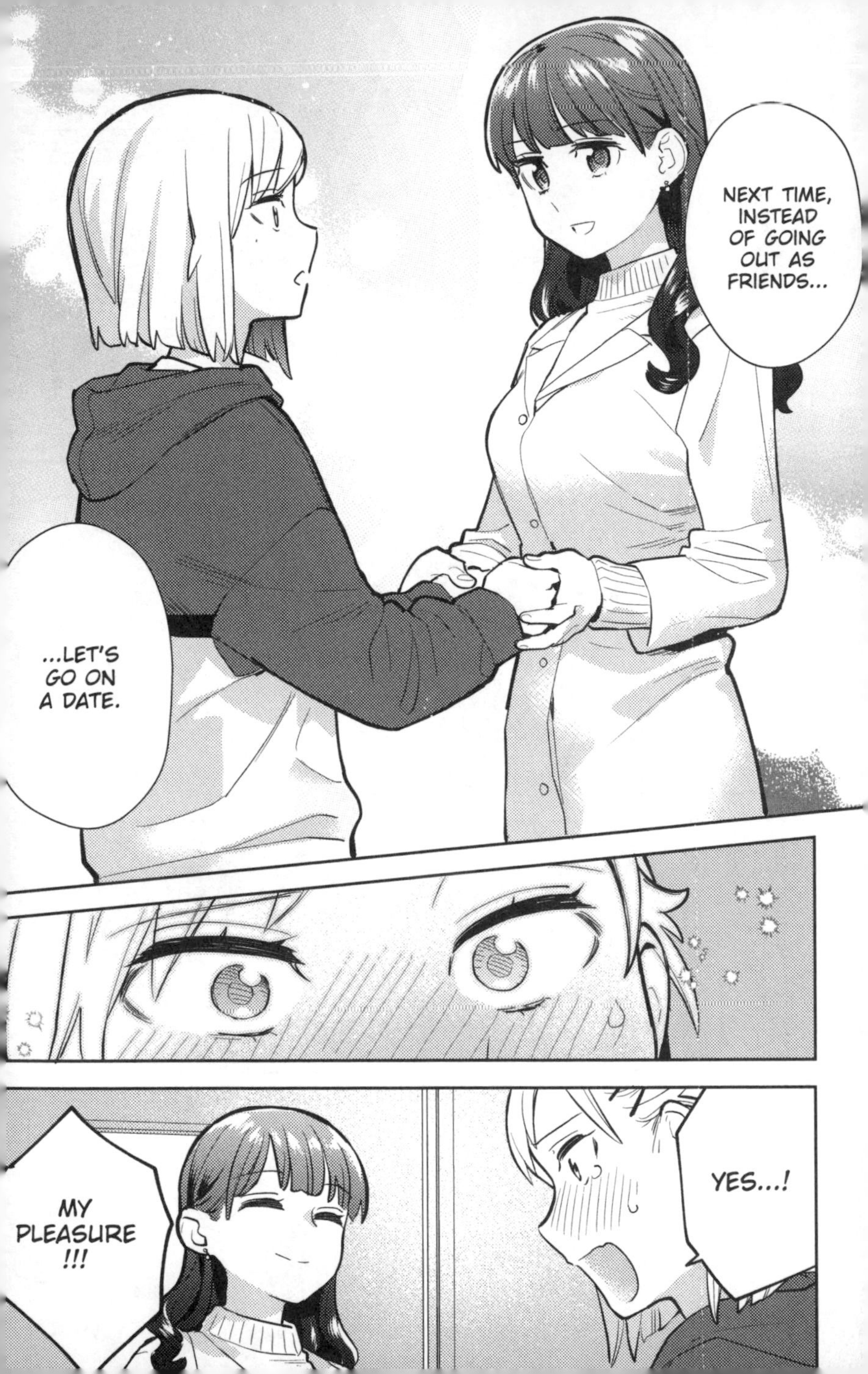
NEXT TIME, INSTEAD OF GOING OUT AS FRIENDS...
...LET'S GO ON A DATE.
YES...!
MY PLEASURE !!!

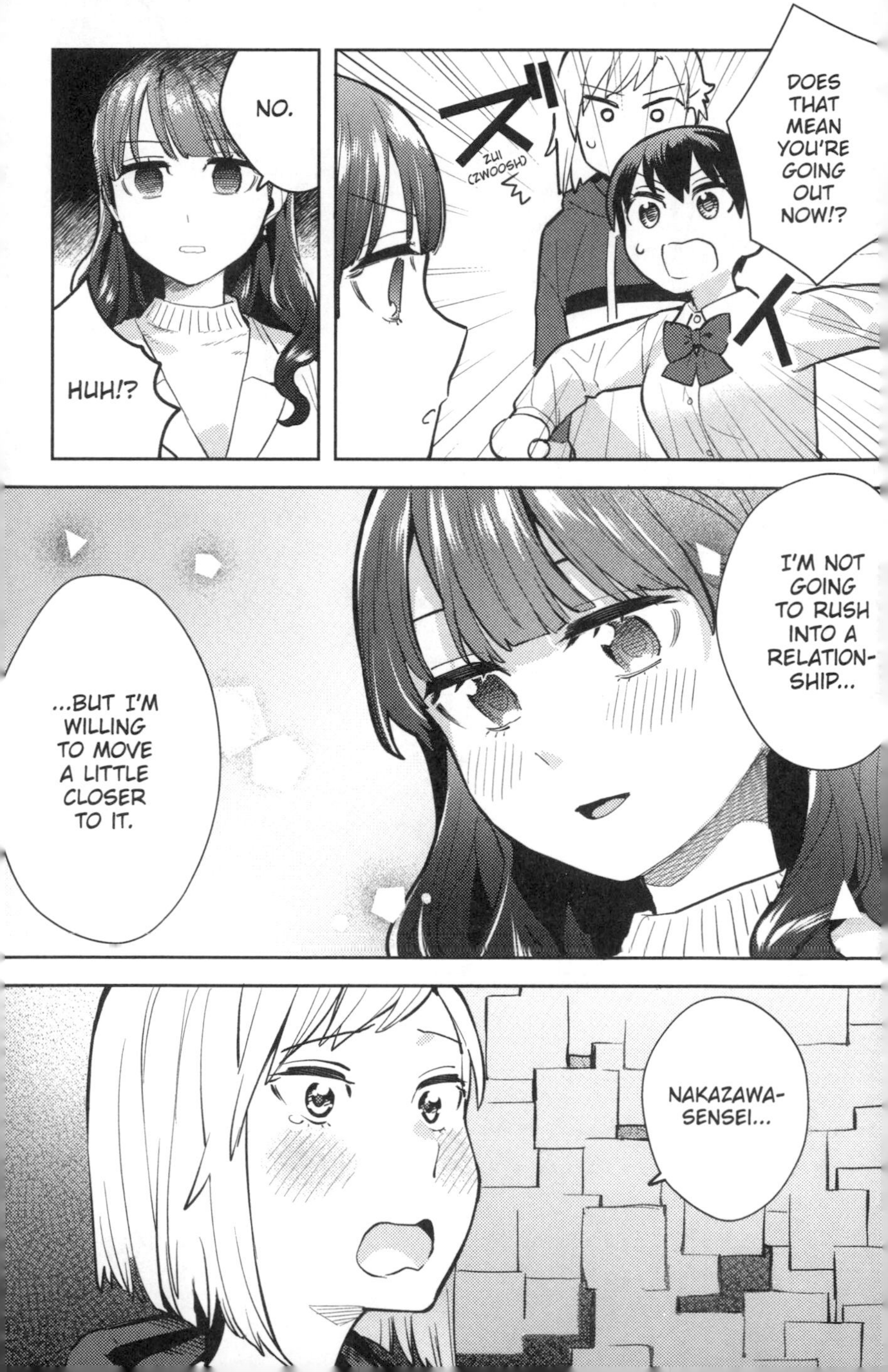
DOES THAT MEAN YOU'RE GOING OUT NOW!?
ZUI (ZWOOSH)
NO.
HUH!?
I'M NOT GOING TO RUSH INTO A RELATION-SHIP...
...BUT I'M WILLING TO MOVE A LITTLE CLOSER TO IT.
NAKAZAWA-SENSEI...

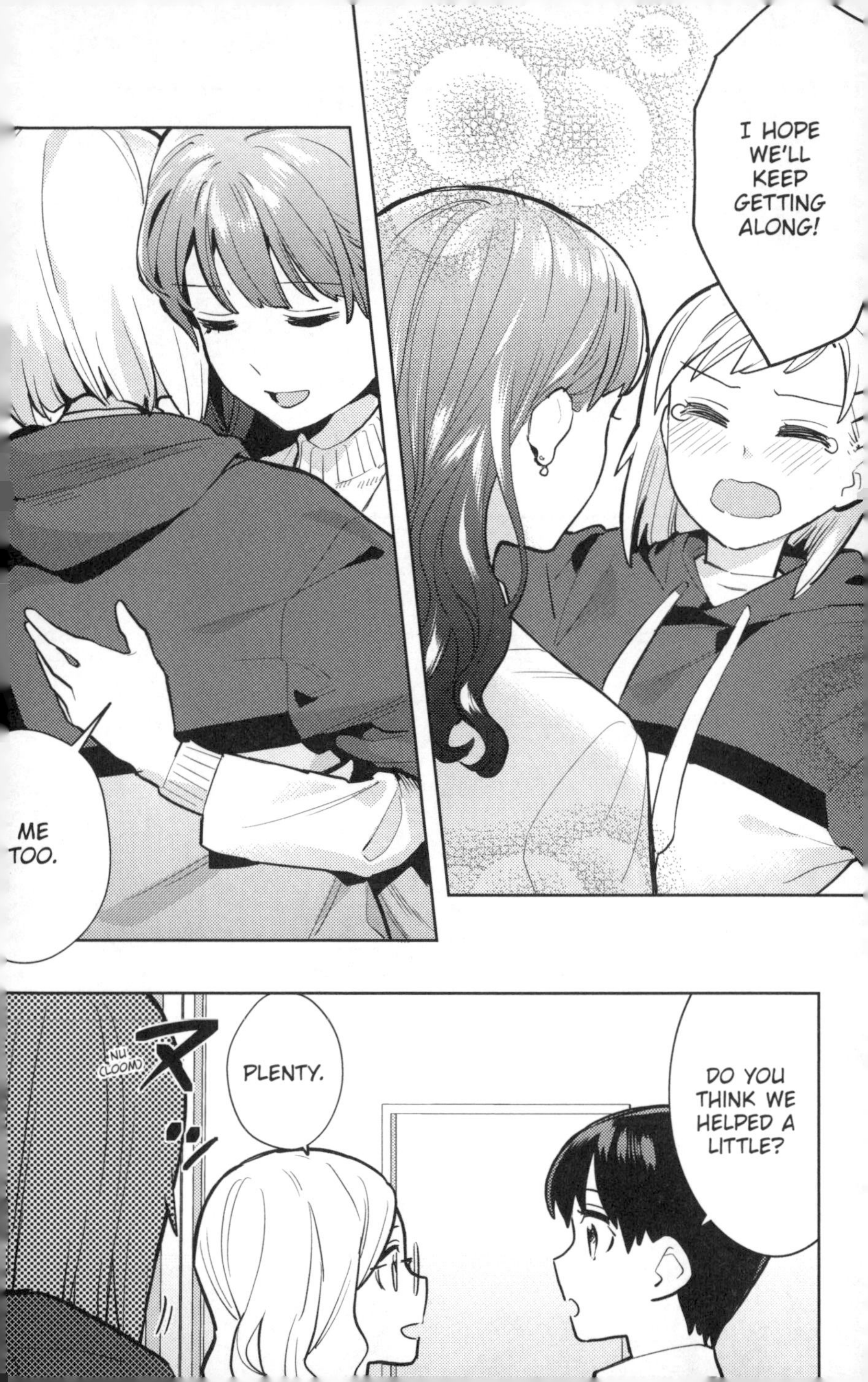
I HOPE WE'LL KEEP GETTING ALONG!
ME TOO.
DO YOU THINK WE HELPED A LITTLE?
PLENTY.
NU (LOOM)

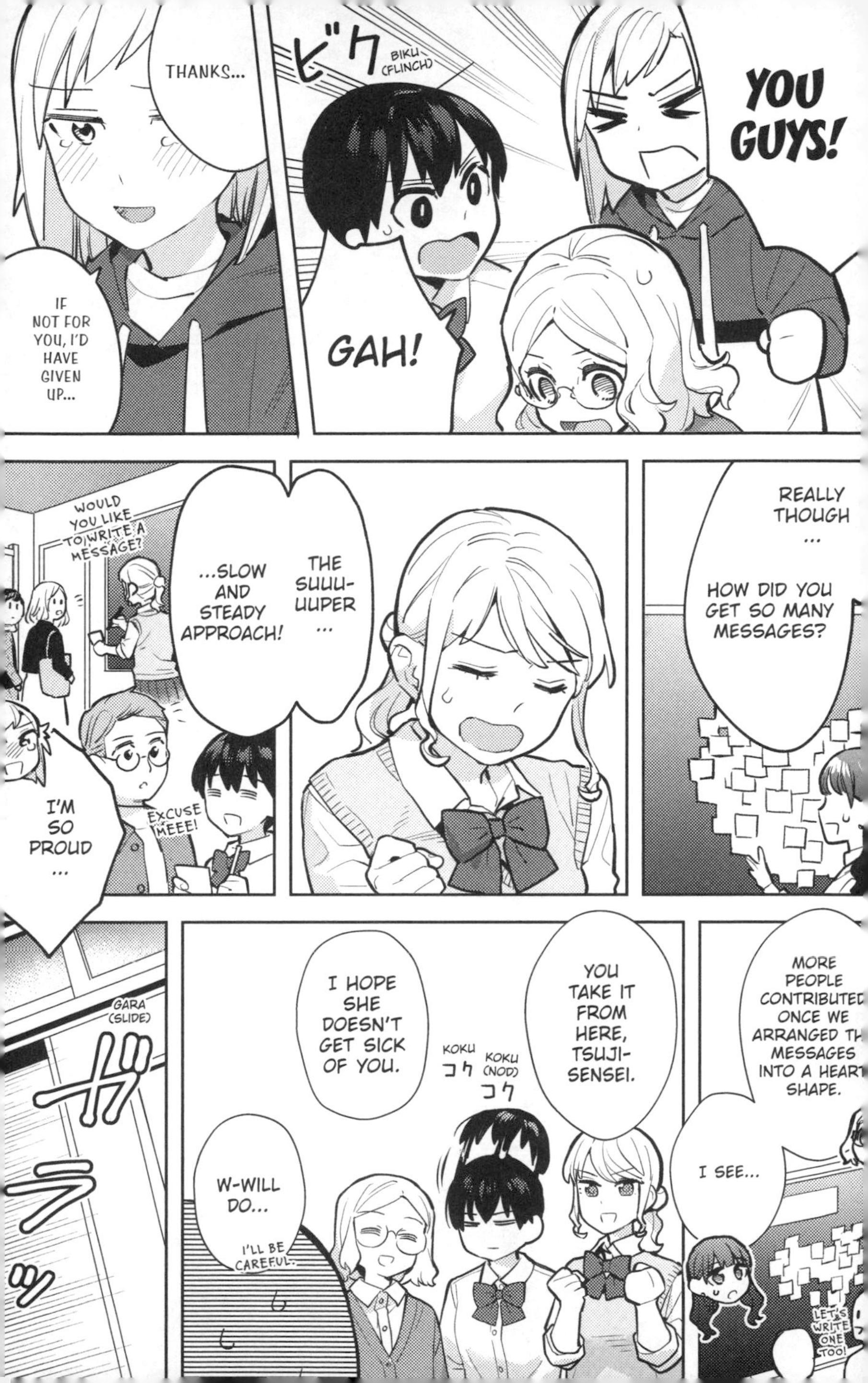
YOU GUYS!
ビク BIKU (FLINCH)
GAH!
THANKS...
IF NOT FOR YOU, I'D HAVE GIVEN UP...
REALLY THOUGH ...
HOW DID YOU GET SO MANY MESSAGES?
THE SUUU-UUPER ...
...SLOW AND STEADY APPROACH!
WOULD YOU LIKE TO WRITE A MESSAGE?
EXCUSE MEEE!
I'M SO PROUD ...
MORE PEOPLE CONTRIBUTED ONCE WE ARRANGED TH MESSAGES INTO A HEART SHAPE.
I SEE...
LET'S WRITE ONE TOO!
YOU TAKE IT FROM HERE, TSUJI-SENSEI.
KOKU コク KOKU (NOD) コク
I HOPE SHE DOESN'T GET SICK OF YOU.
W-WILL DO...
I'LL BE CAREFUL.
GARA (SLIDE)
ガラッ

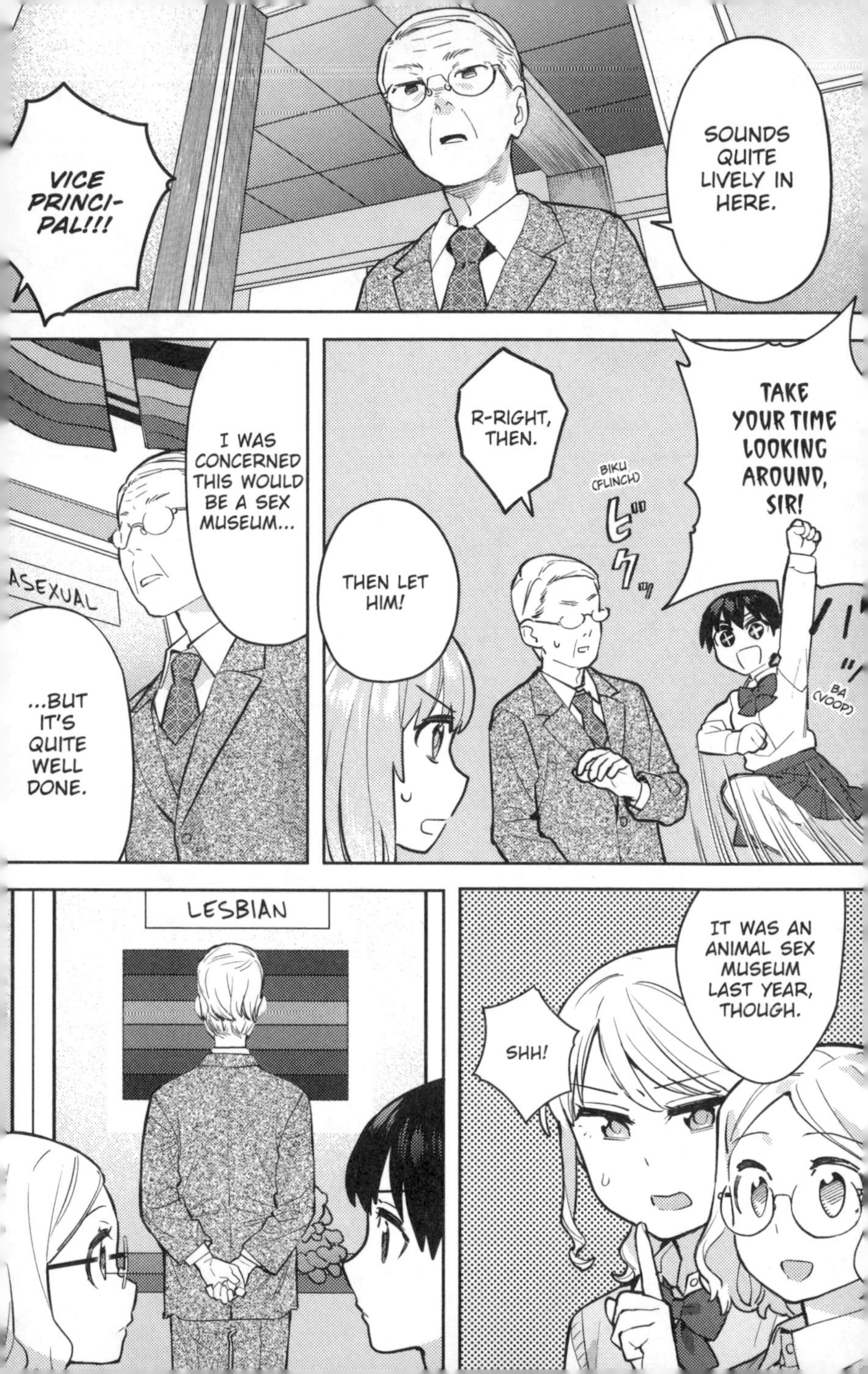
SOUNDS QUITE LIVELY IN HERE.
VICE PRINCI-PAL!!!
TAKE YOUR TIME LOOKING AROUND, SIR!
R-RIGHT, THEN.
BIKU (FLINCH)
BA (VOOP)
THEN LET HIM!
I WAS CONCERNED THIS WOULD BE A SEX MUSEUM...
ASEXUAL
...BUT IT'S QUITE WELL DONE.
IT WAS AN ANIMAL SEX MUSEUM LAST YEAR, THOUGH.
SHH!
LESBIAN

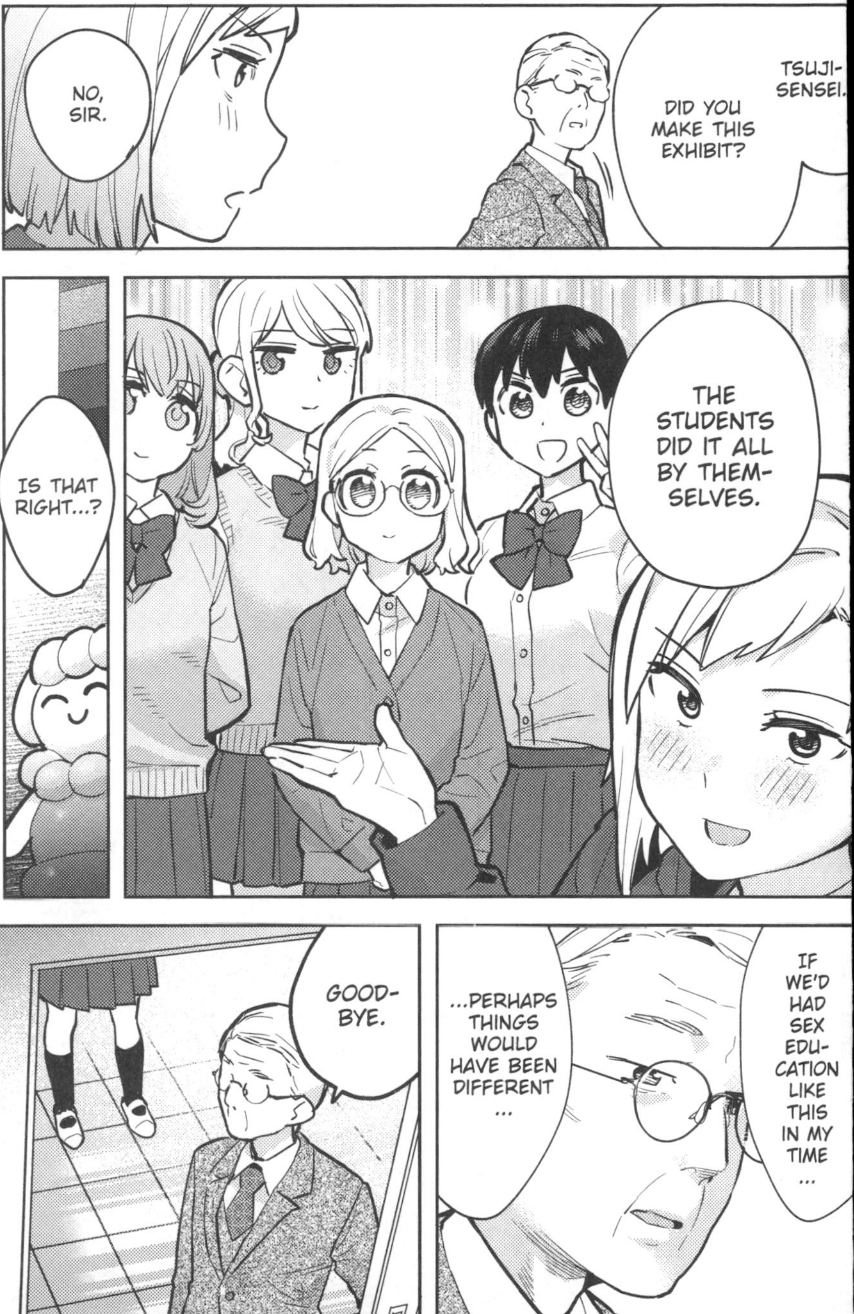
TSUJI-SENSEI.
DID YOU MAKE THIS EXHIBIT?
NO, SIR.
THE STUDENTS DID IT ALL BY THEMSELVES.
IS THAT RIGHT...?
IF WE'D HAD SEX EDUCATION LIKE THIS IN MY TIME...
...PERHAPS THINGS WOULD HAVE BEEN DIFFERENT...
GOOD-BYE.

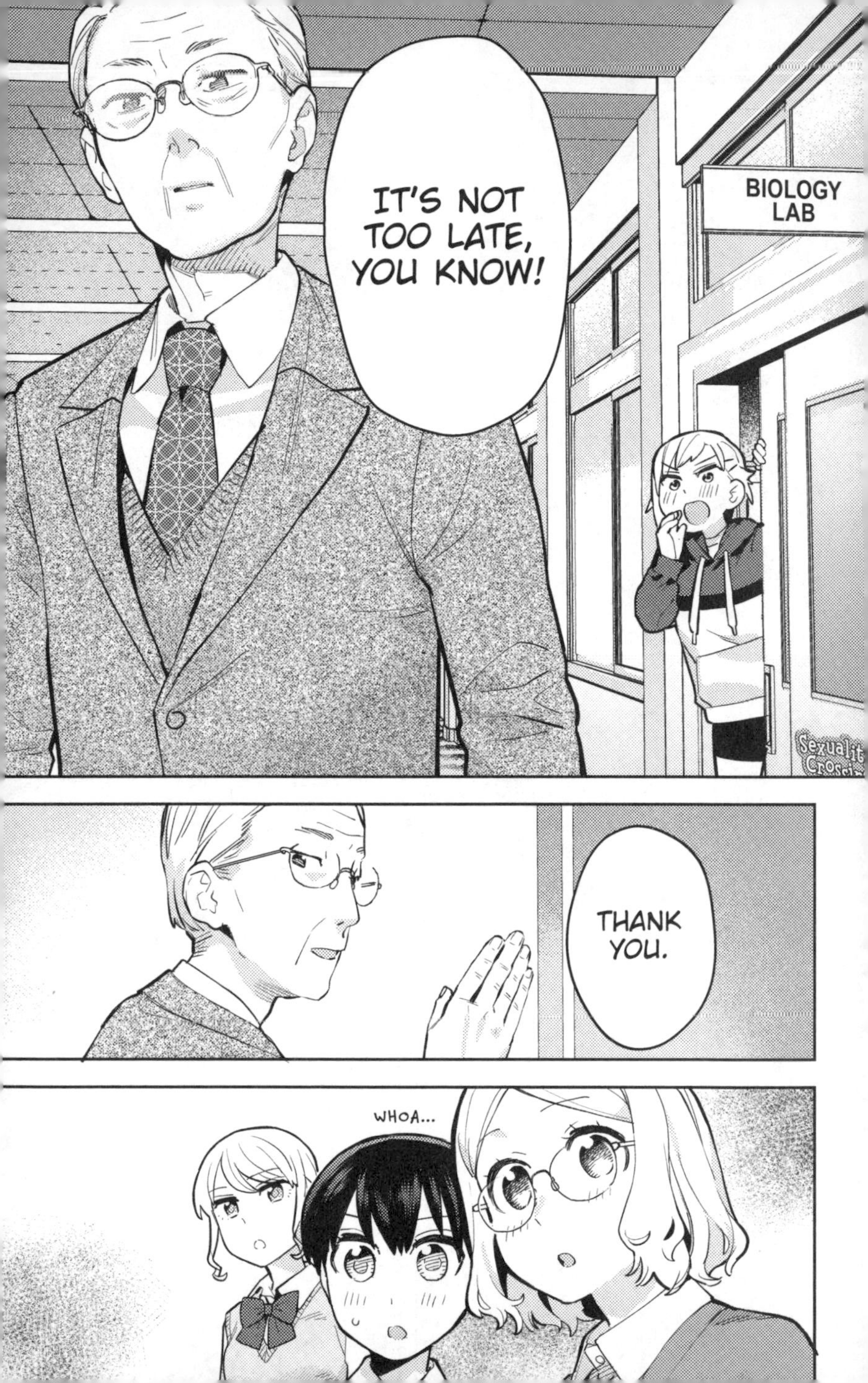
BIOLOGY LAB
IT'S NOT TOO LATE, YOU KNOW!
THANK YOU.
WHOA...

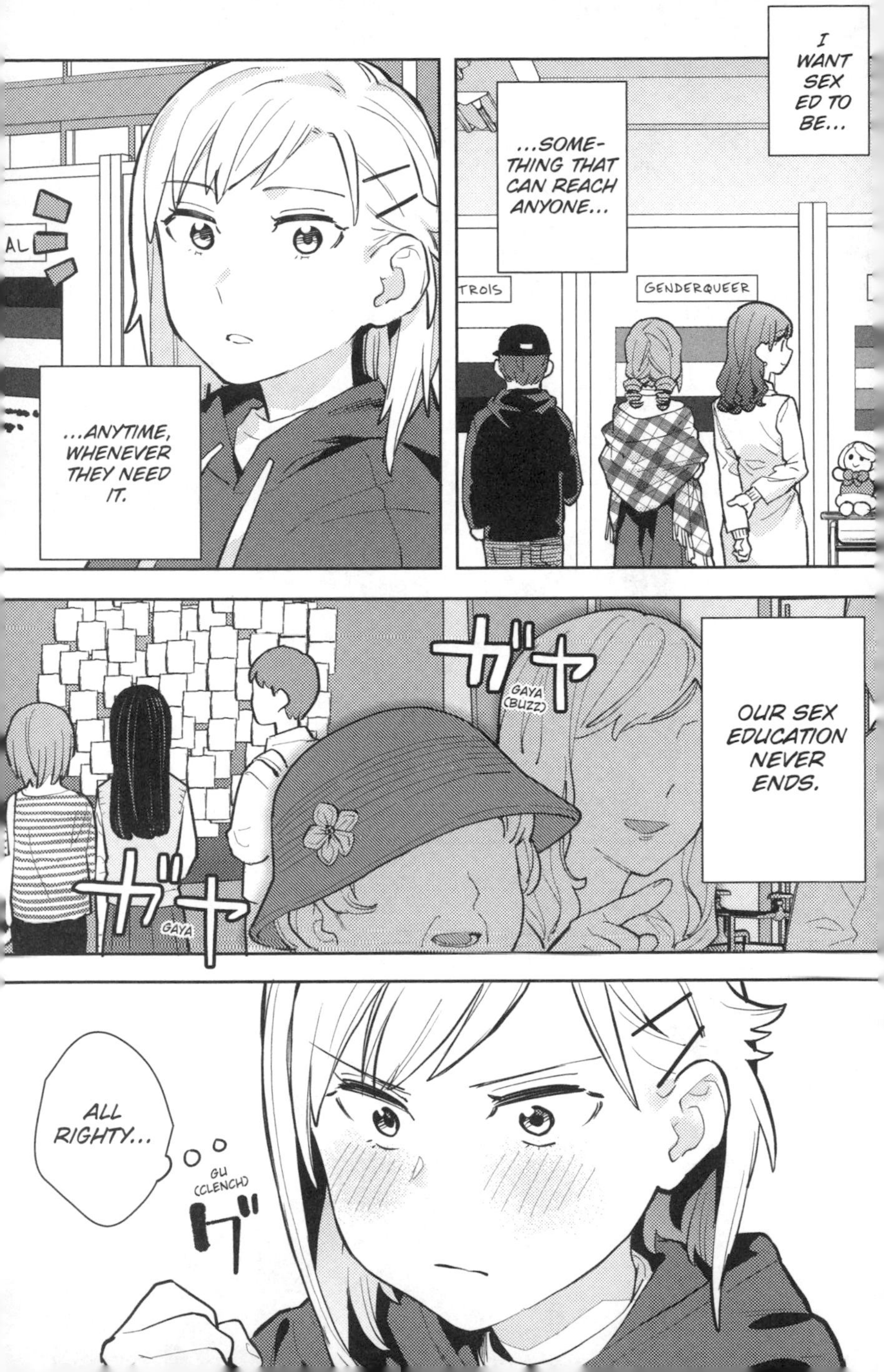
I WANT SEX ED TO BE...
...SOME-THING THAT CAN REACH ANYONE...
GENDERQUEER
TROIS
...ANYTIME, WHENEVER THEY NEED IT.
AL
OUR SEX EDUCATION NEVER ENDS.
GAYA (BUZZ)
GAYA
ALL RIGHTY...
GU (CLENCH)

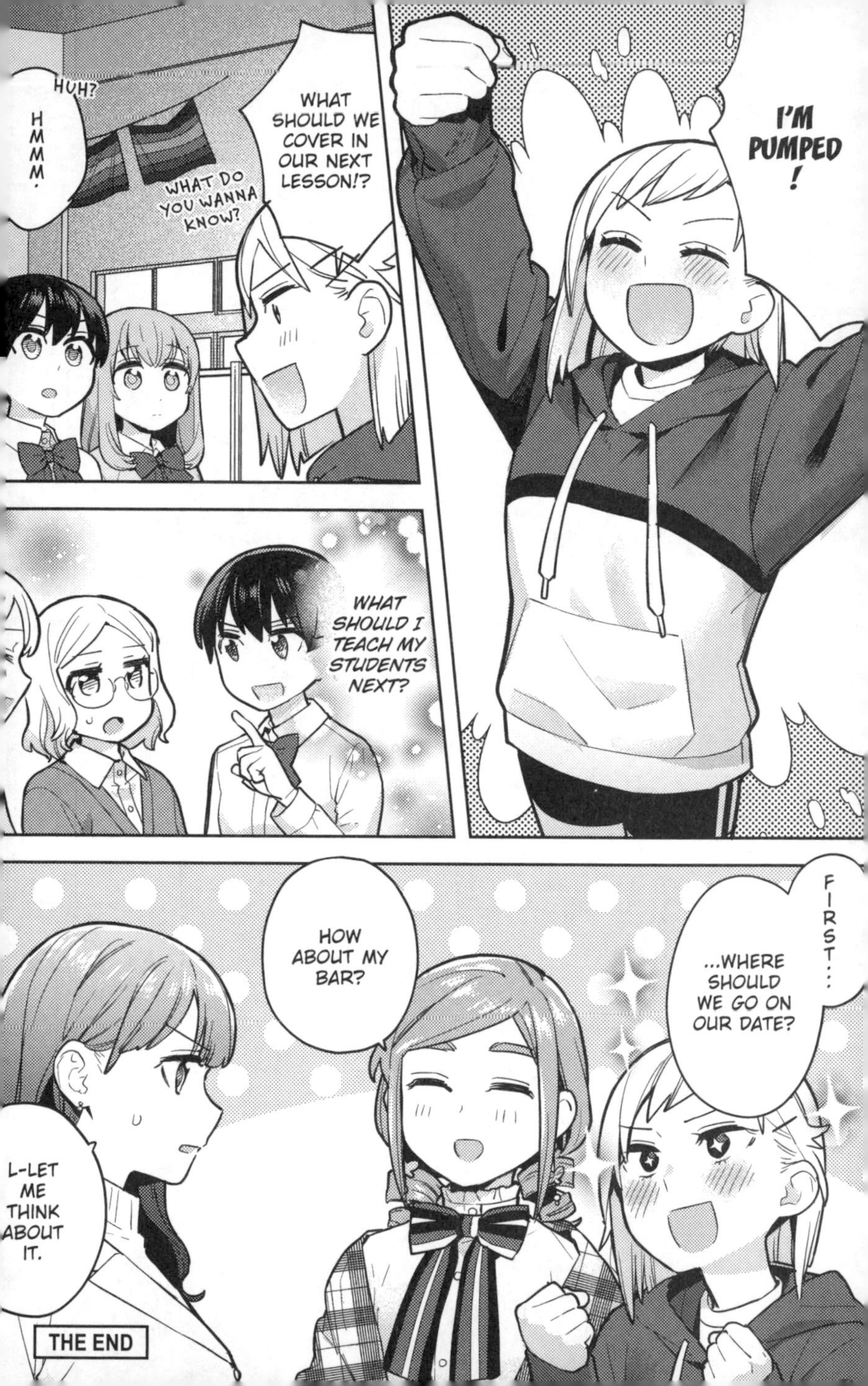
I'M PUMPED!
WHAT SHOULD WE COVER IN OUR NEXT LESSON!?
WHAT DO YOU WANNA KNOW?
HUH?
HMMM.
WHAT SHOULD I TEACH MY STUDENTS NEXT?
FIRST...
...WHERE SHOULD WE GO ON OUR DATE?
HOW ABOUT MY BAR?
L-LET ME THINK ABOUT IT.
THE END

Extra Lesson 16

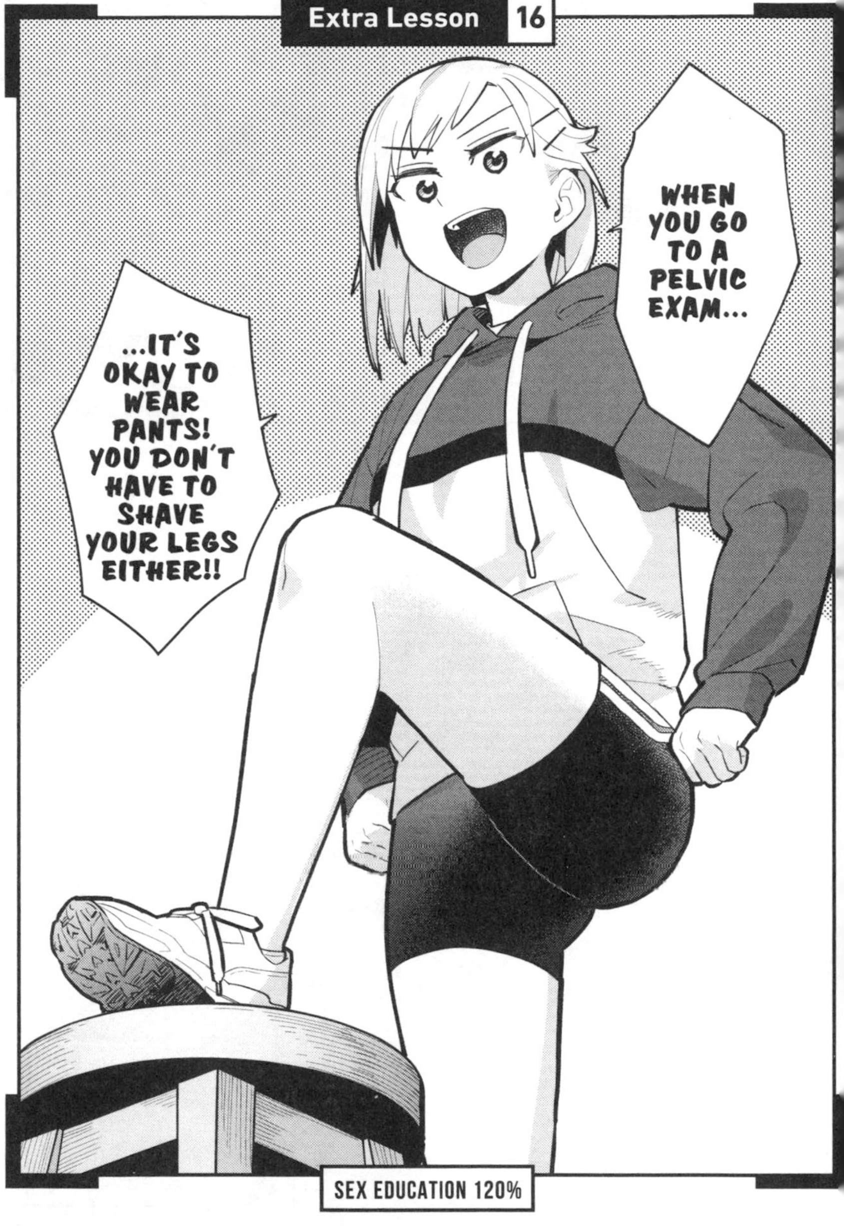
WHEN YOU GO TO A PELVIC EXAM...
...IT'S OKAY TO WEAR PANTS! YOU DON'T HAVE TO SHAVE YOUR LEGS EITHER!!

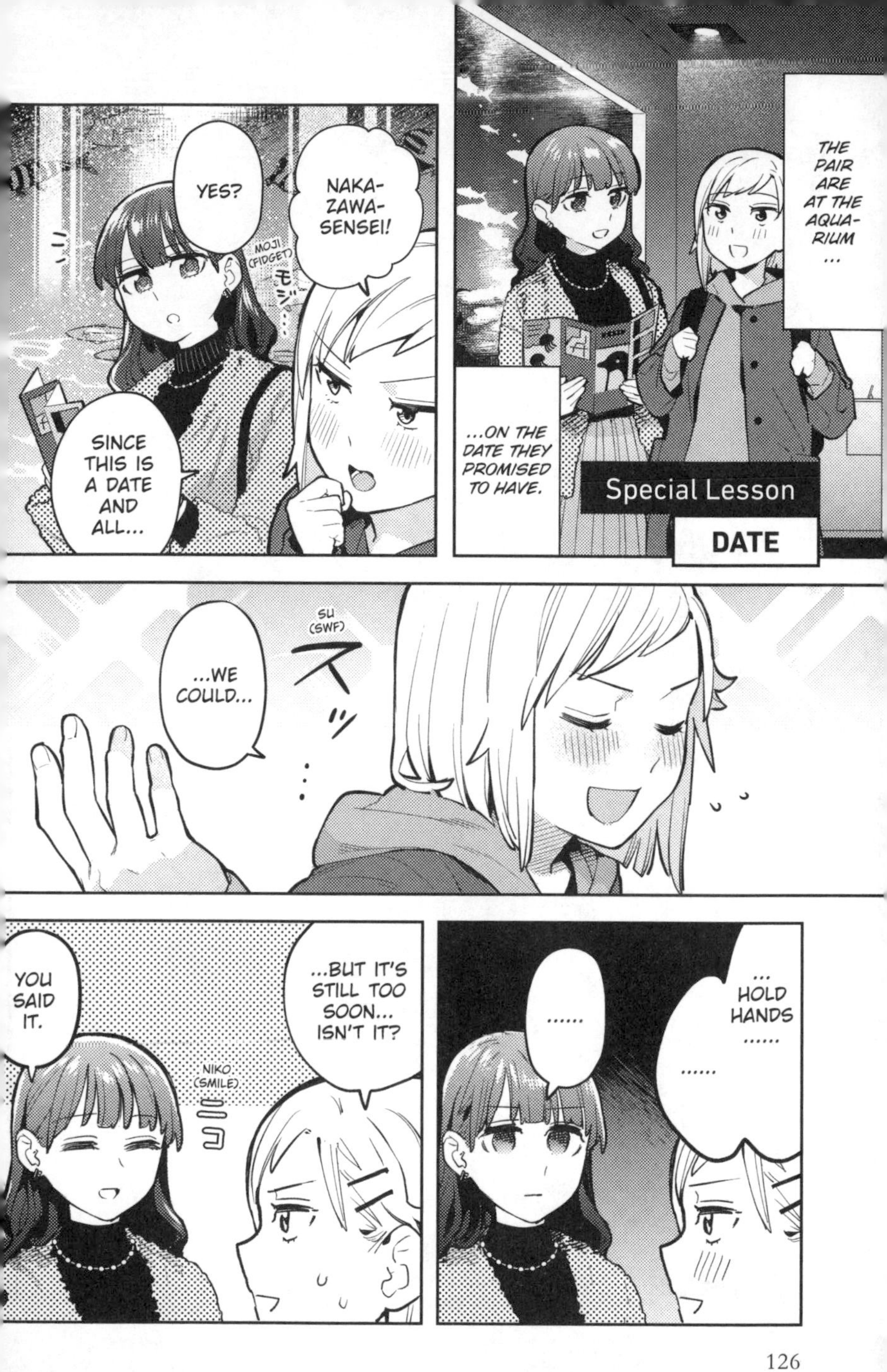
THE PAIR ARE AT THE AQUARIUM ...
...ON THE DATE THEY PROMISED TO HAVE.
Special Lesson
DATE
NAKA-ZAWA-SENSEI!
MOJI (FIDGET)
モジ...
YES?
SINCE THIS IS A DATE AND ALL...
SU (SWF)
スッ
...WE COULD...
... HOLD HANDS ......
......
......
...BUT IT'S STILL TOO SOON... ISN'T IT?
NIKO (SMILE)
ニコ
YOU SAID IT.

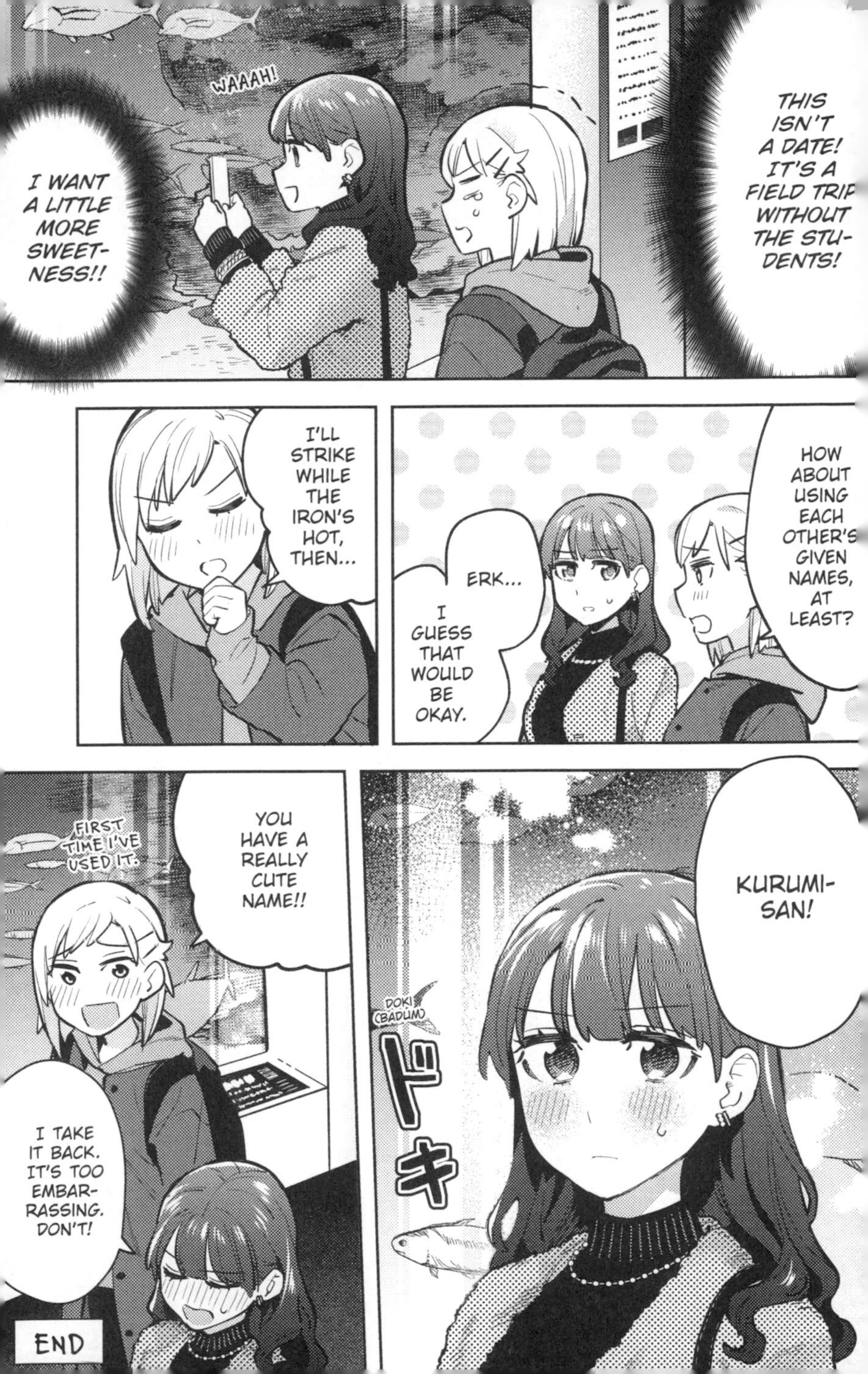
THIS ISN'T A DATE! IT'S A FIELD TRIP WITHOUT THE STUDENTS!
WAAAH!
I WANT A LITTLE MORE SWEETNESS!!
HOW ABOUT USING EACH OTHER'S GIVEN NAMES, AT LEAST?
ERK...
I GUESS THAT WOULD BE OKAY.
I'LL STRIKE WHILE THE IRON'S HOT, THEN...
KURUMI-SAN!
DOKI (BADUM)
ドキ
YOU HAVE A REALLY CUTE NAME!!
FIRST TIME I'VE USED IT.
I TAKE IT BACK. IT'S TOO EMBARRASSING. DON'T!
END

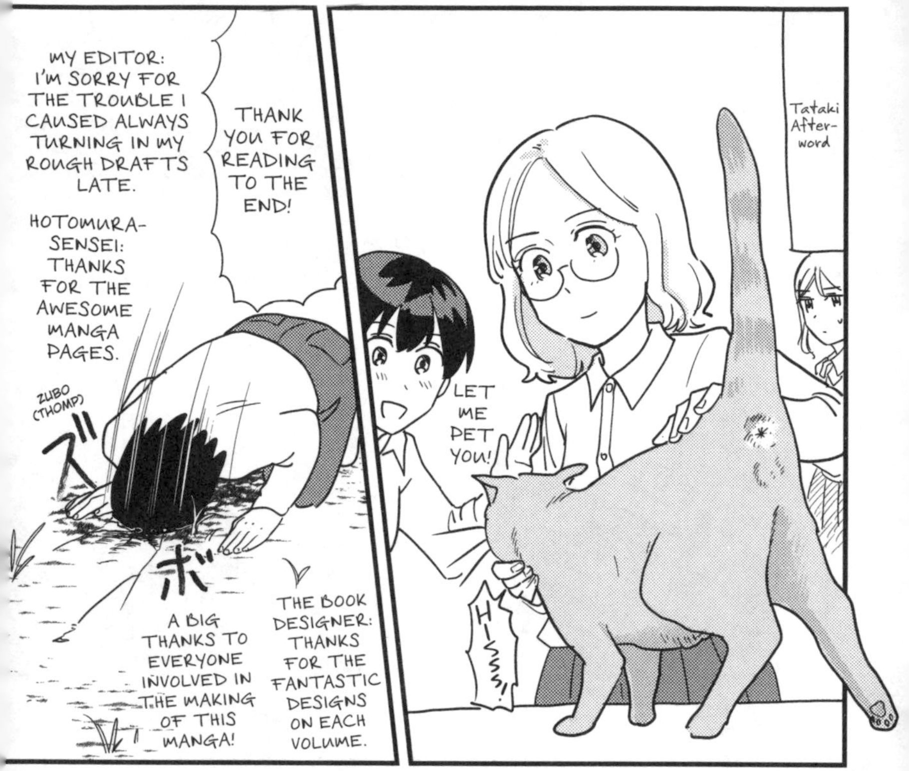
Tataki Afterword
LET ME PET YOU!
HISSS!
THANK YOU FOR READING TO THE END!
MY EDITOR: I'M SORRY FOR THE TROUBLE I CAUSED ALWAYS TURNING IN MY ROUGH DRAFTS LATE.
HOTOMURA-SENSEI: THANKS FOR THE AWESOME MANGA PAGES.
ZUBO (THOMP)
ズ
ボ
THE BOOK DESIGNER: THANKS FOR THE FANTASTIC DESIGNS ON EACH VOLUME.
A BIG THANKS TO EVERYONE INVOLVED IN THE MAKING OF THIS MANGA!

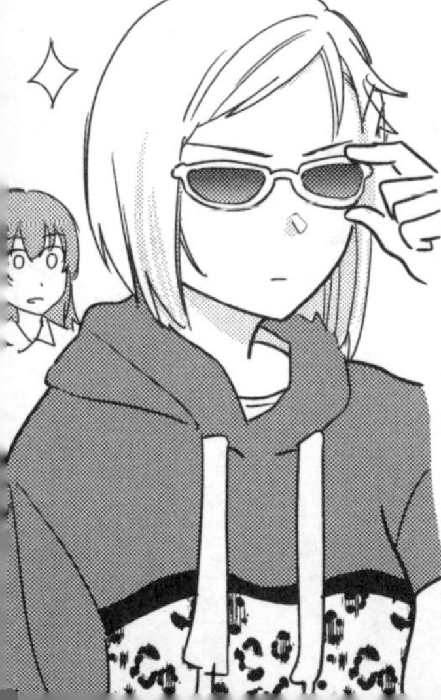

CHAPTER 13
Hashimoto, Noriko; Sekiguchi, Hisashi; Tashiro, Mieko. *Everything You Should Know About Sex by 20 (2nd ed.).* Otsuki Shoten.
The Council for Education and Study on Human Sexuality. *The Study of Human Sexuality, Updated Edition. Surveying the State of Sex Ed: Japan and the World, Connecting and Expanding.* Otsuki Shoten.

CHAPTER 14
Understanding Children's Mental Development Series, Book 7. Gender Dysphoria in Children: Transgenderism, SOGI, and Sexual Diversity. Compiled by Kou, Jun. Godo Shuppan.

CHAPTER 15
Moriyama, Noritaka. *Reading into LGBT: Introduction to Queer Studies.* Chikuma Shinsho.
Pohlen, Jerome. *Gay and Lesbian History for Kids: The Century-Long Struggle for LGBT Rights.* Translation by Kitamaru, Yuuji. Thousands of Books, Inc.

BONUS PAGE
Blackledge, Catherine. *The Story of V: Opening Pandora's Box.* Kawade Bunko.

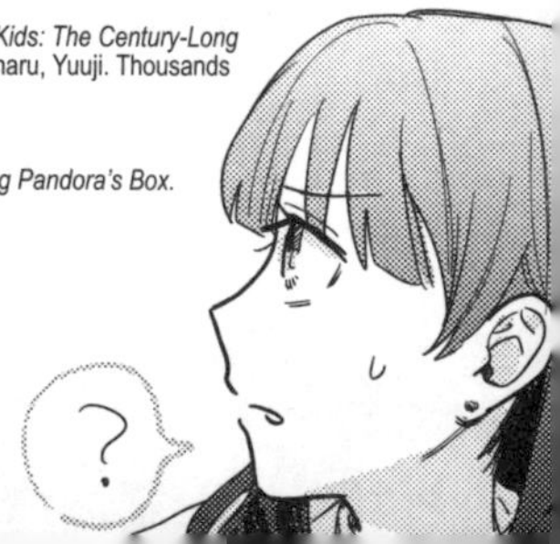
?

AFTERWORD

A BIG THANK-YOU TO EVERYONE WHO READ THIS FAR AND TO ALL THE PEOPLE INVOLVED IN THE MAKING OF THIS MANGA. TO TATAKI-SENSEI AND THE EDITOR, MY APOLOGIES FOR CAUSING SO MUCH TROUBLE...I WAS HAPPY TO HAVE THE HONOR OF DRAWING A MANGA THAT WAS NOT ONLY FUN, BUT ALSO SO EDUCATIONAL.

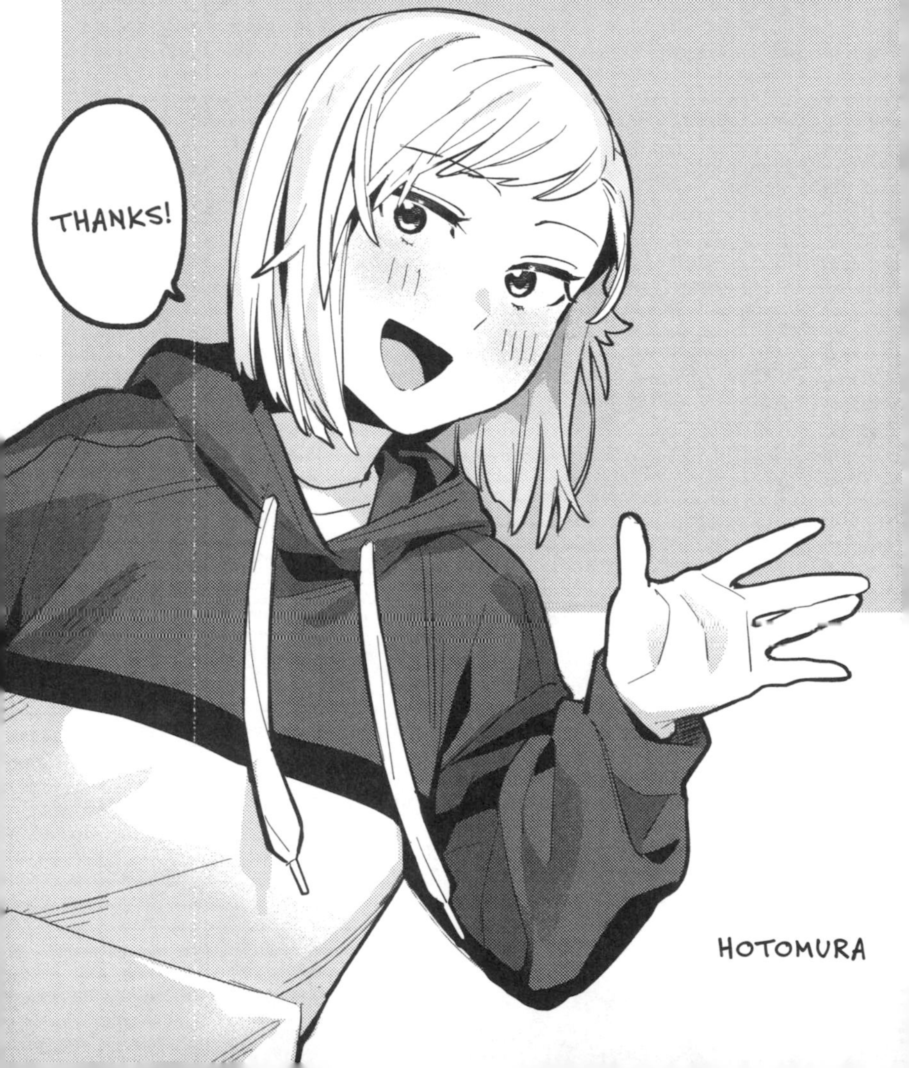
THANKS!

HOTOMURA

SEX ED 120%

STORY BY KIKIKI TATAKI
ART BY HOTOMURA

[VOL.3]

Translation: **Amanda Haley** | Lettering: **Sara Linsley**

SEIKYOIKU120% Vol. 3

First published in Japan in 2021 by KADOKAWA CORPORATION, Tokyo.
English translation rights arranged with KADOKAWA CORPORATION, Tokyo
through TUTTLE-MORI AGENCY, INC., Tokyo.

Yen Press
150 West 30th Street, 19th Floor
New York, NY 10001

Visit us!
yenpress.com • facebook.com/yenpress • twitter.com/yenpress
yenpress.tumblr.com • instagram.com/yenpress

First Yen Press Edition: February 2022

Yen Press is an imprint of Yen Press, LLC.
The Yen Press name and logo are trademarks of Yen Press, LLC.

The publisher is not responsible for websites (or their content) that are not owned by the publisher.

Library of Congress Control Number: 2020951827

ISBNs: 978-1-9753-3669-1 (paperback)
978-1-9753-3670-7 (ebook)

10 9 8 7 6 5 4 3 2 1

LSC-C

Printed in the United States of America